# AMERICAN CINEMA

one hundred years of filmmaking

# AMERICAN CINEMA

## one hundred years of filmmaking

jeanine basinger

RIZZOLI
NEW YORK

First published in the United States of America in 1994 by
Rizzoli International Publications, Inc.
300 Park Avenue South, New York, New York 10010

Editor and project manager: Charles Miers
Copy editors: David Brown, Cathryn Drake,
Philip Reynolds, and James Schulman
Compositor: Rose Scarpetis
Designer: Alex Castro

The American Cinema project is a thirteen-
week television course from the
Annenberg/CPB project.

Major Funding from
The Annenberg/CPB Project

For further information about the course,
call 1-800-LEARNER. Major funding for the
American Cinema project has been provided
by the Annenberg/CPB project. Additional
funding has been provided by the National
Endowment for the Humanities and the
National Endowment for the Arts.

Library of Congress Cataloging-in-Publication Data

Basinger, Jeanine.
American Cinema : one hundred years of filmmaking / by
Jeanine Basinger.
        p.        cm.
Includes bibliographical references and index.
ISBN 0-8478-1814-4
1. Motion pictures—United States—History. 2. Film genres—
United States. I. Title.
PN1993.5.U6B314  1994                         94-12263
791.43'0973—dc20              CIP

Printed in Japan

# Contents

# Acknowledgment

I would like to thank two of my former students who played key roles in the creation of this book: Sasha Alpert, who first involved me in the New York Center for Visual History television series that is the book's companion, and Sarah Projansky whose research and basic write-ups form the foundation of the factual his torical material this book contains. Without Sasha I would never have started to write this book, and without Sarah it would never have been completed. I also want to thank Mary Lea Bandy of The Museum of Modern Art for her counsel and support in all matters. I am indebted to the personnel at *The American Cinema Project* and the New York Center for Visual History, notably Lawrence Pitkethly, Executive Producer; Greg Martinelli, Senior Producer; Molly Ornati, Senior Producer; Rita Maté, Senior Producer; Shana Swanson, Series Associate Producer; and Caroline Rubens, Research Assistant. I would like to thank the excellent staff at Rizzoli: Rose Scarpetis, Philip Reynolds, David Brown, Belinda Hellinger, and Elizabeth White. I especially thank my editor, Charles Miers, for his conceptualization of the book; the book's designer Alex Castro, who has a marvelous eye for movie stills; and Antonio Polito for his initial enthusiasm. Thanks also go to Howard and Ron Mandelbaum of Photofest, Bob Cosenza and Fiona Jackman of the Kobal Collection Jeremy Arnold for basic research, and Strauss Zelnick for his support. Finally, as always, I thank my hus band, John, and my daughter, Savannah, for everything they always do to help me with my projects.

The New York Center for Visual History wishes to recognize the following individuals for their help: Alan Yentob and Michael Jackson at the BBC; Bill Kobin, Steven Kulczycki and Phylis Geller at KCET; Mara Mayor and Lin Foa at the Annenberg/CPB Project; James Dougherty and Barbara Sirota at the National Endowment for the Humanities; and Brian O'Doherty and Laura Welsh at the National Endowment for the Arts. The Center also wishes to thank John Wyver, Chris Rodley, and Steve Jenkins in the United Kingdom and Ferdinand Habsburg in Germany. The Center would particularly like to thank Sydney Pollack, Martin Scorsese, Jack Lemmon, Sam Fuller, Oliver Stone, Lawrence Kasdan, John Bailey, Robert Towne, John Waters, Julia Roberts, Arthur Penn, Clint Eastwood, Dede Allen, Richard Sylbert, Eva Marie Saint, and Rosemary Mankiewicz. And very special thanks are extended to Steven Spielberg, Hugh Hefner, Ray Stark and Suzanne Weil.

The Center also wishes to recognize the following for their cooperation and support of *The American Cinema Project:* ABC/Capital Cities; the Brooks Clift Collections; Carolco; Castle Rock Entertainment; CBS Entertainment; Circle Releasing; Columbia Pictures; the Estate of Marilyn Monroe; the Estate of Bette Davis; EuroFilms; Films du Carosse; IRS Releasing; Island Pictures; Tom Kalin; Kino International; Geechee Girls Productions; Levy, Gardiner & Lavin Productions; Lumiere Pictures; Lucasfilms Inc.; Miramax; NBC News Archives; New Line Cinema; NSB Pictures; Ed Pressman; Republic Pictures; RKO; Gena Rowlands; Sandcastle Five; Robert Altman; Spelling Films International; Turner Entertainment Company; Twentieth Century Fox; United Film Enterprises; Universal Pictures; the University of South California; Walt Disney Company; Warner Bros.; Weiss Global Enterprises; Worldview Entertainment; and Zoetrope Studios.

For their cooperation and contributions to the series the Center wishes to thank all those interviewed; Dede Allen, Lindsay Anderson, Gregg Araki, Paul Arthur, John Bailey, Peter Bart, Jeanine Basinger, Lawrence Bender, E.E. Bernds, Albert Bezzerides, Katherine Bigelow, Peter Biskind, Budd Boetticher, Peter Bogdanovich, David Bordwell, Richard Brandt, James Brooks, Henry Bumstead, Niven Busch, Raymond Carney, Charles Champlin, Ethan Coen, Joel Coen, Peter Coyote, Julie Dash, Alan Daviau, Brian DePalma, Andre De Toth, Ira Deutchman, Edward Dmytryk, Richard Dyer, Clint Eastwood, Michael Eisner, Nora Ephron, Douglas Fairbanks, Jr., Peter Falk, Harrison Ford, John Frankenheimer, Carl Franklin, Gray Frederickson, Leonard Fribourg, Otto Friedrich, Samuel Fuller, Paul Fussell, Teri Garr, Todd Gitlin, Martin Goldsmith, Douglas Gomery, Nick Gomez, Jean-Pierre Gorin, Bob Gosse, Ron Goulart, Jane Greer, Sidney Guilaroff, Molly Haskell, Norman Hatch, Amy Heckerling, Charlton Heston, Paul Hirsch, Jim Hoberman, John Irvin, Richard Jameson, Jim Jarmusch, Tom Kalin, Lawrence Kasdan, Harvey Keitel, DeForest Kelley, Howard W. Koch, Sr., Gary Kurtz, Charles Lang, Jack Lemmon, Elmore Leonard, Joseph Lewis, Ray Liotta, George Lucas, Anthony Lukeman, Sidney Lumet, A. C. Lyles, Karl Malden, Garry Marshall, Joseph L. Mankiewicz, Delbert Mann, Todd McCarthy, Frances McDormand, Thomas McGuane, Larry Meisterich, Harold Michelson, Gene Michaud, Lynda Miles, John Milius, Matthew Modine, Errol Morris, Joe Morton, Walter Murch, Mace Neufeld, Rick Nicita, Tim O'Brien, Bill Orr, Alphonse Ortiz, Robert Parrish, Arthur Penn, John Pierson, Janey Place, Sydney Pollack, Abraham Polonsky, Sam Raimi, Julia Roberts, Cliff Robertson, Henry Rogers, Fred Roos, Gena Rowlands, Jonas Rosenfield, Al Ruddy, Jane Russell, Eva Marie Saint, Nancy Savoca, Stephen Schiff, Thomas Schatz, Paul Schrader, Martin Scorsese, Susan Seidelman, Henry Sheehan, Ed Sikov, Joel Silver, Gene Siskel, Richard Slotkin, Annick Smith, Wayne Smith, Steven Soderbergh, Aaron Spelling, Anne Stark, Oliver Stone, Richard Sylbert, Jonathan Taplin, Quentin Tarantino, Bertrand Tavernier, Robert Towne, Catherine Turney, John Turturro, Christine Vachon, Sylvia Wallace, Eli Wallach, John Waters, Haskell Wexler, Richard Widmark, Arthur Wilde, Meta Wilde, and Rudolph Wurlitzer.

Jeanine Basinger

# BEGINNINGS:

## ONE HUNDRED YEARS OF MOVIES

Only one hundred years? I thought it was forever, and, of course, for most of us alive to celebrate, it *has* been forever, since there was never a time in our lives when the movies were not there to comfort us, outrage us, and entertain us. There was never a time in my life when the movies weren't there for me, and, with any luck at all, there never will be. It has, however, only been one hundred years since film was born, and only recently has that birth date been agreed upon. That is because at first no one really took movies very seriously. It was thought that they were a fad, and everyone was having so much fun making them that they forgot to keep track of what was happening.

*Fred Ott's Sneeze*, one of the earliest known motion pictures, in which the action is simply a few seconds of Thomas Edison's assistant Fred Ott sneezing. The date of the kinetoscope is copyrighted as 1894. In the next quarter-century, the technical and aesthetic foundations of filmmaking were laid.

**Opposite: By 1915 D. W. Griffith was able to present in film an epic, two-and-a-half-hour-long story of two families during the Civil War and Reconstruction era, *The Birth of a Nation*.**

**Previous pages: The Little Tramp copes with the vicissitudes of the machine age. Charles Chaplin directed and acted in *Modern Times*, which he made in 1936 as a silent film, although the transition to sound had already occurred. He composed his own music to accompany the images and created a soundtrack that included special sound effects and an amusing and memorable gibberish song.**

The idea of a "history" of the movies seemed like a joke, so nobody wrote anything down. For years, most people just assumed there was a simple starting point for movies because, after all, movies required the invention of specialized equipment and such inventions could surely be dated. The movie business itself contributed to this sense of simplicity about invention—one man, one machine—with biographical movies that trivialized such processes. Using Hollywood's own models, it was easy enough to construct a scenario for the invention of movies: a handsome man in a white coat stands around in a laboratory assisted by someone—preferably a highly attractive female he can later marry—and *eureka!*, he invents the movies. A calendar near his desk clearly reads FEBRUARY 3, 1895. For clarification, he writes in his diary (also dated February 3, 1895): "Invented movies today."

In reality, an international labyrinth of inventions and experiments developed the motion picture and its technology, so much so that scholars and archivists have had to conduct many discussions in order to agree upon the "date of birth," which was finally announced by FIAF (the International Federation of Film Archives, a group consisting of representatives from the world's major film archives) to be 1895. To decide on that date required a definition of what was meant by the term "movies" and a reconstruction of what happened in the beginning. What *did* happen?

Well, in the beginning, Fred Ott sneezed. Officially, he sneezed in 1894, because the motion picture today called *Fred Ott's Sneeze*, originally known as "The Edison Kinetoscope Record of a Sneeze" resides in The Library of Congress copyrighted as a photograph on January 9, 1894. Some historians feel that it might have been shot earlier because Thomas Edison, Ott's boss, demonstrated his "kinetoscope" to the National Federation of Women's Clubs in May 1891 by showing them an image of Fred Ott sneezing. While Ott was sneezing, the Lumière brothers in France were shooting their first film, *Workers Leaving the Lumière Factory*, dated 1895. At about the same time, others were playing with the concept of the motion picture, and almost all of this activity was taking place simultaneously. Robert William Paul and Birt Acres were experimenting with film in England, and Max and Emil Skladanowsky were showing their "Bioskop" invention in Germany.

The date of 1895, however, is the result of a specific definition of "the birth of the motion picture" as the successful adaptation of a moving image to a projection device. This definition helps to determine the date, because two inventions were involved: the moving picture and its projector. If the movies are to be defined *only* by the projection of an image, then the movies were born in the seventeenth century and known as "the magic lantern." If "movies" *only* means the commercial selling of images to an audience, then probably Thomas Edison's peephole kinetoscope of 1894 marks the beginning. If motion itself is what counts, then the mutoscope—a kind of peephole flip-card device—was around in the late 1800s and was operational on a fairly wide basis in the early 1900s. But if what we call "cinema" or "movies" or "film" means the projection of photographed moving images, then the best date of birth is probably 1895. This is the date of the Lumière brothers film as well as of Edison's American peephole movie, *The Execution of Mary, Queen of Scots.*[1]

From 1895 to approximately 1907, movies were made that provided audiences with one of five kinds of visual presentation: factual records of the important events of

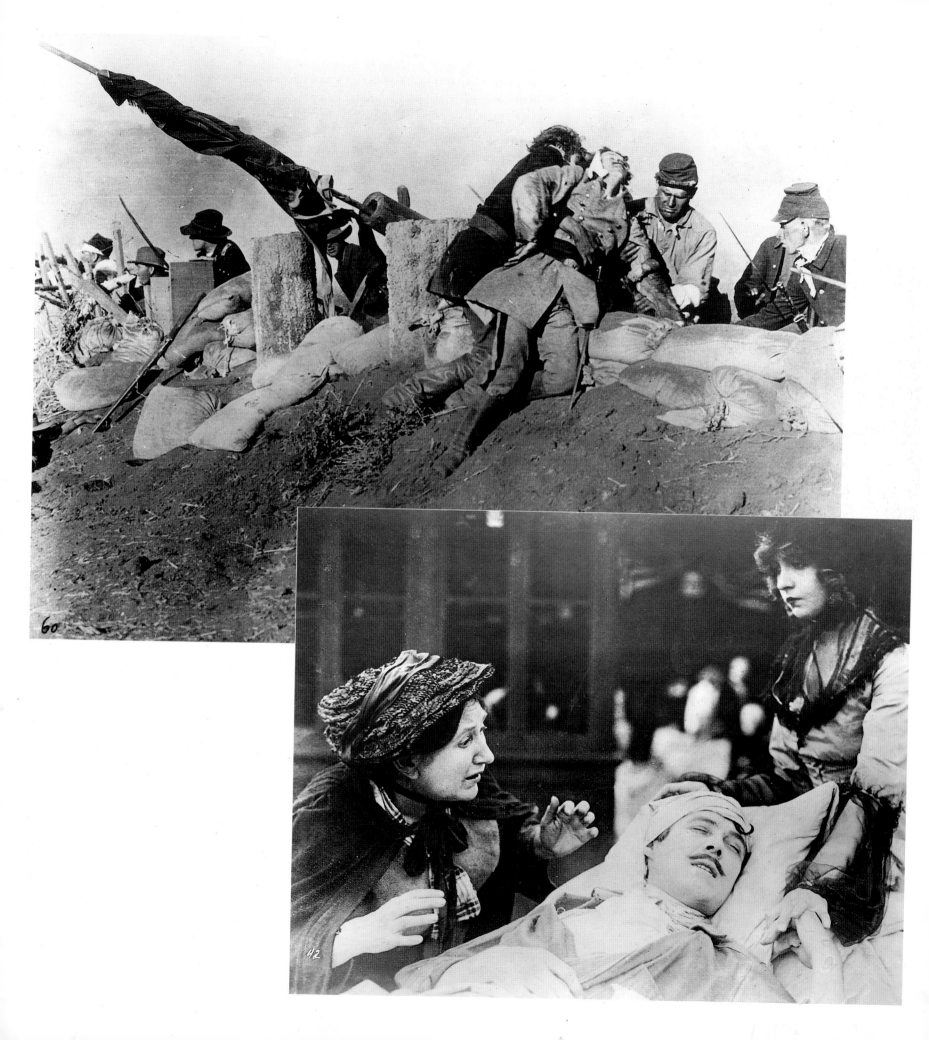

A publicity portrait of Rudolph Valentino, the film world's sex symbol of the 1920s. When he died of a burst appendix, female fans went crazy with grief and his legendary status was assured.

Right: The lavish settings and costumes were a large part of the appeal of *Ben Hur* (1926), one of the most ambitious of all the silent film spectacles. Years in production, the finished film was reputed to cost over $4 million, but its enormous and lasting success at the box office justified the expense.

the day (for example, *McKinley Taking the Oath*, 1897); re-creations of specific historical events (*The Corbett–Fitzsimmons Fight*, 1897, a restaging of the event for the cameras); picture-postcard presentations of beautiful scenery for those who might never get there (*Rapids above American Falls*, 1896); the depiction of ordinary daily events for posterity, as a kind of microhistory (*Feeding the Doves*, 1896); and the beginning of telling invented stories for amusement (*Love's Young Dream*, a comedy of 1897).

Between 1907 and 1915, cinema began to emerge as a sophisticated narrative form. The rapidity of the development is astonishing. In short, the movies progressed from something like *Scenes of Convict Life* in 1907—which is just exactly what its title says it is and nothing more—to D. W. Griffith's masterly epic re-creation of an era, *The Birth of a Nation*, in 1915. In these years, the means of exhibition changed from nickelodeon peepholes to large movie houses in which full orchestras could accompany the film. The business went from a knockabout endeavor engaged in by scalawags and get-rich-quick artists to a well-regulated industry with registered trademarks, patents, defined censorship systems, and well-paid executives. These years also brought on the emergence of the star system, the arrival of the full-length storytelling feature film, and the growth of what is today called "the grammar of film." Filmmakers began to experiment with editing techniques, camera movement and positioning, film lighting, special effects, and various aspects of performance.[2]

From 1915 until the addition of sound to films in the late 1920s, the motion picture moved forward to take its place as a major American industry, a complicated social, cultural, and technological business with enormous influence over the populace. Lavish movie palaces were built. Film genres were defined. Stars were born and became household names. The foundation of what became the studio system was put into place.[3] That famous entity developed that most people call by one name and one name only: Hollywood.

In America, the word *movies* is synonymous with the word *Hollywood* even though many movies of all kinds are and have always been made elsewhere in the United

States. Hollywood was and is the center of commercial American cinema, however, and its own history can be traced. In 1887 a man named Harvey Henderson Wilcox registered his 120-acre ranch in a beautiful area just northwest of Los Angeles, fancifully proclaiming it "Hollywood." By 1903 a village of the same name had grown up around the ranch and was eventually incorporated as a municipality. By 1910 its residents—about five thousand people—voted to become a district of Los Angeles in order to secure their water supply. Slightly before this incorporation and then following it, motion-picture companies began arriving and setting up shop in the area, attracted by the warm climate and by the geographical variety of mountains, deserts, oceanside, city streets, farmland, palm trees, and orange blossoms that were all available within a short driving distance. Labor was cheaper than in the East, and there were different ethnic groups available to play extras and small parts. In addition, it is said, the filmmakers were close to the Mexican border should escape be necessary for any financial or legal reason!

*Hollywood* meant certain story conventions. A pie in the face, a slip on a banana peel, a happy ending. Westerns with handsome heroes on their horses photographed against a magnificent landscape. Melodramas in which men were cruel and women suffered. *Hollywood* also meant certain famous faces that the public identified as their favorites and made into great stars: Charlie Chaplin, Buster Keaton, and Harold Lloyd, three original comics, each with his own style of humor and his own definitive comic character; Mary Pickford, "America's Sweetheart"; Lillian and Dorothy Gish; Rudolph Valentino, one of the first sex symbols; and Douglas Fairbanks, an energetic and brash swashbuckler. *Hollywood* also meant the magnificent film artistry of D. W. Griffith, the great storytelling of Cecil B. DeMille, and the European sophistication of Ernst Lubitsch. Writers, cinematographers, designers, artists of all kinds contributed to the glory of the silent film, taking moviemaking to the level of art at the same time as they entertained people and shaped popular culture. Hollywood became the average person's arbiter of all that was desirable, tasteful, real, and important, and it also became a major definer of the concept "American," a cultural and social force, a creator of national myths.

**American Cinema** is not a formal history book; rather it is a discussion of how movies make meaning, what kinds of movies are made in America, and how the studio system that made these movies functioned in a changing world. I focus primarily on the years after the transition to sound—by the end of the silent film era, Hollywood was

The richness of silent film is illustrated by these two examples of its variety of stories and sets. Opposite: In this scene from *Lady Windermere's Fan* (1925, directed by Ernst Lubitsch from a play by Oscar Wilde), May McAvoy and Ronald Colman play the rich and well-groomed.

D. W. Griffith's 1921 *Dream Street* (above), was a heavy mixture of allegory, melodrama, poetry, and superb cinematic style. Its female star, Carol Dempster (center), played a gyspy dancer of the streets caught between two brothers of opposite natures: a bully (Ralph Graves; left) and a sensitive soul (Charles Emmett Mack; right).

Opposite: Buster Keaton, one of silent film's most inventive and significant comic players, ever played the mournful and spurned suitor; here he finds his ring being returned to him by Kathryn McGuire in *Sherlock, Jr.* (1924), which Keaton directed and in which he plays a movie projectionist.

Four of the greatest stars of the silent era were Mary Pickford ("America's sweetheart" and one of the most renowned stars and producers), Douglas Fairbanks, Sr., and Charlie Chaplin (above), and the exquisitely beautiful Lillian Gish (below), one of D.W. Griffith's favorite stars.

already big business. The things that moviegoers today associate with movies were in place: the star system, the familiar storytelling patterns, the pressure of money on creativity, the system that manufactured movies and sold them, distributed them, and exhibited them. The end of the silent era brought about one other major change: the requirements of early sound recording more or less drove filmmakers indoors, where they could control all aspects of production on giant soundproof "stages." The loose, in-the-field quality of many early silent movies gave way to a more controlled, confined, business-dominated environment. The filmmaking process became a complex organization, divided into separate departments with specialized labor skills. Those responsible for sound, for instance, were grouped into different areas: music arrangers, composers, performers, sound mixers, sound dubbers, and equipment maintenance people. This departmental labor force became the filmmaking business now known as the studio system, which thrived during the 1930s, 1940s, and 1950s, or the "golden age" of Hollywood.

# 1 HOLLYWOOD STYLE AND THE AUDIENCE

"Everybody has two businesses. Their own, and the movies."

This famous remark, attributed at various times to everyone in the film business except Lassie, has never been more true than it is today, when the whole world has quick and cheap access to movies. All kinds of films—old and new, foreign and domestic, fictional and factual, animated and experimental—are available on television, on videotape, on laser disks, and at multiplex theaters around the world. The mass popularity of movies, once threatened by television and sports, is secure.

In addition to wanting to *see* movies in a variety of formats, audiences want to know more than ever before about the business and the people who work in it. *Time, Newsweek, New Republic, Vanity Fair, Esquire, Vogue*—all cover the film business on an in-depth basis, while specialized magazines such as *Premiere, Movieline,* and *Entertainment Weekly* are thriving. Even small-town newspapers carry the weekly lists of movies with the highest box-office receipts, information that used to be found only in trade papers. Every publication that considers itself in tune with the world has a film critic, and every television station has a local reviewer. Siskel and Ebert are household names. Bookstores have whole sections devoted to "Movies and TV." Guides are published to identify all the films available on more than fifty cable channels. Special documentaries on the history of the movies have appeared, covering everything from

favorite movie stars (James Cagney, Barbara Stanwyck, Gary Cooper) to humanistic issues ("Hollywood and the Native American on Film") to studio histories ("The MGM Story") to studies of directors' works (Todd McCarthy's biography of Preston Sturges) to real-life events ("World War II on Film"). Is there anything left to say on the subject?

Curiously enough, almost none of these books, magazines, newspapers, documentaries, and articles ever deal directly with one of the most important factors in the development of the Hollywood movie: the audience. Although some social studies about people's tastes have been written and some studies of box-office hits are available, no one seems to approach the subject from the point of view that it was all planned with the viewing audience in mind.

The glory of the Hollywood commercial cinema was always its desire to reach the audience—to please it, to capture it, to hold its attention, and, of course, to get its money in return. The ability to entertain a broad audience is the defining characteristic of American cinema. All the glamour, all the beauty and power, all the drama and all the slapstick, all the closeness that grew in the dark—it was audience-driven. The history of the Hollywood cinema is the story of how filmmakers learned to manipulate the medium in ways that drew people into the story and kept them there. The job was to get the audience to care about the movie and its characters, to fall in love with its stars, and to stay in their seats, just dying to know how it all would turn out. Have you ever started watching on television an old movie late, late at night only to fall asleep before it ended? The next morning—you moan, "Oh, I wish I knew how it had turned out." You ask around. "What happened? Does anyone know?" You watch for it to repeat some other night, and when it appears, you sit down to watch. You *know* you do . . . because Hollywood knew its business.

When you watch a movie, you willingly enter a filmed universe that has been written, photographed, designed, performed, cut and processed, advertised, and delivered to you by individuals whose combined purpose was to involve you in it in some specific and planned way. It's not always the same way from film to film. Sometimes you are asked to sit back and judge, just observe. Sometimes you have a romantic experience, and sometimes you have a great hoot. You might get scared, learn a lesson, gain new information, see a historical event re-created. Whatever it is, the people who made the film had to know in advance what they wanted you to do to help them make it all work out. They then collaborated toward this goal.

A great deal has been written about this collaboration. Who wrote a film, and who directed it, and who was responsible for its success and/or failure? Who designed it, and who photographed it? Whose idea was it in the first place? How did the individuals working on it interact? What does the movie they made mean to us culturally, historically, generically, sexually, psychologically, or economically? And was it an effective communication or not? Movie collaboration is constantly analyzed, explained, and judged, often by critical standards that are seldom explained and almost never spelled out.

> *"Hollywood makes you pay attention to the pictorial world, not the means by which it brings it to you."*
>
> Richard Sylbert

There is another collaboration involved, however. It is the collaboration between the film and the audience. You may not even realize how much your response was planned, how much you were manipulated. And if you do realize, you still may not understand how it happened. You're usually having such a good time at the movies that you may not even see how hard you are working, because no movie running through a projector in an empty theater is really a movie. It needs a viewer to complete it. You supply part of the film yourself by following the guidelines the movie sets out for you. You invest yourself in the situation. You become a part of the storytelling process.

In an intuitive way, we all know this. In America, it's as if we were born at the movies. Nobody has to teach courses on "How to Buy a Movie Ticket" or "The Etiquette of Filmgoing" (no matter how much we might need it in some cases). We may not be able to read a transportation timetable or follow a simple recipe, but we can certainly use a movie schedule or the *TV Guide*. We can get to the video store and find a tape or a disk. When we go to the movies we know what to do: Go in and sit down in the seat, with or without a box of popcorn. Glue our eyes to the screen and wait for the curtain to open. And then, let it happen. Enter in. Participate.

Right from the earliest days, Hollywood movies reached out to audiences this way. One kind of moviemaking was straightforward, linear storytelling, with an "invisible" editing technique that sought to be as clear and "real" as possible. Movies like this welcomed you and made you comfortable. The other kind—the cinema of such film directors as Rouben Mamoulian, Orson Welles, Samuel Fuller, and many others—did the opposite. These directors experimented with the medium. Hollywood, after all, knew you went to the movies as often as possible. To keep movies fresh and to play with you, they made another kind of movie alongside the classical ones: movies that innovated and manipulated in new ways. These movies challenged you and caught you by surprise, but both kinds were planned with the audience in mind. As Jean-Luc Godard observed about the American cinema, "All movies have a beginning, middle, and end, but not necessarily in that order."

Although movies are a unique art, people often try to explain them by comparing them to other art forms. Movies tell stories, like books and short stories. They have actors speaking lines of dialogue while moving around inside a framed space, like plays. They are loaded with subtext, like poems, and they can be lyrically beautiful. They move through time and space, like music. They have composition and framing and color like paintings. To finish out such descriptions, it is usually pointed out that they are *not* like television. (They're better, say such people.) It's not that simple, of course. Movies aren't really like novels or plays or poems or sonatas or even television (although they appear regularly on the small screen). They're different. Film scholars usually start out by telling everyone how movies are *not* like books and plays and paintings. The question that is interesting is not whether they are different, or even how they are different, but what are they? How do they make meaning, and how do they make you feel and think what you feel and think when you are watching them? Analyzing these questions for American cinema means thinking about how movies manipulate audiences, because that is the primary definition of the classic style of Hollywood filmmaking.

The romantic aura and glamour of classic Hollywood love stories enveloped audiences in elegant passion: Henry Fonda and Bette Davis (whose love affair is never fulfilled) in director William Wyler's *Jezebel* (1938).

## Hollywood Style

People today often say that Hollywood movies aren't what they used to be. (What is?) What they are talking about is that in the old days Hollywood aimed its product at the mass market. One movie tried to fit all. Today movies are target-marketed and aimed at specific audiences: the teenagers or the "over-forty crowd." During the golden age of the studio system in America, it was assumed that a teenager and a couple in their fifties could and would enjoy the same story. The old movies were after every dollar, every dime, from every pocketbook.

To get everyone into the theater, the classical Hollywood movie did two things. It was ambivalent enough to appeal to all sides of any argument or relationship, to show both sides even if one won out in the end ("Crime Does Not Pay," says the finale, after showing all the glamour and violence of crime in action) . . . and it created a relationship with the members of the audience that allowed them to play a role in the story in some way.

Although the first part of this formula is now often eclipsed by the specifics of marketing to specialized constituencies, the second principle is still the basic guiding light of the business: get viewers in and hold them. American movies were, and still are, audience-driven. There is still a place for you in the picture. You have to make deductions, think out relationships, and decipher conversations about tuna-fish sandwiches that are really about the end of a love affair. You have to watch everything carefully, because what is being said might be the opposite of what is being shown. A good movie treats you as if you're an intelligent, grown-up person. As you sit down and begin to watch, it does what Humphrey Bogart does to Claude Rains at the end of *Casablanca* (1942). It throws an arm around you and says, "This is the beginning of a beautiful friendship." And you, for your part, go along with it, giving it a fair chance.

Movies know how to draw you into the story by various means. It might be through a character you can really love or really hate, such as Cody Jarrett, a psychopathic hero played by James Cagney in *White Heat* (1949). He's nuts and he's dangerous, but when he gnaws on a chicken leg while he pumps six bullets into the trunk of a car, giggling demonically and yelling to the victim inside, "Here's some air holes for you!" he's got your attention. When he blows himself up at the end of the movie, shooting bullets into gas tanks and screaming, "Top of the world, Ma!" he's atomic in his charisma. Robert De Niro as Travis Bickle in *Taxi Driver* (1976) and Al Pacino in the remake of *Scarface* are similar central characters who are violent and disturbed, but fascinating. On the other hand, you might be deeply touched by the simple beauty and dignity of Jane Wyman, playing a deaf girl in *Johnny Belinda* (1948), when she first "hears" music by placing her hand on a violin that is vibrating. A similarly sympathetic heroine is played by Holly Hunter in *The Piano* (1993) or by Sally Field in *Places in the Heart* (1984) and *Norma Rae* (1979).

*"The distance between your life
and that life in film was enormous;
that was part of the success."*

Sydney Pollack

Sometimes movies draw you in by casting an actor or actress that you love and want to see over and over again, even in a bad movie. You went to see John Wayne improbably playing a Mongol warrior in *The Conqueror* (1956) because you liked John Wayne, and you sat through Jack Lemmon in *Under the Yum-Yum Tree* (1963) because he was so good in *Some Like It Hot* (1959) or Jack Nicholson in *Man Trouble* (1992) because of *Chinatown* (1974).

Another method to involve you is that of telling you a darned good story of the kind you have seen before and want to see again—a familiar genre such as a western or gangster film—or by telling you the facts about the life of a real-life hero . . . or by telling you that darned good story in a specific way that intrigues you and holds you, by cleverly repressing key information until the end or telling you the story out of chronological order. Controlling what you know through revealing and repressing information keeps you enthralled, keeps you paying attention.

A primary way movies have of involving you is by using the technical tricks of the trade, such as lighting, composition, cutting, and camera angles and movements, including a series of subjective techniques that filmmakers are masters of, such as point-of-view shots, music on the soundtrack that warns you danger is coming or that tells you to cry or laugh, sounds that make you jump, and voice-overs that talk directly to you in a one-on-one storytelling mode.

In *The Searchers* (1956), perhaps director John Ford's finest movie, there is a wonderful scene that asks viewers to understand subtle visual storytelling. John Wayne, playing a drifter, has come to his brother's house, an isolated ranch in the great western landscape. When word is received that there are Indian uprisings, the two brothers prepare to investigate. The information has been brought to them by the character actor Ward Bond, who waits for Wayne and his brother to get ready. During this scene, the brother's wife, played by Dorothy Jordan, goes into a bedroom to get Wayne's coat for him. The scene is simple, but eloquent. After Ward Bond kicks the front door shut, he is left alone in the main room of the ranch house. He is relaxed and casual, with a doughnut in one hand and a coffee cup in the other. He takes a position in the back of the frame, his back to the audience. As he turns and walks toward the camera, he glances to frame right. A cut shows the viewer what he is privileged to see: the wife removing Wayne's coat from a chest, but taking time to stroke it tenderly, lovingly. Another cut restores the view of Ward Bond looking toward (and obviously seeing) the action just witnessed. Bond makes no face, says no word. John Wayne enters from the back of the frame and goes to meet his sister-in-law as she brings him his coat. As she hands it over, Wayne chastely kisses her forehead, a kiss appropriate for his brother's wife. Just the slightest moment of hesitation occurs between them, and then Wayne turns to leave. Jordan follows him and is framed for a moment in the doorway, looking out. During this action, Ward Bond never looks toward either of them. He has carefully averted his eyes from any action between them. His face reveals nothing.

Two of the silver screen's most popular and glamorous figures, Gary Cooper and Audrey Hepburn, starred in director Billy Wilder's 1957 love story, *Love in the Afternoon*, in which a middle-aged roué is captured by a virginal young cello player. The "invisible" barrier between them was a mark of classically effective filmmaking.

After they have parted, Bond himself turns and goes out the door, walking around the wife as he exits.

Bond's careful aversion of his eyes, following the solidly established moment of privileged information that places you, the viewer, in the same position he is in, tells you the story of the hidden, unspoken love between John Wayne and his brother's wife. Although there have been a few other subtle hints earlier, no information about this relationship has been or will ever be stated or confirmed in the movie. Yet, when you realize that John Wayne, an outsider to family life, spends the rest of the film searching for his niece, Debbie, this moment becomes a powerful motivation to the story of *The Searchers*, an unspoken explanation of Wayne's passion to find the child of the woman he loves.

Of course, it may be possible for someone to watch *The Searchers* and miss the implication of this moment. The film story still works, but not as fully, because the story is about the search rather than the love. However, the organization of the movie—including its cut to the secret view of the mother with the coat—is intentional. It asks you directly to understand. This is a great example of movie storytelling and characterization. It exists through the careful manipulation of physical action and cutting, rather than through dialogue, exposition, or bombastic acting; and it is designed specifically to make you think for yourself. Although I have not met anyone who did not see the moment, I have met many people who thought they and they alone were the only ones who had noticed it.

This ability to create a seemingly secret little relationship with an individual in an audience is basic to good moviemaking. During the 1960s, people who had grown up going to the movies were asked by *Films in Revue*, a movie magazine for serious buffs, to list their "favorite movie moments." The survey was supposed to reveal everyone's private little viewing secrets. What a surprise when it turned out that everyone listed the same ones! People remembered how Elizabeth Taylor, startled, suddenly turned to the camera and cried out, "Are they watching us?" in *A Place in the Sun* (1951) and how Audrey Hepburn, walking out into the sunlight without her nun's habit for the first time in years in *The Nun's Story* (1958), paused to keep the long skirt she was not wearing from tripping her. They remembered Paul Muni fading back into the shadows in *I Am a Fugitive from a Chain Gang* (1932), explaining how he was able to survive: "I steal." They remembered Lana Turner's walk down a village street in *They Won't Forget* (1937) . . . and much, much more. Those little privileged discoveries had all been planned by moviemakers. They were a built-in part of the moviegoing experience.

Silent movies laid the foundation for this process. Since actors could not talk directly to the audience, filmmakers told the story so that the audience had to participate closely in order to follow events. An example of how this process was continued, and made specific, can be found near the end of *The Two Mrs. Carrolls* (1947). In this movie, Barbara Stanwyck has impulsively married Humphrey Bogart without knowing he has murdered his first wife to be free for her. When he meets a third woman (Alexis

Smith) that he likes even better than Stanwyck, he naturally sets out to follow his usual procedure of eliminating an unwanted spouse: poison. Stanwyck has caught on, however, and, although nervous and frightened, has managed to throw the tainted milk Bogart has given her out the window when he was not looking, although she does not notice some of it has spilled onto the windowsill.

This is where things stand when the movie presents a key scene in which you are required to observe action, deduce thought processes, and understand motivations without dialogue. At first, Bogart and Stanwyck are together in the frame, and Bogart, observing her nervousness, keeps asking her if something is wrong. She reassures him and leaves the room. After her departure, Bogart goes to the window to close it because it has started to rain, and the wind is blowing the curtain. As he shuts the window, he sees the poisoned milk on the windowsill. Bogart examines the sill. We watch him figure it out. Since you have been shown Stanwyck dumping the milk in the previous scene, there can be no doubt about what Bogart is thinking. You have had the privilege of seeing what he can only deduce. He has to imagine what you have already seen. Using your privileged information, you see that he catches on. This is a simple level of the use of audience knowledge to create a sense of understanding of how a character thinks. (In a novel, such a scene would need to be explicitly described to explain what is happening to readers. At a play, the audience could not be brought up close to the spilled milk. This type of "showing" and directly guiding the audience's thought process defines cinema as a different method of storytelling.)

Bogart, distressed, turns back into the room and picks up the daily newspaper, on which he sees the headline "STRANGLER STALKS LOCAL WOMEN." (Characters have been discussing this strangler throughout the film.) Impatient and upset, Bogart throws the newspaper into the roaring fire that Stanwyck has laid in the fireplace.

**Powerfully complicated plots manipulating levels of knowledge have often engrossed audiences in the movies: Barbara Stanwyck and Humphrey Bogart played husband and wife in *The Two Mrs. Carrolls* (1947), with Stanwyck discovering that Bogart murdered the first Mrs. Carroll in order to wed her . . . and then that he has already picked out the third Mrs. Carroll.**

> *"I was raised on American films, which means story and narrative. In most cases, everything is at the service of the narrative, of the story. I think that this may have created what they call the "invisible" style. But it's not invisible! It's very subtle, but it's clear."*
>
> Martin Scorsese

The movie now cuts to a close-up of the burning newspaper inside the fireplace. As the paper curls and burns, only the word "STRANGLER" can be read. The audience is shown a large close-up of "STRANGLER," and the image is held long enough for even the slowest viewer to absorb the information. A series of cuts then unfold. You see how Bogart also focuses on "STRANGLER"; how he looks at the spilled milk and realizes he must get rid of Stanwyck before she tells someone about him; and how he appropriates the idea of strangling her instead of poisoning her, so that it can be blamed on the convenient local killer. Why set up this scene this way? Because it makes you realize that, just when you thought Stanwyck was safe because she thinks Bogart doesn't know she knows, she's not safe at all! She's going to be strangled immediately! It increases the tension and your involvement. It also makes you into a storyteller.

The sense that you are telling the story yourself, and are in control of it, is really another way of wording the definition of the classic Hollywood cinema ("movies manipulate audiences"). The manipulation created the individual involvement that drew audiences in so completely, and what still today makes viewers feel so connected to movies, so much a part of them. Although films seemed to be stressing nothing but story and character, they are actually often complex systems of manipulation.

Today, scholars seek to define these complexities. Some call the old system one of "invisible editing," by which it is meant that the films kept the audience involved in story and characters and hid their devices from them. Others believe invisible editing to be only part of the Hollywood tradition, as some of the filmmaking teams worked in more shocking, or elliptical, formats, making the devices noticeable. Examples can be found for either side of the discussion, but both come down to the same thing: the audience was being directed and shaped, drawn in and involved in the storytelling process. There was a role for them in the movie. They had to pay attention and engage their minds and hearts in the process.

Whether movies are classical and comfortable or experimental and challenging, logical or illogical, fully developed or elliptical, they were and are made for you. They really *are* your business. To get you involved and keep you coming, they are always doing things planned specifically for you. They leave things out, control what you know, use all the tools of their trade, form friendships and identifications for you, and tell familiar stories.

## The Art of Omission

Movies are the art of omission. In the 1942 comedy *Road to Morocco*, Bob Hope and Bing Crosby play out-of-work stowaways who are shipwrecked off the coast of Africa. After a series of madcap misadventures, they end up captured by a desert chieftain. Tied up and placed inside gunny sacks, they are unceremoniously dumped in the middle of the Sahara, where they would presumably, if this weren't a Road picture, die a hot and hideous death. Because it is a Road picture, they struggle onto their bound feet. Still inside the sacks, they begin bunny-hopping gamely forward toward some imagined goal of safety. This is a surreal image. Two sacks—apparently mobile and very vocal—jumping across an empty, sandy, and seemingly endless landscape, exchanging one-liners as they go. You can only sit and wonder.

Suddenly, however, this image dissolves off the screen in front of you and is replaced by the sight of Bob Hope and Bing Crosby, untied and very jaunty, walking briskly along in the desert, planning what they are going to do next. Hope abruptly stops. "Say," he says, "do you think the audience will wonder how we got out of those sacks?"

"Probably," replies Crosby.

"What shall we do?" asks Hope.

"Let's just not tell them," suggests Crosby. And they journey on.

Well, what can you expect in a movie in which a talking camel turns to you and says right out, "This is the craziest film I've ever been in!" *Road to Morocco* is, of course, a comedy, and a particularly loose one at that. First, you laugh because, since seeing is believing, you have to believe they got out of the sacks because you're seeing it. It's a movie joke: silly, but fun. Second, however, it's also a joke on you because you accept things like this in the movies all the time without questioning them. Didn't you see *The Thirty-Nine Steps* (1935), where the hero was left hanging off a railroad bridge girder one night, alone and hungry, and in the next scene he was walking across the Scottish moors? Well, how did he get down and find his way? Didn't you see *North by Northwest* (1959) and watch Eva Marie Saint start to fall surely to her death off Mount Rushmore, clinging to life only by the hand of Cary Grant? This scene dissolved directly into the next one, in which he was helping her into an upper berth on their honeymoon train trip. You didn't really need to know how they got down or why she didn't fall because *The Thirty-Nine Steps* and *North by Northwest* make the dangers their characters get into give you pleasure. When the danger is over and resolved, you don't need to waste time seeing them climb down from girders and Lincoln's nose . . . although, if you think about it, how did they get down? Do you care? *Road to Morocco* makes a joke about this—and you love it. You're being treated like the wise and willingly gullible moviegoer you are.

The *Road to Morocco* joke illustrates one of the most important ways that movies draw you in and keep you there—by the bizarre contradiction of not telling you things. Leaving things out. Good screenwriting is knowing when not to include an explanation that the viewer doesn't need. It's knowing not to have the character say, "You see, I really love you, Beth, and I always have. Let me tell you about when I first realized my feelings for you."

*"Get the audience by the throat. Don't let them escape. Don't wake them up. Don't let them stop and realize 'this is only a movie.'"*

Billy Wilder

*"All we're trying to do is to get somebody's attention and make them concentrate."*

Robert Altman

Cary Grant gives Eva Marie Saint a hand-up on the face of Mount Rushmore in the climax of Alfred Hitchcock's thriller *North by Northwest* (1959).

Should a film cut directly from the sight of a character packing in his hotel to the sight of him boarding an airplane (or even inside an airplane already in his seat) . . . or should he be seen to leave his hotel, enter a taxi, ride in the taxi, and depart the taxi outside the airport? The answer to the question—Should you show the ride in the taxi or not?—is: no; yes; maybe. How might an audience react in each situation?

*No:* It is irrelevant and the film needs pace and movement . . . the character has already been established as a traveler . . . no danger or problem exists for him in this journey . . . his character is already fully developed, and we do not need to observe him . . . no narrative event is going to happen between the hotel and the airport. *Yes:* If time is needed to develop the character in some way, such as he is nervous, worried, under stress, drunk, angry . . . if some event is going to happen, such as he will be followed . . . if his journey is to be interrupted . . . if the local atmosphere is important . . . or he is going to arrive late, necessitating his taking a different flight, etc. *Maybe:* It all depends on the story the movie is telling and how the filmmakers want to tell it. What do they want from the audience? Although expert screenwriters tell novices always to start as far into any film scene as they possibly can, sometimes scenes that just move a character from place to place *are* necessary.

Have you ever stopped to think about how much movies actually leave out? How many times you accepted an explanation that was not there, but only inferred, that you had to supply for yourself? Movies can cut across time and space in breathtaking ways. Viewers are instantly presented with a new time and a new place, and they have to explain it to themselves. One of the keys to understanding movies—and to making and writing them—is knowing what an audience can understand from what it sees, and knowing what it can't understand. It is knowing what to show and when to show it and how to show it.

*Sleep My Love,* a 1948 film directed by the German expatriate Douglas Sirk, begins dramatically with a frightened woman waking up suddenly on a train that is speeding through the night. She is terrified, screaming, and asking in confusion, "Where am I?" Viewers are plunged directly into a situation they cannot at first understand. No explanation is provided. The audience is put in the same position as the leading lady (Claudette Colbert). You don't exactly say, "Where am I?," but you are immediately brought directly into the story by this lack of an explanation. You know there is a reason she is there, and now you want to know her story.

As it turns out, *Sleep My Love* is about a woman who is constantly placed under hypnosis by her husband, who wants to kill her for her money. He wants everyone first to think she is losing her mind. If this movie began with a scene in which Colbert was shown as a normal woman, happy in her home, and then she turned up on the train, you would see both her and the movie differently. If the movie began with a set of mysterious feet (no faces shown) carrying Colbert's sleeping body onto the train, you would also see her differently. But, no. You see her immediately as a terrified, confused, lost, and possibly mad figure. You are forced to question her sanity yourself, just as the people inside the plot will do. This process not only raises the intriguing question of Colbert's sanity, but also is part of what it is about: waking up without knowing how you got there.

One of Hollywood's most successful writer-directors, Billy Wilder, once told an anecdote that is a great lesson in leaving things out. He and his writing partners, Charles Brackett and D. M. Marshman, were trying to find a solution to a problem in their award-winning 1950 film *Sunset Boulevard.* At the end of the movie, the mentally unbalanced character played by Gloria Swanson wants to shoot William Holden. But where did she get the gun? Why did she have a gun? The writers spent days on this, trying to work the gun subtly into the situation in various ways. Everything they tried was clumsy, wildly telegraphing to the audience that Swanson was going to be the murderer. Finally, they found the perfect solution. At the key moment, Swanson runs toward Holden, waving the gun and shouting, "I have a gun!" After all, do you care where she got it? It's enough that she has it . . . and is going to use it. You can *see* she got it from somewhere, and that's hardly as important to you at the moment as the issue of whether or not she'll get away with using it. (You already know that someone uses it. The movie began with Holden's corpse floating in the swimming pool.) "Movies are about emotions, not logic," Wilder explained. "We just left the explanation out. No one ever missed it."

Claudette Colbert has a classically terrifying problem in *Sleep, My Love* (1948) . . . should she take that drink her husband is offering her? And why does she keep waking up in strange places after she drinks his offerings?

In *Shadow of a Doubt,* a movie he directed in 1943, Alfred Hitchcock omitted any logical development or explanation of a major point in the plot. Teresa Wright, playing a young and innocent girl named Charlie, is happy to welcome her mysterious Uncle Charlie (her namesake) to town for a visit. Unbeknownst to her and her family, her uncle is the notorious "Merry Widow" murderer, who strangles wealthy women and steals their money. Two detectives are on the uncle's trail, and they show up in disguise as "survey takers," invading her family's home. One of the detectives (MacDonald Carey) takes Wright to the movies on what appears to be a normal date. They leave the movie, laughing and talking, sharing jokes and happy conversation. Suddenly the image dissolves away from their mundane date into a medium close-up of Teresa Wright, her face twisted in disbelief and shock, saying, "I know what you are . . . you're a detective. You're not a survey taker at all."

Although young Charlie has been shown to have an almost psychic connection to her uncle, the audience has had no specific narrative preparation for this sudden jump across the plot. There has been no scene in which Teresa Wright discusses her dawning suspicions or develops a dislike for her uncle. There has been no scene in which the detective has told her his suspicions. This will all come later on in the story. What happens here is that through a dissolve, a character goes immediately from one point of view—a state of innocence—to another point of view—a fully developed awareness. A dissolve is a filmic device that suggests passage of time, and in this regard, Hitchcock has simply spoken directly to you of what you inevitably know: this young girl will finally have to find out this information. Hitchcock omits laborious plot development through one skilled cinematic device, moving illogically in literary terms but logically in filmic terms forward in the story. It is also a way of further establishing young Charlie's quick and intuitive mind.

*Pickup on South Street* (1953), a tough film noir by producer-writer-director Samuel Fuller, omits much detail, jumping the story across time in dramatic ways. Whole details of plot development are ignored. For instance, the heroine (Jean Peters) and the hero (Richard Widmark), who have just met, are seen insulting one another, with Widmark socking Peters cruelly right on the jaw. Less than a minute later, he is massaging her jaw and kissing her. In this hot scene, which takes place in the isolated fishing shack that Widmark calls home, a large cargo hook is suddenly moved into the frame. The audience sees the couple kissing, but their image is dominated by the hook in the foreground. Peters and Widmark exchanged no pleasant conversation, went on no cute dates to the carnival. They did not tell each other their life stories. They just abruptly changed their relationship. Furthermore, they remain devoted, living and nearly dying for one another, and end the movie totally committed as a couple. But this is all you get for the development of their relationship—a big hook, that stands in for all those story lines you've seen in other movies.

This movie, which omits so much about Peters and Widmark, does the opposite with Thelma Ritter, playing a down-on-her-luck grifter. She has to walk home alone at night, trying to sell cheap ties to construction workers as she goes. This scene contains no actual plot development; just Ritter, a great character actress who was nominated for a Best Supporting Actress Oscar for the part, walking home trying to sell ties. But it sets up what is to follow—Ritter's murder—in which she poignantly says to her killer, "The way I feel right now . . . you'd be doin' me a favor." Without the prior short sequence that shows why she is tired and

Gloria Swanson plays silent film star Norma Desmond in the 1950 film *Sunset Boulevard*, a story about the inside of Hollywood made by Hollywood insiders.

how tired she is, neither the murder nor the line would have the same poignancy, the same resonance or sense of honest tragedy. Sometimes leaving things out for you can be used to make something left in all the more important. And because so much is left out of *Pickup on South Street*—the love story is nothing but a hook—the time spent on Ritter selling ties is all the more powerful and meaningful. Omission enhances later development.

Every Hollywood movie leaves something important out. That's how American movies tell their stories: by omission and through making audiences connect things. You'll allow yourself to jump willingly from an island in the Caribbean to a hotel room in Paris. You'll take it on faith that Grant and Saint got down from Mount Rushmore. You'll notice all the little things that are carefully planted to be seen, like a wink of the eye or a note passed secretly or a shadow that falls over someone's face. Every time you're given a privileged glance at something only one character can see, you'll make note. Every time something important is not there, you'll think it up for yourself.

Leaving things out holds you in your seat.

## Control

When it comes to controlling the audience, movies have it easy. When you read a novel, you can page ahead and read the end first. When you watch TV, you can change channels. When you're at a play, no matter how much the director has tried to block the actors to keep you looking at the leading lady sitting by the poisoned bottle of wine, if you want to you can look at your Aunt Tilly who's playing the maid standing over by the curtains. But at the movies, you see only what you are allowed to see, in the way you're supposed to see it. You can't look at Aunt Tilly if she's not in the frame. In fact, the movie can make you look at the leading lady *through* the poisoned wine in the bottle.

Good moviemakers ask themselves what they want you to see in a scene and how do they want you to see it. They consider what they want you to know about what you see and how they want you to feel about it. They plan for how they want you to react and for what they want you to carry forward from one scene to the next. They reveal and repress information so that it is discovered only when it is supposed to be. A bad movie is a movie in which this process breaks down, and what's coming can be guessed. An audience becomes bored and soon doesn't care anyway.

A masterful example of how a film is organized to control your understanding of—and response to—the story is Alfred Hitchcock's 1959 movie *North by Northwest*. In it, Cary Grant plays a sophisticated ad man who is mistaken for a political agent named George Kaplan. Grant spends most of the movie trying to find out who is trying to kill him and why. As it will turn out, the "who" are revealed early, and the "why" doesn't really matter. Because the story is told in a series of exciting events involving danger to Grant, no one really cares much about the why. The dangers are made strongly apparent. You can see them in almost every

*Pickup on South Street* (1953), directed by Samuel Fuller, is one of the best film noirs of the postwar period. Jean Peters (above) is threatened by FBI agents who have been trailing her. Her sense of confusion, heightened by threatening possibilities, is the fundamental essence of noir.

sequence. What is not as apparent is the clever way you are manipulated and controlled in the storytelling process itself. You are led to identify with Cary Grant, only to have that relationship shifted without your really noticing. At first, you know what Cary Grant knows. Then, you find out more than he knows. After that, you will be surprised to learn that you know less than he knows.

When you know what Cary Grant knows, it is an ordinary day and Grant sets out to the Plaza Hotel in Manhattan for lunch. His name is Roger Thornhill, and he's a successful Madison Avenue ad man. During his lunch he gets up to make a telephone call at the same time a man named George Kaplan is being paged. Grant is taken forcefully at gunpoint by two men who think he is Kaplan. Grant is not Kaplan. They've made a mistake. He knows that and you know that. Who are they? He doesn't know, and you don't know. Grant is taken to a Long Island mansion, interrogated, and set up to die. A full bottle of Scotch is poured into him, and he is put at the wheel of an automobile that is started down a long, dangerous, winding drive alongside the sea. This is a nightmare! You are put in a position that is the same as Cary Grant's for the majority of the trip downhill, except he's drunk and you're sober. You're in the car and struggling at the wheel—it's a hair-raising rush forward, totally out of control.

As the movie progresses, you begin to know more than Cary Grant knows. While Grant tries to figure things out, he is implicated in a murder at the United Nations and has to run for his life. While he is running, you are shown a scene in which government agents discuss the fact that there is no such person as George Kaplan. Kaplan is a decoy, a dummy agent that has been invented to lure the enemies and keep them occupied. You now know Grant is in danger from two sources: the police, who want him for murder, and the enemy agents, who think he is George Kaplan. He is going to try to find Kaplan, but you know this is not only wasted effort, but very, very dangerous. Grant boards a train in New York that is heading to Chicago, but authorities are searching the train. He is helped by a beautiful woman, played by Eva Marie Saint. She hides him, and he believes she is a friend, but you are allowed to discover she is secretly allied with Grant's enemies. In the morning, when they reach Chicago, Saint tells Grant he is to meet Mr. Kaplan at a destination that turns out to be a deserted cornfield. During this part of the film, your knowledge of what is happening is superior to Grant's.

In a later sequence, you know less than Cary Grant knows. At this point in the movie, you are allowed to assume that your knowledge and Grant's are reunited. He is rescued by the government agents, who explain the situation to him. Saint and Grant meet at Mount Rushmore. She quarrels with him when he obviously sees her as a glorified whore who slept with him for political reasons, and she shoots him. Later, you learn that Grant is not really dead or wounded. Saint only pretended to shoot him. This scene was faked for the enemy agents who were lurking in the Rushmore cafeteria to lead them to believe that Saint is still on their side and that Grant/Kaplan has been removed. Hitchcock has cleverly controlled your knowledge of what is going on and used it against you. Confident that you know more than Grant, you naturally do not expect his "death." Having seen it, you are so surprised that you do not have time to think it is a trick. Before you have too much time to doubt it or think about it, the truth is revealed. The ploy works because you trusted that you fully understood the situation.

*North by Northwest* ends with an extended sequence in which Cary Grant comes to a house atop Rushmore in order to rescue Saint. This sequence deploys everything that

Cary Grant runs for his life outdoors . . . the film's labyrinthine plot notwithstanding, the wide open spaces offer no safety and no place to hide in *North by Northwest* (1959). This is one of film's most famous chase scenes.

has happened before about what you know and do not know. Grant sneaks up on the house and climbs a ledge outside in order to look in a picture window and spy on the occupants. Just as if he were a member of a movie audience, like you, he sits watching. He sees one of the two villains (Martin Landau) shoot the other one (James Mason). What he sees is a fake shooting, just like the one you saw between Grant and Saint, because Landau is using Saint's gun in order to show Mason *they* can't trust her. Even though you had just seen one fake shooting, you still believe this one is real.

*North by Northwest* achieves a high level of suspense with every turn. In the film's most famous sequence, Grant has followed Saint's instructions to take a bus to meet "Kaplan" at a location in Indiana. When he gets out of the bus and stands in a wide open space under a beautiful sky, you *could* feel complacent, but because you now know more than Grant does, you are anticipating danger. You are nervous and prepared for anything. Every single thing that happens—a car that drives by, a man who arrives to wait for the bus—could be the source of murder. The use of moments of silence as Grant waits, Hitchcock's own reputation as a master of suspenseful films, the imaginative cutting of the sequence—all contribute to your response. Hitchcock has given you one subjective romp in the careening car when Grant was drunk. Now he gives you a different, more subtle scare.

This type of thing is a trademark of Alfred Hitchcock's work. He explained it numerous times in interviews by citing the example of his movie *Sabotage* (1937). In this movie, a little boy is carrying a package with a bomb in it, but, of course, he does not know that. The boy boards a crowded bus, and you are forced to wait for the inevitable explosion. Hitchcock makes the point over and over again that this is the definition of involved suspense—knowing something is going to happen but not knowing when—as opposed to movie shock, just having it suddenly happen. You know that both things are effective. Whereas you *can* jump out of your seat at an unexpected explosion. You also know that Hitchcock is right. Knowing a bad thing is about to happen keeps you, as they say, "on the edge of your seat."

The kind of maneuvering of knowledge in *North by Northwest*—the subtle shifting of your relationship to the information given out by the story—sounds academic when described on paper. When you are watching *North by Northwest*, however, it is anything but pedantic. The movie is pure entertainment, and it was a highly successful box-office draw when first released. Cary Grant and Eva Marie Saint's "pickup" love scenes on the train are wonderfully modern and sexy, and the adventure holds your attention even though it is utterly meaningless. *North by Northwest* has an exceptional cast, director, collaboration team, screenwriter, and top-notch production values. It epitomizes how Hollywood movies controlled the flow of information, or story release, to keep you totally involved and entertained while watching it.

Perhaps one of the easiest ways to show how Hollywood films controlled audiences is to examine the famous storytelling device, the movie flashback. A simplified definition of the term *flashback* is this: "A scene in which a return to action that happened before the film began is shown." Actually, in order to cover all the possibilities of the flashback, it might be better to say: "A return to a visual past from a visually established present for some specific narrative purpose and from a consistent point of view, with a further understanding being given about how much time passed both within and outside of the flashback itself."

The flashback was one of Hollywood's most trusted devices for telling a story that created a very specific relationship with the audience. Flashbacks were used only when they could accomplish something that presumably could not be achieved if the story were told straightforwardly in linear fashion. There has to be a reason to tell the story by giving the ending first . . . or by presenting events out of the order of their chronological sequence. The main reason was a simple one: flashbacks can also deceive.

Think about how flashbacks work. First of all, you are being told right at the very beginning of the situation how the movie turns out, or at least where a character stands in life, or in the plot. The flashback appears to be saying to you, "Let me tell you how this happened." or "Let me explain things to you." It also seems to be saying, "Let me tell you the truth." Audiences were quick to find out, of course, that it was not that simple. Often enough, the ending that appeared at the beginning *was* straightforwardly explained. But sometimes it was denied. It was all a dream and it never really happened! Or, the character dying in the gutter and telling his story was miraculously cured and lived on anyway. Sometimes the movie was left ambivalent—what really *had* happened, or what really was going to happen next—after the lights came back up?

If you went to the movies regularly when flashbacks were popular, you learned soon enough not to be certain which of these things was going to happen. Going to the past for the "truth" was no guarantee that you knew where things stood. What you did come to understand was that the story was being told in a context of a final event that mattered. You knew you were watching a story that was being told with an attitude or from a specific point of view. This was further made true by the fact that most flashbacks were narrated or told from the perception of one particular character.

When a story is being "told" to you by a narrator, you tend to believe it. The voice creates an intimate relationship with you. Of course, a narration can also be a distancing device, in that it can say that events happened years ago or that no one knows if it ever happened or is really true and it can take a "voice of God" or "historical presentation" stance. Typically, however, a narrating voice is that of a character inside the story that is going to be told. It can be a minor character, or it can be the hero or heroine. It might also be a child telling parents, or the voice of a "reporter" who has gathered facts and will share them. What counts is that the voice of the narrator is established to bring you under its control. You allow it to tell you "the truth."

In Orson Welles's *Citizen Kane* (1941), the story is told in overlapping flashbacks out of chronological sequence. The model for this format occurred earlier in the lesser-known movie *The Power and the Glory* (1933), written by Preston Sturges and directed by William K. Howard. *Kane* is presented as a puzzle: newspaper magnate Kane's final word before he died was a hoarsely whispered "Rosebud." But what is "Rosebud?" A reporter seeks the answer, slowly putting the pieces of a puzzle together. A newsreel at the beginning of the movie actually tells the superficial details of Kane's life—who he married, who he didn't marry, how he got money and made more money, how he ran for office and didn't win. These facts, however, do not really tell his story. As the people who knew Kane tell the private events they witnessed, his life has its outer layers stripped away to show the messy part underneath. Still, Kane's story remains an enigma, and the meaning of "Rosebud" is never discovered—except, of course, by you.

You find out the big secret at the very end of the movie as the camera takes you—and only you—inside a burning furnace for a privileged peek: "Rosebud" was his childhood sled, a symbol of his lost family life. This information becomes an ironic comment on the inability to understand fully what motivates any man. To tell Kane's story any other way would destroy the main point the movie is making.

*Laura* (1944), directed by Otto Preminger, opens with the unmistakable voice of Clifton Webb saying, "I shall never forget the weekend Laura died. A silver sun burned through the sky like a huge magnifying glass. It was the hottest Sunday in my recollection. I felt as if I were the only human being left in New York. For Laura's horrible death, I was alone. I, Waldo Lydecker, was the only one who really knew her. I had just begun to write Laura's story when another of those detectives came to see me. I had him wait. I could watch him through the half-open door. I noticed that his attention was fixed upon my clock. There was only one other in existence, and that was in Laura's apartment, in the very room where she was murdered."

This voice-over has been discussed and debated by film connoisseurs for years. The movie ends with Lydecker's death; but since the film opens with him seemingly speaking in present time about past events, is this the voice of a dead man? The movie cleverly draws you in and conceals from you the fact that Webb plays the murderer, largely through this controlling narration. We assume that if he is telling the story and the story is a search that will end with the finding of the murderer, he must not have been the murderer. This narration also refers to the clock, which has a duplicate in the murder room. Boldly, the film has introduced both the murderer and the place where he hid the murder weapon. It is a "purloined letters" plot. With Webb's obsession with Laura out in the open and with the hiding place directly referred to, your doubts and suspicions are erased accordingly. The voice-over also helps to convince you that Laura is dead, but she isn't.

Opposite: A dramatic signature image of *Citizen Kane*, a film that uses overlapping, out-of-sequence flashbacks.
Above: Ray Collins abandons a frantic Welles (as Kane).
Right: The young Charles Foster Kane (Buddy Swann), his beloved sled, *Rosebud*, in hand, is introduced by his mother (Agnes Moorehead), to the banker (George Coulouris) who will take him away from his childhood world of love and security. His hapless father (Harry Shannon) looks on.

Making the audience think that Laura has been murdered is accomplished with more credibility in this manner of storytelling. An important part of the movie's ambience concerns the detective (Dana Andrews) and his growing obsession with a portrait of the beautiful Laura. When he falls asleep in Laura's favorite chair under her portrait in her apartment, he has apparently fallen totally under her spell. When she unlocks the door and calmly enters the room, awakening him, his sight of her becomes more than the news that she's not dead. It confirms the lyrics of the title song that Laura "is only a dream." This organization of the story makes the movie more than an ordinary mystery. It creates an ambience and an atmosphere that is truly haunting and obsessive. Through voice-overs and flashbacks and concealment you surrender to *Laura*'s atmosphere and to its control of your knowledge of Laura and her friends.

The reason filmmakers choose to use a flashback is that it is a device that provides maximum control over what you know. When you look at a movie that has one, you can ask yourself—would it be the same story without the flashback? Would it have had the same effect on me? Unless the movie is a botched job, the answer would have to be no.

Novels, of course, also use the device of returning a reader to a past event, but films have the possibility of manipulating a viewer's sense of time in a unique way. For instance, in *Out of the Past* (1947) Robert Mitchum drives a car from a small town in California to Lake Tahoe. As he drives, he tells the story of his life to his passenger. In the twenty or so minutes it takes for the film to pass through the projector in real time, several years of his life are covered, and he and his passenger have passed the night away, from dark to dawn.

In *Ruthless* (1948), a story is shown on the screen that technically does not take any time at all to tell. A man strikes a match, and you fade into the story. When you come out of it, the match has flared up and is being used to light a cigarette—no screen time has passed at all. But about twenty minutes passed while you sat in your seat. And years passed within the narrative dilation.

In *The Locket* (1946), Laraine Day plays a beautiful young woman who is about to marry a rich man. The film opens with an elegant reception to celebrate their coming nuptials. An uninvited guest arrives (Brian Aherne) who proceeds to tell the would-be groom (Gene Raymond) a hideous story about how Day's character is a psychiatrically disturbed woman who only seems to be normal.

This idea is not so unusual, but the way it is told to the audience *is* unusual. Brian Aherne tells how he met and married Day and everything was fine until the day her former lover, played by Robert Mitchum, came to see him to tell him about *his* experience with her. Inside Aherne's flashback about Day, Robert Mitchum begins to tell *his* flash-

An unusual flashback structure defines *The Locket* (1946).
Opposite: Shadows fill the world of an artist's (Robert Mitchum's) garret for a meeting with Laraine Day.
Above: Mitchum and Day are desperate and trapped, having just found a dead body; below, a world of party-goers admire one of Mitchum's paintings, innocent of events above.

back about her. A flashback within a flashback! And as if that weren't convoluted enough, inside Mitchum's flashback comes a moment in which Day tells *him* a story of a traumatic event of her childhood in which she was accused of stealing a locket from the daughter of the rich household in which her mother was employed. A flashback within a flashback within a flashback. Furthermore, the audience is not taken back to the present abruptly. Instead, Day's flashback returns to the "present" of Mitchum's flashback, which in turn returns to the "present" of Aherne's flashback and then to the actual present.

Why tell you the story this way? In this case, the movie is about a woman whose traumatic childhood experience turned her into a liar, a murderer, and a thief. On the surface, however, she is beautiful and seemingly honest. You can't tell if Aherne is crazy himself or telling a lie because he still loves her or what. You have to go down to the inner layer of her story, or strip away her surface protections, to find out. Having found out, you feel only sympathy for her and need the rest of the story (the layers that move back to the present) to find out how sick she really is. The unusual format carries out the theme of the movie and keeps the audience in total suspense. It also provides an excellent way of concealing information and controlling your conclusions about whether Day is really crazy and evil or just maligned.

One of the most unusual and controversial flashbacks is in Hitchcock's *Stage Fright* (1950). It comes immediately after the film opens and tells a story that turns out to be a lie. Since it lays a foundation for everything you are going to believe in the plot, it's a bold example of controlling what you know. For years, *Stage Fright* was written off by critics because "it cheats." "You cannot tell a lie in the movies like that," people said. Film, of course, is the liar's medium. It always tells lies. The question is—can a movie tell a lie in a flashback and be fair to you? Has the film broken faith with you?

It *is* fair if hints are given to you along the way, and in that sense, *Stage Fright* plays fair. First of all, its story is all about lies and liars, performers and performances. Everybody in the film is deceptive at some point, and nearly everyone takes on a role other than the one they are playing. Layers and layers are piled on. The well-known actress Jane Wyman plays the role of the character called "Eve." (Already a deceit, since she's not Eve, of course. She's Jane Wyman.) Eve pretends to be "Doris," disguising herself as another character to get information about the murder. And in case you are paying close attention, Jane Wyman as "Eve/Doris" walks around wearing a smock with the name "Nellie" embroidered on it. Marlene Dietrich plays an actress who is as adept at giving a performance off-stage as on, and Alastair Sim as Wyman's father is a lying old reprobate.

In *Stage Fright* (1950) killer Richard Todd traps the innocent Jane Wyman. A story with a lying flashback and a film with intense close-ups cut by a light that illuminates fear and desperation.

This beautiful image from director William Wyler's *The Heiress* (1949) is one example of the skillful use of the language of film throughout the production. Olivia DeHavilland played a spinster chased by a fortune-hunter, a story based on Henry James's novel *Washington Square*.

You are also given other clues. At the very opening of the movie, a stage safety curtain is slowly raised up after the credits. After it rises, you see—not a stage set— but a real street with a real car on it. Or, if you want to be serious about it, not a real street, of course, but a picture of a real street with a real car. Suddenly, you see that same "real car" racing along against what is obviously a fake rear projection. Curtains going up announce to you that things are not real, but fake, and curtains keep getting raised and lowered all through the movie.

The flashback itself comes to you before you have a chance to know either of the two characters involved: Wyman, who is hearing the story, and Richard Todd, playing the liar who tells it. Since you can have no judgement about either character, you just take the flashback as truth. However, as the film unfolds, Todd is never protected from your suspicion. He is seen to be emotional, unreliable, selfish, and, well, *suspicious*. He tells lies. He also disappears from the action for a long time, which any skilled viewer of murder mysteries knows is a way of hiding who-done-it.

## The Tools of the Trade

In one of their most bizarre short films, the Three Stooges find themselves in jail. Learning they are to be executed the next morning, they realize they must devise a foolproof plan to get out of their cell. But how? They are in a cramped space with only one small bed and an unreachable window. They scratch their heads and grimace. They pace and wonder. Suddenly, one of them has the answer: "I know!" he cries out. "We'll use the tools!" He triumphantly goes to the bed, turns back the mattress and reveals a convenient set of high-level tools suitable for any form of jail break. They pick them up and are soon out on the streets. It's a lesson to us all. The tools are always there if you know where to look, and Hollywood filmmakers knew where to look.

During the golden age of the studio system in Hollywood, the finest talents in all areas of movie production were under contract, available to contribute creatively to any film on a daily basis, six days a week. As many as 450 to 500 feature films per year were made, not including newsreels, cartoons, shorts, and previews. The war in Europe further motivated the best talent from France, England, Germany, Scandinavia, Italy, and Spain to come to Hollywood to live and work. It was a time in which everyone in America went regularly to the movies more than once a week. Since so many films were made, and since so much money was available and the audience was practically guaranteed, there was more experimentation in movies than there is now. Contrary to popular belief, Hollywood in the old days often took chances, and studios let many artists try things. Although anyone who ran over budget was in trouble, the people who ran Hollywood *did* let some filmmakers play with their tools.

Today, the result of this development of the medium is the "language of film," the practical use of the filmmaker's tools in editing, camera movement and angle, lighting, composition. This "language" also includes performance, sound and music, dialogue, sound effects, costumes, settings, and locations. Most important, it means the complicated interaction of all these things as applied to whatever kind of story is being told. Like a brain surgeon, a filmmaker has to learn to use the right tool at the right time, and the choice all depends on what is wanted from the audience. The way to understand movies is this skilled use of tools—the basis of Hollywood style.

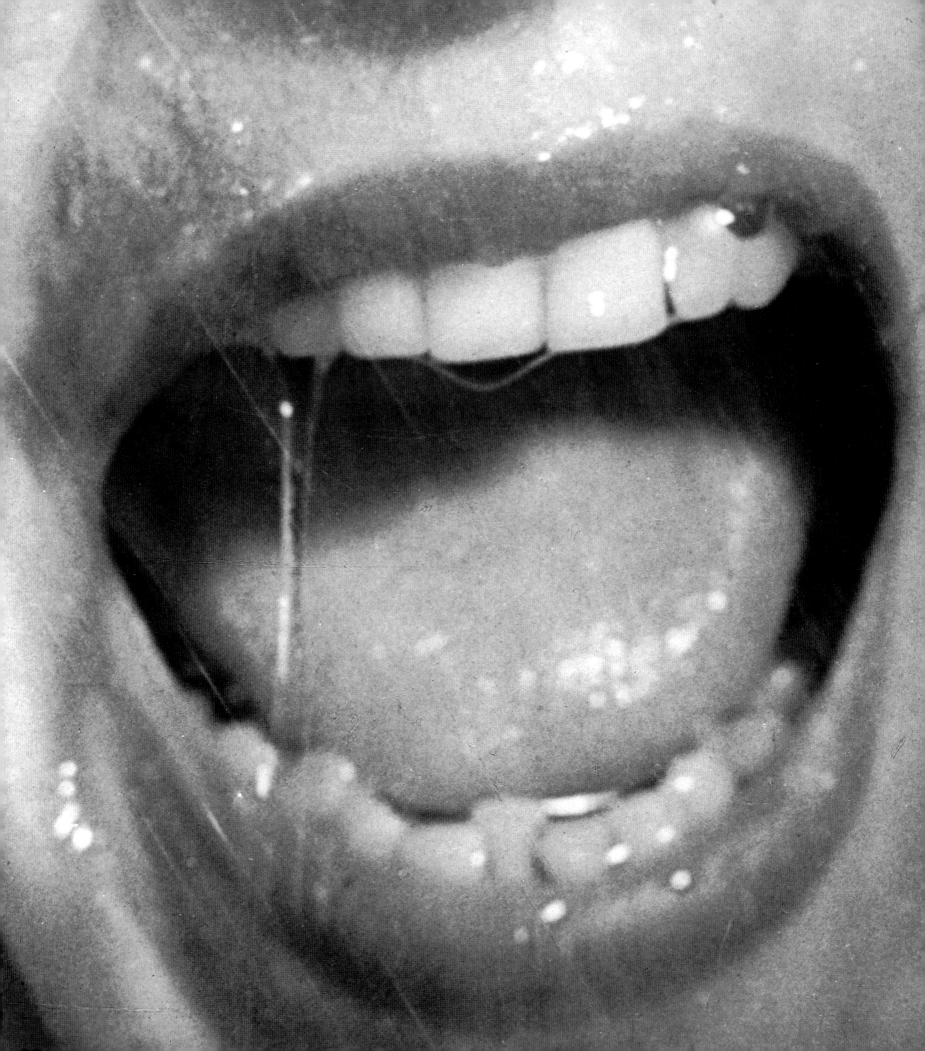

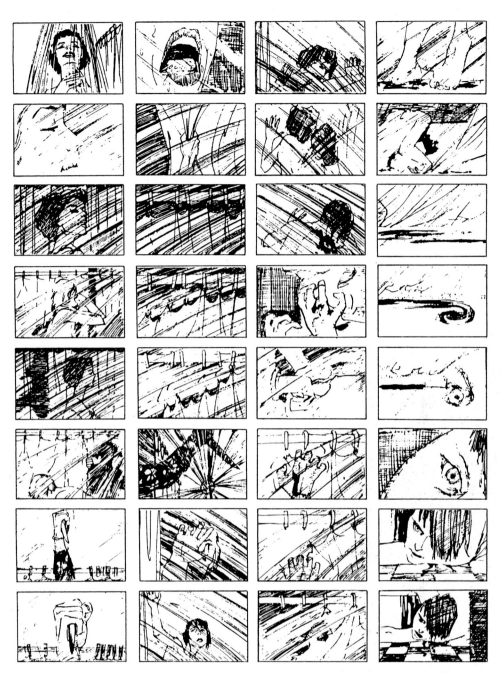

One of the most famous sequences in film history, the shower stabbing from Hitchcock's *Psycho* (1960). Opposite: Janet Leigh's desperate scream as she is attacked. Above: The original storyboards for the sequence to be shot.

## Editing

"The two things we constantly juggle in editing are character and narration. When should one supersede the other and when are they in tandem? When is one outweighing the other? The interesting thing about editing is that you can analyze a script a number of times before it's shot, and yet it's a completely different thing once it's shot. Everyone has brought their own quality to it, and then the adjustments are actually very subtle."

Carol Littleton

*Psycho:* The film cuts dynamically between the mysterious unidentified stabber . . . and the victim (Anthony Perkins in drag and Janet Leigh in the shower).

One of the unique tools of filmmaking is editing, or the organization of visual material for you so that you see a character, follow a plot development, understand a motivation, or respond emotionally or intellectually to what you are seeing on the screen. Various strategies for editing a film exist—continuity editing, point-of-view editing, and so on, but let's take a simple look at what happens for you as you watch according to the choices that are made for you in this regard.

Suppose a movie has a simple piece of action to show you: an unknown assailant will enter a bathroom and stab a woman to death in her shower. This is not an uncommon scene in the movies. Now suppose the filmmakers are deciding how to shoot and cut this scene. Which tools to use? Here is where the filmmaker clearly thinks about how the audience is going to see the scene. Suppose it is absolutely imperative that you *not* be able to see who the assailant is. And suppose the woman in the shower has appeared to be the leading character in the movie so far, so that it should come as a huge shock and surprise to you that she is going to die. There are two goals here, but one is a problem—keeping secret who is doing the stabbing. The scene could be shot without much light, but why would a woman take a shower in the dark? And if you are supposed to be really surprised and horrified, you've got to be able to see what is going on, don't you? The scene could be shot from a very, very high angle above looking down, but this is not a Busby Berkeley musical, and the degree of distance might lessen the horror. Also, showing a hideous stabbing with blood against the white shower tiles under a bright light somehow makes it all the more frightening. And there's another thing. You certainly take showers. Showing the murder in this space puts it right in your own everyday world, your own bathroom. The best choice for the filmmakers is to opt to design this film as an exercise in montage, or rapid cutting, in which the scene is cut up into little pieces of film, all broken apart.

Everyone knows this scene. It is one of the most famous in the history of film—the well-known "murder in the shower" sequence from Alfred Hitchcock's *Psycho* (1960). Hitchcock, a director who generally favored montage (editing) over long takes, *could* have shown the shower sequence as a long take, or in two sections. However, by showing it as hundreds of little pieces of film, broken apart, he accomplished several key goals. He suggests a parallel of cutting and hacking between form (the editing process) and content (the stabbing event on the screen); he controls your involvement—making you keep your eyes on the screen by never allowing you to look away. (You are not revolted because what you see is definite, but unspecific. You feel you will miss information if you don't watch. You want to see who the killer is. Your involvement is increased accordingly). He does not allow you a clear look at the killer. And, not unimportant, he also avoided censorship restrictions, as no one frame allows you to see a full view of the naked woman's body.

Hitchcock builds up your participation in the actual stabbing through montage. If the event were presented as a long take, your response would be less emotionally involved and would become more expository. You would be watching primarily for information. You would feel less threatened and would be more critical, more analyti-

cal. By turning the stabbing into an event that is horrible, frightening, sudden, and *unclear*, the movie increases your fear and irrational response while it decreases your chances of "catching on." Most important, it makes you feel like you've been stabbed and yet you were also a voyeur in the position of the stabber.

There is one other thing to realize about what happens when you watch the shower scene in *Psycho*. Although you are deeply involved, your involvement is, by design, almost completely emotional. The scene sweeps over you, riveting you to the screen and blocking the thinking and questioning process out. Other movies use editing to bring you in and start you thinking—while still presenting a highly charged emotional moment on the screen. *Criss Cross* (1949), starring Burt Lancaster, has a very simple scene: Lancaster walks into a bar, goes over to the dance floor, and watches a beautiful woman dance with her partner to a Latin beat. It could be just an ordinary moment, background to a larger story—a kind of pause before important events begin to happen. On the contrary, this sequence is a key development in both the plot, the relationships of the two characters (Lancaster and Yvonne De Carlo, who plays the woman), and the inevitable doom of Lancaster. The scene is a miniature sample of what turns out to be the story, the relationship, *and* the doom: De Carlo is able to manipulate Lancaster to keep him enthralled.

By using cutting, music, lighting, composition, and point-of-view shots, the movie lets you understand four things: Yvonne De Carlo does a hot dance with Tony Curtis while Burt Lancaster watches her . . . De Carlo is aware that Lancaster is watching, but pretends she isn't . . . Lancaster watches her in a way that shows he is helplessly drawn to her . . . he can't take his eyes off her . . . De Carlo controls Lancaster's view of her.

This adds up to the understanding on your part that you have seen how one character looks at another and lusts for her, but you have also seen the dance from three points of view: that of De Carlo, who sees Lancaster but pretends not to; that of Lancaster, who sees her as beautiful and sexy; and your own view of all of this, in which you add up everything for a full understanding of the plot and characterization involved.

The articulation of a full relationship and its implications has taken place. Although the beginning of the movie has shown you that these two have a hot romance (the film opens up on their smooching in a parking lot), this scene is important for understanding how Lancaster got into that embrace in the parking lot in the first place (the movie partially takes place in flashback). The cutting and music work to do something different from the shower scene in *Psycho*. Here, you are asked to both feel *and* think:

The scene begins with a cut to where Burt Lancaster walks into his favorite bistro. He walks the length of the bar, coming to its end just as some Latin music from the dance floor begins. Lancaster is seen turning toward the music, heading to stand at the edge of the floor and watch the dancers.

After the initial cut, which takes you into Lancaster's arriving at the bar to begin his walk, there are thirty-one cuts in slightly more than two minutes of screen time. The scene is played out as an orgasmic presentation, with the music, the cutting, and the frenzy of the dancing increasing in tempo and intensity as the scene progresses.

# CRISS CROSS:    Lancaster Meets DeCarlo

1. Cut to a shot of the orchestra and dancers, the Latin music swelling as the orchestra leader begins to play a high-pitched flute and the rhythm begins to intensify.

2. Cut to a medium close-up of the flute player. As he plays, the camera moves to the frame left to show a close-up of Yvonne De Carlo dancing. Her face is seen over her partner's shoulder, with his back to the camera. She looks up at her partner, and then looks frame right (toward the direction in which Lancaster would presumably be standing by now). A very, very small change of expression, represented by her sudden blink and by a tiny acknowledgment of *something* crosses her face. A small smile she was forming disappears.

3. Cut back to the flute player, now seen from the other side of where he would be on the bandstand.

4. Cut to a medium close-up of Lancaster watching the dancers. His face is immobile but expressing some kind of inner feeling that is both passionate and painful.

5. Cut back to De Carlo dancing, moving around so her partner's face is now toward the camera and her back is to us *and* to Lancaster. She twirls around her partner, then spins again. At the start of this cut, De Carlo seems to be looking toward Lancaster, and after her first twirl, she is looking that way again. Her mouth turns down in a purposeful movement. Then she spins again.

6. Cut back to Lancaster same as in #4.

7. Cut to De Carlo. Dancing freely, passionately, to the Latin music, which is intensifying. She spins, dips, looks only at her partner. She never looks at Burt Lancaster again.

8. Cut to piano player.

9. Cut to the bongo drummers.

10. Cut to a close-up of the piano player's hands.

11. Cut to an intense close up of De Carlo, showing only her head as she spins in dance.

12. Cut back to the piano player's hands. His head enters the frame as he bends down toward his own hands.

13. Cut to close up of Lancaster, watching.

14. Cut to close up of De Carlo, dancing, spinning, not looking toward Lancaster.

15. Cut to piano player's hands.

16. Cut to orchestra member's hands, shaking maracas.

17. Cut to piano player's hands.

18. Cut to hands shaking maracas.

19. Cut to bongo drummers again.

20. Cut to medium shot of De Carlo in dance. She and her partner are concentrating intently on one another as they dance. They move frame right, passing by the spot where Lancaster is now seen standing, watching them. They do not look at him. Other dancers pass, also.

21. Cut back to flute player, same as #3 above.

22. Cut to Lancaster in medium shot, watching, dancers passing by him.

23. Cut to De Carlo and partner again, spinning.

24. Cut to Lancaster.

25. Cut to hands shaking maracas.

26. Cut to flute player, same as in #3.

27. Cut to De Carlo spinning again.

28. Cut to flute player, same as first time we saw him in #1.

29. Cut to bongo drummers

30. Cut to the flute player, who has now stopped playing his flute as music dies down.

31. Cut to sight of audience clapping, turned toward orchestra. De Carlo and partner are among this group.

De Carlo pretends to have one relationship to Lancaster but actually has another. He deals with her as he really feels. In the sense that she is controlling *his* viewing, by making him watch her, she is controlling him. But she appears not to be. Again, this is the story of the film and the story of their relationship.

In addition to the establishment of both characters and their feelings and attitudes toward one another, the editing created an atmosphere of passion and sexual desire. To spend more than two minutes just showing Burt Lancaster watch Yvonne De Carlo dance could be boring. Instead, it is a steamy and very meaningful sequence, and does much to create the sleazy power of the movie and its story. It lays down the meaning needed: she will betray him, and he will be helpless.

This type of cutting to involve you in multidimensional understanding is common to movies today. *Witness* (1985)—an appropriate title—is grounded in a scene in which a little Amish boy on his first visit to a big city accidentally sees a brutal murder. The boy peeks out from one of the stalls in the men's room where the killing takes place. You are shown what he sees from his point of view, and you are also shown how he looks while he is watching. You are shown what is happening from outside the stall as well as from inside it, and you are shown one of the killers searching the stalls after he hears a noise. These different points of view are cut together to create different responses: horror—the violent murder that you see; tension—the boy hiding in the stall and his potential discovery; terror—the boy's fear as he watches; curiosity—the boy has never witnessed anything like this before; pressure—you accompany Danny Glover, who plays the killer who searches. As you watch, you never think how the tools of cinema are being used to switch you from aligning with the boy, to aligning with Glover, to aligning with your own role as audience. Skillful manipulation brings the maximum out of the scene—and brings you the maximum amount of involvement and entertainment at the same time.

## Long Takes

The scenes described, from *Psycho*, *Criss Cross*, and *Witness*, use editing to achieve their goals. Cutting is used to organize time and space and the narrative event. Suppose the opposite is done, and a long take, uninterrupted by cuts, allows you to see the entire action as a unified and coherent event. A famous example of a breathtaking long-take introduction to a movie is in *Touch of Evil*, an Orson Welles film of 1958. A single take runs for nearly three minutes. (A recent homage to this take was the eight-minute opening to Robert Altman's 1992 *The Player*. In the case of *The Player*, however, no actual narrative development takes place other than establishing people in Hollywood making silly deals.)

As *Touch of Evil* opens, you are plunged directly into an event. You see a close-up shot of a man's hands holding a bomb on which is set a timing device. The camera moves back to reveal the man holding the device. It is dark—early evening—and the man sneaks toward an open convertible, where he plants the bomb in the car's trunk and runs away. As he completes his action and departure, a second man and a blonde girl in a strapless dress come into the frame and head for the car. The credits of the film have started to roll throughout this long take, and music on the soundtrack begins as the man and girl approach the car.

The couple get into the car and begin to drive it forward, away from the bottom of the frame. As the car turns left at frame top, preparing to go around a building, the camera moves across the frame bottom to where the man with the bomb had been originally standing, so that as the car turns left, it is turning down toward frame bottom or toward the camera's position. The camera has picked the car up as it moved, rejoining it. The camera begins to track backwards so that you can observe the car moving forward. The car is moving slowly as there is a lot of foot traffic on the street. It is obviously a warm night, and many people are out and about, looking for fun and taking the air. As the car moves and is preceded by the moving camera, it arrives at a crosswalk. The car stops, and the camera turns to pick up a strolling couple, two more unknown characters.

These two are "unknowns" in terms of the story being told, but they are obviously going to be important to the movie because they are recognizable to you as Janet Leigh and Charlton Heston. You automatically know that they are important and probably *not* going to be blown up. The camera begins to follow *them* for you, instead of the car. The car moves out of the frame. The camera continues tracking back until the two couples are seen again together in the frame as they approach the Mexican border crossing. The car with the man and blonde woman is at frame left and Heston and Leigh are at frame right, engaged in a casual conversation with the border guard. As they give him their documents for inspection, they talk about getting an ice cream cone. On the other side of the border, you can see Mexican men are talking to the man driving the car about how he "caught the big boss." The "Grande family" is mentioned. During these two simultaneous actions, the blonde tries to get the guard's attention. She is trying to tell him that she keeps hearing a ticking sound. ("I've got this ticking noise in my head.") Otherwise, all the talk is casual. The camera follows Leigh and Heston across the border, and the car again disappears out of frame. Leigh and Heston stop to embrace, and, as they kiss, a large flash of light covers them. An explosion is heard off-screen. As they turn to look, the first cut of the movie shows you a burning car.

Welles chose to begin the movie with one coherently recorded event, a "long take" that is a miniature story unto itself. It is a piece of clear action that has a beginning, middle, and end of its own.

By allowing the action to unfold within one long take, Welles *pretends* to let you see the two couples as unrelated, as accidentally in the same space. The explosion of the car seems to happen at random in Heston and Leigh's evening stroll for some ice cream. Since the entire movie is about how this event affects their lives and their relationship, it is an excellent statement of theme, done with virtuoso mastery of tools.

By shooting this scene in long take, Welles accomplishes these goals: making the cut, when it does come, of great dramatic importance; increasing your tension because you are never taken out of the situation in which you know the planted bomb is going to explode; establishing of all five characters and showing their proximity to each other by how endangered they all are; introducing two leading characters as living innocently in a dangerous situation not of their creation; establishing two tracks the film will be exploring—that of the story of the bomb and who planted it and why, and the love story of Heston and Leigh (the film is going to interweave these two stories, and show how the love relationship is affected by the other story).

*"The audience wanted to escape— not to a different galaxy, not to a different world—but to their own world as they might have wanted it to be."*

Joseph Mankiewicz

## Camera Movement

The long take of *Touch of Evil* is achieved through imaginative use of tracking shots. (A tracking shot is made by a moving camera that follows the action, either in front of, behind, or beside the moving object or person.) When a movie provides you with an extended, constantly changing view of events, moving forward in a logical, un-broken manner, you are seeing the use of a convenient tool, the tracking shot. Basic usage of such shots can accomplish different goals: exposition (shows you where you are, what it looks like, what the parameters of its spaces are); atmosphere (shows you that you are in a special place, with particular look and attitudes, colors, people and things, and dangers); subjective alliance (puts you behind the eyes of one specific character, shows you how that character sees the space he or she is walking through, or puts you in the position of following one particular character); and all of the above or some of the above.

A beautifully effective tracking shot occurs at the beginning of Otto Preminger's 1965 movie about World War II, *In Harm's Way*. Camera movement brings you slowly into a dance that is being held at the Naval Officer's Club in Hawaii on the night of December 6, 1941. This information is revealed to you first by establishing the music, the peaceful atmosphere, and the glamour of the club and its dance. The camera starts to move outside on a moonlit night, tracking into the area as sounds grow louder. The orchestra is playing Big Band music of the 1940s. Tracking past a table on which are neatly placed white caps of Naval officers, the camera seeks out a chalkboard that announces "Commissioned Officers Mess, Ford Island, U.S. Naval Station, Pearl Harbor, December 6, 1941, Dance." The camera then moves gracefully inside and ironically shows you the carefree, happy couples at their dance. There are no cuts.

Tracking shots are long, elegant camera movements, but not all camera movements track forward in extended spaces. You can receive information in movies from camera movements that do other things. For instance, sometimes the camera moves to show you a new space in the frame or to change your viewing perspective on that space. The camera follows characters for you so you can see what they are doing, where they are going. It moves away from them, watches them, goes ahead of them, always taking you along and placing you in a specific relationship to them. There is a big difference for you, as you watch a movie, as to whether the movie crosscuts between two characters who are talking to each other or instead has them sit opposite one another with the camera moving back and forth between them. The first—crosscutting—puts the char-acters in separate spaces. They seem equal in importance. Or, according to what they are saying—or depending on the angle from which they are seen—one can dominate the other. They are separate. The reactions they have to one another, as well as what they are saying, clearly tell you how to see them, but camera movement is further sug-gesting what is their relationship. You are an observer, and you are also not part of this scene. In the second example, the camera is clearly setting up a "third person" in the action. That person has to be you. As the camera swings back and forth you are objec-tively seeing two people in the frame, and you are placed directly into the situation. You have to decide what their relationship is for yourself.

*"American cinema is international like the fairy tales were international."*

Bernard Tavernier

If you enter a scene as a viewer and see two people sitting in chairs talking to one another for two minutes, and the camera, for the first time, moves directly up close to one of the people, the effect is sudden and dramatic. Camera movements can also be dreamlike, seemingly attached to no human form, floating through space in an ethereal way. The opening of *Rebecca* (1940) has such a camera movement, as a voice-over says, "Last night I dreamed I went to Manderlay . . ." while the camera moves forward along a road that turns, revealing the burned-out mansion. Both the camera and the narrated line suggest a dreamlike state. Camera movements can also be joyous and exhilarating, as when Gene Kelly is dancing in the rain in *Singin' in the Rain* (1952) and the camera takes off up the street in a rush of joyous action. Cameras can stalk, as in countless horror films, and they can seek out. In today's filmmaking world the invention of the Steadicam (a camera that can literally be worn by an operator, so the photographer can move rapidly through spaces of any sort at a high speed), has created newer, freer, even more dramatic uses of camera movement. In the German movie *Das Boot* (1981) the rapid movements of the Steadicam through a cramped U-boat show both the excitement of combat *and* the truly small spaces the men must live in. Another example of Steadicam sustained camera movement is seen in director Martin Scorsese's *Goodfellas* (1990), in which the hero and his girlfriend enter the Copacabana through a downstairs kitchen and wind their way through tiny halls and doorways upstairs into the main nightclub.

## Time

So often people will say, "Oh, I remember that scene! It went on and on. It took forever until the child was rescued." Later they see the movie again and are amazed to realize that the scene really took only seconds. Stanley Cavell has written about this memory phenomenon in his book *A World Viewed*. He describes how films remembered are not the same thing as the films themselves. Your mind stretches out certain scenes, shortens others, and makes its own definitions of characters and motivations. The subtitle of Cavell's book, *The Ontology of Film*, places this phenomenon, well-known to moviegoers and planned in advance by filmmakers, in suitable academic terms, legitimizing what is one of the fundamental relationships to the audience that is being described here. Most of these memories, inaccurate in all but emotional recall, have to do with time—the subtle play films make with it, stretching it out and closing it up, cheating its reality.

In movies, there are three kinds of time for you: the amount of real time it takes for the film to run through the projector, the running time itself (actual time); the amount of time that is supposed to be taking place inside the story that is told on the screen, for instance, a twenty-four-hour period, ten years, a century, or whatever (chronological story time); and the way you experience the events, in what film theorist Bela Balaz defined as "psychological time—your impression of the duration of what you see." Seldom do the second and third categories correspond to the first, but two famous Hollywood films in which they correspond are *High Noon* and *The Set-Up*. Both of these movies cleverly establish time as an essential narrative issue.

In director Robert Wise's *The Set-Up* (1949), an aging boxer is getting ready for yet another tough fight in a sleazy town called Paradise City. In seventy-two minutes of "real" time, he prepares for the fight, argues with his wife, discovers that his manager has promised he'll take a dive, and takes the ring against a scrappy youngster. He feels he can win and thereby gain enough money to buy the contract of a younger fighter and transform his life by becoming a manager. He has seventy-two minutes to prepare, discover, and form his resolve with his entire future in balance.

In Fred Zinnemann's *High Noon* (1952), the sheriff learns at ten-thirty in the morning that, at exactly noon, a man he sentenced to prison is returning to town to kill him. He has about ninety minutes to get ready. Time is everything in *High Noon*. Time is the title; time is the psychological pressure on the hero; and time is the physical reality of his existence. The theme of time is present in that the past dominates all characters and their decisions . . . and that a past grudge is the motivation for the villain's actions . . . and the consideration of what will happen in the future to the town and in all people's lives motivates events, too. Time is also the dominant formal device, the dominant thematic device, and the thing that made *High Noon* famous. Every interior contains a clock, prominently displayed, and constant returns to close-ups of clock faces, swinging pendulums, and other reminders of time occur and recur. And, of course, the film runs eighty-five minutes and the screen action takes eighty-five minutes . . . an honest-to-goodness real-time experimentation. However, it is not quite that simple. You are only tricked into believing it is. The film appears to have a perfect temporal unit: a running time of eighty-five minutes to match the time of the action of the story. You begin watching at 10:35 A.M. on the clock and progress to high noon and slightly beyond. But the movie plays with this "real time" within the film. It is *not* a perfect experiment that says eighty-five to eighty-five, that's all folks. Time in parts of the story is in fact closed up and stretched out for narrative purposes within the real-time structure of eighty-five minutes.

## Space

There is only one space in the movies, and that is the space inside the frame. Although it varies slightly according to the aspect ratio the movie is being projected at, the space is fundamentally the same from film to film. The stagecoach racing to safety in John Ford's *Stagecoach* (1939) is rushing through the same space that Fred Astaire and Ginger Rogers are dancing across in *Follow the Fleet* (1936). Paul Henreid roman-

**With the clock constantly reminding us of the march of time, Gary Cooper, who won an Oscar for his role as Sheriff Will Kane, shelters his screen wife, the beautiful Grace Kelly, in the western *High Noon*.**

tically lights two cigarettes in the same amount of space in which James Cagney is blown to smithereens at the top of an oil tank. Greer Garson discovers radium right about where Frankenstein's monster offs a little village girl. No one ever thinks of this, and for good reason. Moviemakers know how to keep that fact a great secret. They know how to redecorate. Movie space is, in fact, one of the most deceptive and mysterious aspects of film. People who make movies create an entire world within the frame, and that world varies spatially according to the type of movie being made.

To realize how flexible the movie frame is, think about two opposites: movies in which there is seemingly unlimited space (westerns) and movies that are exercises in limited space (several Hitchcock films). Your relationship to what you are seeing in these opposites is a basic definition of film space.

Nobody enjoyed the challenge of limited space inside the movie frame more than Alfred Hitchcock. Four times he made movies in which he set himself the difficult task of keeping you entertained within limited space: *Rear Window* (1954), in which James Stewart is confined to a wheelchair inside a small apartment; *Rope* (1948), in which all the action takes place inside one apartment; *Dial M for Murder* (1954), in which almost all the action takes place in one apartment, shot in 3-D; and *Lifeboat* (1943), in which nine people take refuge inside a lifeboat after their ship is torpedoed during World War II.

*Lifeboat* is a great example of how you are tricked into accepting the space inside the frame as being only the size of an actual lifeboat—while you are still kept looking at a constantly changing, ever-interesting spatial situation. After the opening shot, which shows a ship sinking, followed by a panning camera movement over to a lifeboat,

In *Follow the Fleet* (1936), one of ten films in which they explored the use of space in film, Fred Astaire and Ginger Rogers face the music and dance, dance, dance.

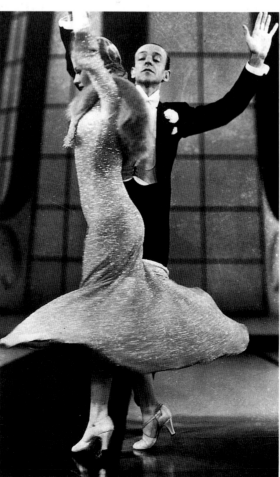

*"I want this picture to be a document, holding a mirror up to life, a picture of dignity, a true canvas of the suffering of humanity . . ."*
*"But with a little sex in it?"*
*"Yes, a little sex in it."*

*"You have to coat the pill with candy."*

the camera only leaves the lifeboat twice. Once the boat is shown in long shot sitting on a tranquil sea, following a huge storm. The other departure is a joke—the camera goes underwater to show a huge fish swimming up to take the bait it is being offered, Tallulah Bankhead's diamond bracelet. Space is defined as limited, but kept mobile through a series of ingenious ideas with which Hitchcock finds room for all the characters to mingle, interact, argue, separate, and hide things from you.

How does he do this to you? Why is it that, instead of feeling cramped in limited space, you feel you are moving around in space while rocking up and down in a boat that has plenty of room for both you *and* a cracking good story?

Well, you never stay in one position for too long. One minute, you are down in the bottom of the boat, where Bankhead and Mary Anderson are having a conversation about life as they try to fall asleep. The next, you have climbed onto the edge of the boat with Anderson, as she begins a talk with Hume Cronyn while he steers the boat. You are constantly put in a new place with a different character, and a new relationship. Although the camera actually just moved your view up a tiny space, your whole relationship to the frame and what is in it has changed.

*Lifeboat* cleverly creates different spaces inside the boat this way. There's a bottom layer, an outer rim, and a middle space. Characters lie down, climb up, and stand or move back and forth, end to end. Sometimes you see just the edge of the boat, or its tiller, in the frame, and outside of it, the widest imaginable space: the entire ocean! Sometimes you see just the ocean, but always from inside the boat. (Ten times in the movie you see the ocean and no part of the boat in the frame). Twice we leave the boat, but only twice. While you are watching the movie, you have no sense of how *really* limited you are.

When a character is shown in close-up against the open sky, with perhaps the sight of the ocean behind, there is a sense of looking at someone in a wide-open space instead of inside a cramped lifeboat. Hitchcock has created a sense of space by actually eliminating space! By taking away the sight of the small boat from time to time, and placing characters against sky or ocean, he makes you feel as if there is room, plenty of room. All through the movie, he keeps shifting the point of view and our potential involvement with characters, grouping them two with two, or all together, or alone, so everything shifts in a fresh and fluid manner. This is a good example of what people call "cinematic art." The boat *is* small, but the film is never cramped.

## Lighting and Composition

Lighting and composition have played an integral role in every scene that has been described so far. When certain dramatic examples of editing are pointed out, as in the *Psycho* shower scene, or long take, as in the beginning of *Touch of Evil*, lighting and composition have been carefully planned and executed to help bring off the effect. Lighting and composition turn a filmed event into an attitude that you are asked to assume or accept.

Lighting is a flexible tool for moviemakers. It can make what you see bright and cheerful, or dark and gloomy. It can take you outside on a sunny day into the hot glare. It can put you on a sleazy street at night, under the glow of neon. It can create shadows

**Two versions of the potential of the movie frame: six people in the corner of a crowded lifeboat in Hitchcock's exercise in limited space, *Lifeboat* (top; 1944), and the unlimited space of the American West in the silent film *Covered Wagon* (below; 1923).**

Left: Henry Fonda as Tom Joad in John Ford's adaptation of the John Steinbeck novel *The Grapes of Wrath* (1940).

Right: The art direction of Richard Day, combined with skillful lighting and cinematography, helped to create this magnificently composed city set for 1937's *Dead End*, a Samuel Goldwyn production directed by William Wyler and adapted for the screen by Lillian Hellman from Sidney Kingsley's Broadway play.

that are menacing or that provide safe hiding places. You can be out on a night under a shaft of moonbeams that brings you love and romance, or under a powerful, overbearing moon that warns it's the wolfman's night to howl. Lighting can show you all the furniture, because you're in a glamour film about clothes and fashion, or it can hide the squalor from you. Why go on? Lighting is something you know about. And it's never got your attention more than when it isn't even there, as in a dramatic moment in *The Ministry of Fear* (1944), directed by German expatriate Fritz Lang and photographed by Henry Sharp.

*The Ministry of Fear* contains a climactic scene in which a completely black screen is used. The hero and villain have struggled over a gun, but with the villain's sister (Marjorie Reynolds) to help him, the hero (Ray Milland) has prevailed. Reynolds is holding a gun on her brother (Carl Esmond) while Milland demands he hand over his coat, in which a stolen microfilm is sewn. While Milland searches the coat, Esmond seizes the moment to run to the wall and turn off the overhead lights. While you stare at an absolutely black screen, edge to edge, top to bottom, you hear Esmond's voice saying to Reynolds, "You wouldn't shoot your brother, Carla." Esmond opens the door to the hallway, and a shaft of sharp light floods in across the black frame. Then he goes out quickly and slams the door, returning the screen to black. The sound of a gunshot is heard, and a tiny pinhole of light appears on the screen, right where the bullet would have gone through the door. Milland opens the door and is seen in silhouette, framed against a rectangle of light. The white light is from the brightly illuminated hallway, and lying there dead is Carl Esmond. Three-quarters of the frame is still totally black, representing the room in which Reynolds stands, presumably with a smoking gun in her hand. All the drama and power of the scene for you comes from the fact that you can't see! It's a great use of no-lighting.

*Criss Cross* has an excellent scene to illustrate how lighting and composition create tension and paranoia. The movie is all about double crosses within double crosses. Watching it, you see characters actually crossing in front of each other in the frame

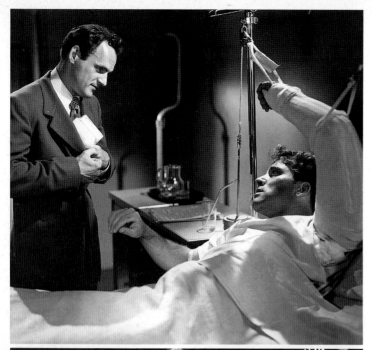

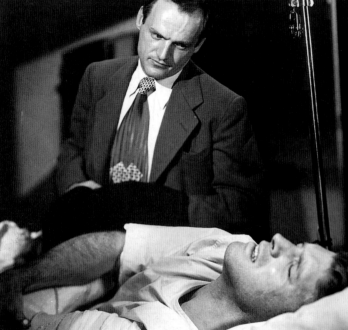

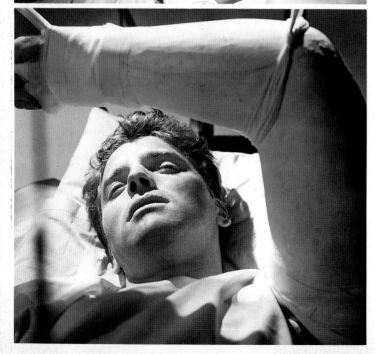

from time to time, and a fight between the hero (Burt Lancaster) and the villain (Dan Duryea) that turns out to have been faked, staged to provide an alibi for a big robbery. The hero has been double-crossed in the robbery before he could pull off his own double cross, and now he lies incapacitated in a hospital bed. He has been accidentally double-crossed by the press, who, misunderstanding his role, have declared him a hero.

You've watched an hour or more of all kinds of crosses and fakery. Now you are going to see a scene in which the helpless hero, trussed up in a hospital bed, his arm and shoulder in a sling, begins to worry about what the villains who escaped after the robbery will do to him. How to shoot the scene? What tools to use?

*Criss Cross* primarily uses lighting and composition to show Burt Lancaster, immobile and tense, trussed up like a turkey in his hospital bed. To stress his helplessness, the situation is seen primarily from his own point of view—in compositions that are tightly restricted and limited because he is confined to his bed. At first you see faces looking down on him, surrounding his bed. You are then shown Lancaster with his arm stretched high above him, supported by pulleys and encased in a heavy plaster cast. He looks dazed, even drugged. His family and friends show him a newspaper headline proclaiming him a hero. The image in the frame fades out and the voices disappear into a blurred dissolve that indicates Lancaster has fainted.

When Lancaster is awake again, a brief expository scene occurs in which a detective tells him that chief villain Dan Duryea also lived through the robbery and will be coming after him. "You see that door?" asks the policeman. "He'll send a gunman for you right through that door." While his voice is heard saying this, you see Lancaster's reaction. You see his stunned face, the shadow of his helpless arm falling over it. Then you are shown Lancaster's point of view: the door to his room is slightly ajar, the hallway partly obscured by a hospital screen. Before the detective leaves, he tells Lancaster he will not put anyone outside to guard him but will leave him to his fate. As the policeman speaks these lines, he goes to get his hat, moving in front of an old-fashioned chest of drawers with a mirror on top of it. This cleverly establishes the presence of a mirror through which Lancaster can see into the hall. Again, you see what Lancaster sees: part of the hall outside his room, reflected in this mirror, with the shadow of a man sitting in a chair clearly visible. As the detective leaves, he closes Lancaster's door, shutting both him and you off from any look at the hallway. No cuts take you outside to show you who the man out there is.

Lancaster is left alone. He is perspiring heavily. Straining his head to look toward the hallway, he can see only the transom above his door. Across it shadows move. Footsteps are heard. The music on the soundtrack intensifies, indicating danger. Lancaster watches intently but can only see shadows and hear footsteps. You are allowed to see no more than what Lancaster can see. The tension builds. Suddenly, you can see the door beginning to open, and in comes—a nurse! Furthermore, a nurse

above suspicion, an old fuddy-duddy nurse that anyone would trust.

Lancaster visibly relaxes. The scene could end here, having already given you enough tension and anxiety, but it goes further. When his nurse tells him that she will be going off duty after she gives him his sleeping medicine, Lancaster again looks into the mirror over the chest. He is now able to see the hallway again, since she left the door open. He sees the shadow of a man sitting in a chair outside his door, still there and obviously waiting. Lancaster begs the nurse to elevate his bed. His new point of view reveals to him the man outside his door. Who is that man? What does he want?

The nurse tells Lancaster that the "poor man" has been there all day because his wife was "hurt in an accident." "He's from Bakersfield," she cheerfully volunteers. Lancaster insists on the man being brought into the room. Lancaster, nervous and sweaty, is clearly suspicious of the man, worried about him. The man begins to tell the story of how he was driving and feels guilty . . . the nurse leaves the room, and Lancaster waits to see what will happen. The man tries to make Lancaster more comfortable, pulling his night table closer to the bed. Lancaster, not mollified, studies the man, noticing a bulge in his jacket. "What've you got there?" he asks, and the man slowly pulls out an order book, a bulging wallet, and a sheaf of order forms. "I've got a home sales hardware business." Lancaster, now relieved, asks the man to close the door and watch over him during the night. He begs him to stay, to wait through the night, and the man finally reluctantly agrees.

During this long sequence, you have never left Lancaster's room. You have never seen the entire hallway. You have remained riveted almost to the bed Lancaster is in, or you have seen the space only from his point of view in limited range and only partially lit. It is a tense and nerve-wracking situation. After the man sits down in a chair in Lancaster's room, a dissolve takes you into the deep of night. You see both Lancaster and the man sleeping. Now the room is lit in the film noir tradition of deep, entrapping shadows, with shafts of light that cut across Lancaster's bed. The man awakes and looks at his watch, getting up and going to the window to peek out through the Venetian blinds. He goes out into the hallway, leaving the door open. The movie allows you to watch his actions only through the mirror above the chest. Again, you do not leave

Ralph Feinnes and Liam Neeson—two Germans, two visions of Hitler's "final solution"—enlighten each other in Steven Spielberg's black-and-white tribute to Holocaust victims, *Schindler's List* (1993).

Lancaster's room. Again, you are trapped in shadows and half light. You watch in dawning horror while the man "from Bakersfield" calls the elevator, looks around to be sure he's alone, and draws up a wheelchair to transport Lancaster. He rudely wakes Lancaster up to take him to Duryea. "I waited," he says cynically.

There are many ways of shooting and lighting this sequence, but probably none could be as effective as the one chosen. It is completely true to its narrative meaning in the way it is placed in front of you. Every choice made in lighting and composition constantly stresses Lancaster's helplessness and his paranoia. And in a movie in which people constantly trick and double-cross one another, the man from the hall also is a double-crosser.

## Sound

Most people can't describe the sound track of any movie they have just seen, except to tell whether or not it had a score or a hit song. You can remember "Raindrops Keep Falling on My Head" from *Butch Cassidy and the Sundance Kid* (1969), the ragtime music from *The Sting* (1973), and Fred and Ginger singing "Let's Face the Music and Dance." But were there sound effects, and if so, what were they? Did they come from offscreen, from an unidentified source, or from something or someone you were watching?

The key to sound is really to understand whether it is coming from somewhere on the screen you are looking at, or whether it is coming from somewhere offscreen, out there in the implied space of the movie. Filmmakers constantly manipulate the audiences through these two basic ideas. Both onscreen and offscreen sound can scare you, soothe you, give you information, lull you, or make you laugh. The point is that movies treat sound as if it is everywhere—and can come from anywhere, for any reason. Everyone has heard the story of the snotty critic who asked a famous director where—for heaven's sake—did the full orchestra come from that was playing for a small boat that contained only two people who had no musical instruments and who were adrift on the open ocean? The director answered shrewdly: the orchestra came from the same place the camera did.

A good example of how offscreen sound controls events for both you and the character in the movie occurs in *Dark Waters* (1944), starring Merle Oberon as a young girl

who has recently survived when the ship she was taking to America was torpedoed during World War II. Oberon was the only survivor of this disaster, in which her own parents died. Left alone and orphaned, she has been seriously traumatized and only recently released from an asylum. Oberon goes to the movies and is forced to watch a newsreel in which it is reported that another ship has been torpedoed. Viewing this deeply upsets her, but the way a viewer is shown this is unique. You never see the newsreel she sees. The sight of the torpedoed boat with its survivors never appears on your screen, only in hers. You learn about it only through sound. You *hear* the newsreel while you watch her reaction to it.

You might think of a scene such as this as being a clever gimmick, a nice variation to the usual way of presenting events. But consider what it does to you. All your choices have been eliminated except the one that makes you watch Oberon's pain and fear. You can't get interested in the newsreel. You can't see it! You have to watch her suffer. Sound is providing you with all that you need to know, and it is also dictating your reaction. The scene wouldn't work in the same way if you didn't hear what she is seeing, because you wouldn't know why she was upset. It wouldn't work if you watched the newsreel instead of her, because then you'd be dealing with action on the screen instead of emotion on her face. Sound forces you to involve yourself deeply in Oberon's emotions.

A dramatic use of sound to scare you to death appears in one of Val Lewton's low-budget RKO productions, *Cat People* (1942), directed by Robert Wise. The situation on the screen couldn't be simpler. It's nothing except a woman walking along at night. She's alone, and she's walking through Central Park. (That was believable in 1942.) Of course, it is only fair to point out that the story has set up a situation that is ominous and eerie for you, but still, the scene works with very basic, simple tools.

What happens is this. Jane Randolph is walking home very late at night. She feels unsettled, as recent events have led her to feel threatened. Suddenly, she hears footsteps echoing from behind her. She stops to listen. The footsteps also stop. Standing under a streetlight, she looks backward into the inky blackness of night. She can see nothing. She can hear nothing. There is no sound. She starts walking again, leaving the security of the streetlight. Once again in darkness, she hears the sound of footsteps behind her. Every times she stops, the footsteps stop. Every time she goes forward, they go forward. The faster she goes, the faster they go. "They" are, however, only sounds. This continues until she is terrified and rushing forward toward frame right. Suddenly, hideously, a loud screeching sound—not unlike that of a large, attacking and vengeful jungle cat—is heard coming from off screen. This sound, I promise you, will lift you up out of your seat. When a city bus then pulls into the frame from the right, stopping to pick Randolph up and take her home, you feel total relief as you realize the screech was the sound of the bus brakes being floored. This use of sound was so effective at scaring audiences that Lewton forever after referred to any similar effects he achieved as "buses."

Another frightening, highly unusual use of sound is found in *Shock Corridor* (1963). This movie, directed by the iconoclastic Samuel Fuller, who often used his tools in ways that no one else would have dreamed of, tells the story of a newspaperman (Peter Breck) who wants to win a Pulitzer Prize more than anything. He

On the set of *Second Honeymoon* (1937), the sound boom moves into place as stars Tyrone Power and Loretta Young get ready for their takes.

concocts a scheme whereby he will pretend to be insane and get himself committed to an asylum in which an unsolved murder took place. It is his plan to find the killer, write the story, and win the Pulitzer. This is a crazy idea, but everything in this movie is crazy. (Though it all fits.) At first, Breck is a sane man in an insane world, and sound is one of the tools used to communicate his situation. As you watch Breck behave unpredictably, you hear his voice on the soundtrack, discussing what he is doing in a rational manner. Sound defines his inner sanity for you.

One of the most bizarre experiences Breck has with a fellow inmate is also defined through sound. Breck is awakened during the night by "Pagliacci," the man in the next bed, who loves opera and who murdered his wife. Breck awakens to see the large man looming over him and waving his arms. What is he doing? You have no idea. However, by carefully manipulating sound, Fuller lets you understand. The camera moves upward toward "Pagliacci's" face, and a full orchestra is heard. It moves down slightly and sound is eliminated. Moving back and forth this way allows you to absorb, as Breck absorbs, the information that the insane man is hearing music in his head and is waving his arms to conduct it accordingly. There is, of course, no sound in the room at all, only in his head.

## Putting It Together: Hollywood Style

All these things—leaving events out, controlling what you know, and using the tools of cinema—fit together. The goal of a good movie is always to reach audiences in a specific way, but filmmakers had differing definitions of how to do that. They knew what the choices were because they knew what their intentions were. Movies, which cost lots of money and require lots of people to complete, do not happen by accident (no matter how much they sometimes seem to be train wrecks). Every cut is the result of a confident choice or detailed decision on someone's part.

All the tools of cinema, used effectively and put together into the "language of film," can put you in a world that is totally unlike your own, but that seems real and powerful while you watch it. While you are in the darkened movie theater, it's the only world there is. A film that achieves the sense of an alien, dangerous place is *Kiss Me Deadly* (1955), directed by Robert Aldrich and based on one of hard-boiled crime writer Mickey Spillane's Mike Hammer stories. When Hammer (Ralph Meeker) arrives home at his own apartment, he sneaks into it as if he were breaking and entering. His world is so violent, so chaotic and filled with treachery and uncertainty, that no place is safe for him. He treats his own apartment as a potential trap. One other effective sequence shows him going out late at night to follow up a clue. It begins with a close-up of the handwritten address: Ray Diker, 121 Flower Street, Los Angeles, California. A real street in a real city. But Meeker's journey there is a surreal and violent excursion, participated in by him in a most matter-of-fact, ho-hum way.

It begins with Meeker parking his European sports car, backing into the space while your eye is allowed to pick up a man standing in a doorway, reading a newspaper, far back in the frame, seen in deep focus. This man will notice Meeker and begin to follow him. You have no idea who this character is or what he is doing there. You can

> *"It was a world you created; it was not a world you went out and found."*
>
> Richard Sylbert

assign various logical explanations to him, but, really, he is an unidentified assailant of the sort who awaits Mike Hammer everywhere. Meeker walks along toward Flower Street, followed by the man. A clever mixture of tracking shots and cuts keeps you aware that the man is following and that Meeker knows he is. You are kept constantly aware of how far apart they are by the tracking shots that show their relationship to one another physically in the space as they go. The cuts to medium close-ups of both men in profile as they walk—as well as to their walking feet—keep up the tempo and tension for you. Meeker stops first at a newsstand, then at a popcorn vender's, and then at a gum machine to check his assailant's progress. You have a clear marker yourself, because Meeker passes a clock that is illuminated. At 2:10 he pauses to buy popcorn. At 2:15 he walks away with a bag full. At 2:20 the other man walks by. There is casual dialogue—Meeker asks the newsman the way to Flower Street and asks the popcorn man "How much?" The assailant casually strikes a match and begins to smoke as he follows.

The speed picks up with the tempo of the cutting and the sound of the arrythmic, atonal music on the track. Finally, you see the man reach into his pocket and draw out a knife. Meeker whirls on him, throwing the popcorn in his face, commanding, "Drop the knife!" Meeker beats this man viciously, banging his head against the concrete wall behind them. As the man sinks slowly down, looking stunned and disbelieving, Meeker picks up the knife, calmly puts it in his pocket, and keeps on walking. The man inexplicably gets up! He follows again, and the incredibly violent fight continues, culminating with Meeker pushing the man down sidewalk steps. As you watch the man literally bounce out of the frame, Meeker turns his back indifferently and walks away.

No explanation for this sequence is ever given. By combining the music, cutting, tracking camera, lighting, and composition, you are given to understand that this is a day at the office for Mike Hammer. Brutal action—vicious attacks from unknowns—that's his job. The tools used in the sequence switch back and forth, from a tracking camera that clearly shows you the two men and their spatial relationship, over to cutting that cheats you from knowing when the follower will attack. Although a newsstand, popcorn maker, and vending machine could all logically be in that place with those men out there at night, everything has been strategically located and placed to pace out the action for you. The scene flows forward into a violent, but meaningful culmination.

Two movies made in Hollywood tell a story about a beautiful, cold, sexy, dangerous woman. A blonde, of course. She's married to a man with money, and it seems pretty obvious his money is exactly why she's married to him. Another man, a kind of emotional drifter, comes into her life when he begins to do business in some way with

Gary Cooper, a.k.a. Longfellow Deeds, suggests Hollywood's vision of what the rich do for fun in director Frank Capra's 1936 award-winning comedy, *Mr. Deeds Goes to Town.*

her husband. She lures this new man into a murder plot, in which he is going to be framed. Although he survives to tell the story to us in a voice-over, she ends up dead.

This is the crude outline of events in both *Double Indemnity* (1944) and *The Lady from Shanghai* (1948). These movies tell a similar story, but they tell their stories so differently you have to stop and really think about it to make the connection. They are both about evil blonde women who wreck the lives of the men who get involved with them, but the storytelling choices are very different even though both are classified as film noir and they were made within a few years of one another.

*Double Indemnity* is a coherent movie, a big box-office success that is well remembered by the moviegoers of its day. It is based on a story by James M. Cain, a revered member of the crime-writing elite. It was directed and adapted for the screen by Billy Wilder (along with Raymond Chandler, another elite detective writer).

Wilder's career spanned five decades, from 1930 to 1980, successfully. He is a respected member of the Hollywood community and has won every major award America has to give a moviemaker. The three stars of *Double Indemnity*, Barbara Stanwyck, Fred MacMurray, and Edward G. Robinson, also had long careers. They were never associated with scandal and never in any serious slump. In particular, Stanwyck and MacMurray thrived. They were as successful in television as in films and died with their reputations intact. *Double Indemnity* got favorable reviews and was nominated for seven Oscars (Best Picture, Best Actress, Best Director, Best Screenplay, Best Cinematography, Best Sound Recording, Best Score).

*The Lady from Shanghai*, on the other hand, was allegedly based on a potboiling novel, but was perhaps made up on the spot in a telephone booth by its director, Orson Welles. Welles's career was a well-known disaster because he lost the opportunity to continue making his type of magnificently visual films after he was labeled "unreliable" and "wasteful" in his early studio projects. Rita Hayworth, who had been his wife, also lost her fame and popularity, and her life ended sadly. *Lady* received lousy reviews and did not make money. It received no Oscar nominations. Even today, people reject it, although it is one of the masterpieces of American cinema.

The reason for the different way these films were received at the time reflects the attitude they take toward the viewer. *Double Indemnity* tells its story through a flashback, but everything about the situation is made clear. Fred MacMurray, dying from a bullet wound, goes to his office and speaks into a dictaphone. He is telling the story to Edward G. Robinson, to whom he addresses the report he is "writing." As he bleeds slowly to death, he talks all through the night, telling the events of how he met the dangerous Phyllis Dietrichson (Stanwyck) and helped her murder her husband. When he finishes, it is dawn. As he describes an event, it is seen as a flashback introduced by his narration. Everything you see in the past is clearly explained and clarified. No loose plot ends are left. No questions are left unanswered. In the end, MacMurray dies. There are no trick endings.

Two blondes, two men, two tales of murder and sex: *Double Indemnity* (1944) with Fred MacMurray and Barbara Stanwyck (above) and *The Lady from Shanghai* (1948) with Orson Welles and Rita Hayworth (opposite).

To remind you of what you are watching, the movie leaves the past to go back to MacMurray and the dictaphone six times. The narrative structure is constantly reestablished. You are reminded of where you were when the movie started.

*The Lady from Shanghai* begins with a narration from nowhere, a voice-over. As with *Laura*, you aren't sure where the character is speaking from. Presumably he is speaking directly to you out in the audience, but there is no establishment of where he is telling the story, or when, or why. Rita Hayworth is introduced as an enigma. In the

opening scene, Welles has to rescue her from attackers, but was the attack real or faked for his benefit? A great deal of the story makes no sense, and most people can't follow the plot easily on the first viewing. In the end, the hero walks out into the sunshine. He is not dead, but where he is going is as unclear as where he was telling the story from.

The way the two leading women die illustrates perfectly the difference between the movies. In *Double Indemnity* you have known all along that Stanwyck is a killer, and the mode of storytelling has already informed you that MacMurray is shot and dying.

An impeccable assembly of Hollywood society: Jimmy Stewart, John Howard, and Cary Grant share a moment with Ruth Hussey and Katharine Hepburn in director George Cukor's *The Philadelphia Story* (1940).

You are further allowed to see that Stanwyck, who awaits MacMurray in a darkened, shadowed room—the very living room of her home in which she first lured and attracted him—has a gun hidden under her lace handkerchief. With these two characters, the film has, from the beginning, made it clear that sex and murder are the same thing. MacMurray will shoot Stanwyck while holding her in an embrace. You see this in medium close-up, and it is the logical conclusion to what has gone on in their other embraces: they are out to destroy one another. It's a no-win love affair. A modicum of surprise is afforded you in that, since you know MacMurray is wounded throughout the telling of the story, you have to wonder what will happen to her in the final scene. The method of showing the action on the screen is true to the tone of the film and its main event—their unholy alliance in death—but you are allowed to see where the two characters are in relationship to one another. You know they both have weapons. You know they both can commit murder if they have to (you've seen them do it). And you know one character will end up shot and dying.

What you see is that MacMurray and Stanwyck are in an embrace. What you hear is a gunshot. As they stare at one another, you can ask yourself who shot who? But where they are standing in relation to each other, the definition of the space they are standing in, the fact that they both have guns and are using them, that he is going to die and she is no good—none of this is unclear. Your attention is held by the gunshot until the moment later when you learn MacMurray shot her—which she didn't expect—but everything is being made clear to you visually.

*The Lady from Shanghai* has a finale that carries out its overall enigmatic presentation. In one of the most visually stunning—and famous—conclusions in motion picture history, Rita Hayworth and Everett Sloane shoot at one another in a fun house hall of mirrors. Everything you see is distorted and multiplied. Furthermore, you don't know where any one of the three characters in the scene (Orson Welles as the hero is also present) is actually standing in relation to each of the other two. As image after image is shattered and broken, you can't tell what's real and what's not real. You don't know who's getting shot and who's surviving. You see big Hayworths and small Hayworths, and a long horizontal set of crippled Sloanes, inching forward on his walkers like some kind of strange insect. It is a fitting end to a movie that has provided no logical explanations, and which has not made anything clear. Whether or not Hayworth is really the villain is withheld until this ending.

The choices made by the filmmakers create two very different viewing experiences. *Double Indemnity* is an audience-friendly movie, and *The Lady from Shanghai* is often appreciated only by connoisseurs of the medium who can understand what a great movie it really is, how imaginative and innovative. Both of these movies are made by masters, and they show clearly the two types of Hollywood filmmaking that coexisted: the classical, *Double Indemnity,* and the experimental, *The Lady from Shanghai.* When Hollywood was a factory system, in the golden age of the 1930s, 1940s, and into the 1950s, efficient business practices allowed for at least some

development of a product that was different from the ordinary. (In chapter seven of this book, this system is discussed in more detail.)

Who has not seen *Casablanca*? People love it or people hate it; people call it art or they call it kitsch; people say it's calculating and people says it's an accident of casting and writing that was never meant to happen. (How do they know it wouldn't have been just as great with Ronald Reagan and Ann Sheridan in the roles played by Bogart and Bergman?) Consider how carefully, how purposefully *Casablanca* is constructed in its opening eight minutes. Those who made the movie knew what they were doing. It's a perfect film to think about to conclude an understanding of how Hollywood never forgot the audience when it made a movie. It perfectly defines classic Hollywood style. All decisions were aimed toward one purpose—the maximum pleasure for the audience. With a movie like *Casablanca*, they got a bonus. Setting out to make some big money and get people in to come see it, they made a movie that has touched generations, that is as alive today as it ever was. This probably should not have happened—why did it?

 *Casablanca* is based on a then unproduced play entitled *Everybody Comes to Rick's*. In a movie like that, the café called Rick's would be the primary setting, and the whole story would take place there. Rick's would represent the world, and the story would be one of those isolated romances that Hollywood made plenty of for gullible audiences. When Hollywood decided to rename the movie *Casablanca*, they made a decision that changed the emphasis. They decided to make "*Everybody Comes to Casablanca*," and in fact, the opening narration of the movie tells you exactly that. Everybody in German-occupied Europe is going to Casablanca in order to try to get from there to Lisbon, and then to the free world. The change reflects intention. Instead of an ordinary little movie like other movies, *Casablanca* becomes bigger, more topical, more relevant (especially at the time of release). It becomes more political. A romance that takes place in this setting is significant, but not as important as the historical events that surround it. The lovers have to think about other issues, or, to use a time-worn cliché, to realize that what is going on internationally is "bigger than both of them." Their world is Casablanca, not Rick's. The movie gives you Rick's, of course, but puts it inside Casablanca.

 In the movie's opening minutes, director Michael Curtiz had to establish these two important worlds. And they have to create a relationship between them that you can quickly understand. In addition, they have a host of characters to introduce, including Nazis, Vichy French, rebel French, immigrants, locals, café employees, and Rick. Two key people are not seen in the first eight minutes: the parts played by Paul Henreid and Ingrid Bergman. The film begins by quickly and efficiently telling you all about things in Casablanca itself, then making a transition through the Nazis over to Rick's:

 *Casablanca.* Casablanca is a real city and it was in the news in 1942. The movie sets out to establish its "real" quality. The film begins with the sight of a spinning globe, various maps of different types, with images from the news superimposed. A voice-over that is clearly patterned after newsreel narra-

*"The thing about writing and directing a film is that you are presenting a view of the universe. Each time, every scene, every line. Every time you put the camera down you are saying here's a version of the universe as I perceive it. And that is being tested by everyone who sees that movie."*

Lawrence Kasdan

> *"The style becomes illusionistic;*
> *the style is saying 'come into*
> *this world.'"*
>
> David Bordwell

tions tells you all about the situation of people heading from Europe to Casablanca and why. You are taken from this "real" establishment down into the city itself, a movie set. In this "city," a policeman receives a teletype saying that "letters of transit" have been stolen and the courier murdered. Police are told to round up suspects. The round-up takes place, showing you how Casablanca is crowded with all kinds of people from everywhere. A man tries to escape and is shot. Then a pickpocket victimizes a naive British couple. You learn it's a dangerous and corrupt place. Then the sound of an airplane—the plane from Lisbon—is heard and everyone looks up to the sky. This sequence has shown you the color, danger, and crime of Casablanca and linked it to reality through maps and newsreels.

*Transition.* The upturned faces take you up to the sight of the plane, which flies in low over a sign for RICK'S CAFÉ AMERICAIN. The plane lands and the Nazis emerge. They talk to Claude Rains, the French policeman, and ask about finding the murderer of the courier. Rains says he'll be at Rick's that night because "everybody comes to Rick's." "I've heard of this Rick," says the head Nazi . . . and you are moved from Casablanca to Rick's smoothly, but also efficiently because the transition was used to establish the Nazis and Claude Rains, as well as the importance of the hero, Rick.

*Rick's.* Now it is night and the sign you saw before is lit. The camera moves forward and approaches the door of Rick's, moving you inside. You are introduced to an interior, private world dominated by Rick and his particular attitude toward life and people and politics. Rick's is a kind of sanctuary for people trying to escape the war. In a series of very brief vignettes—one-liners, really—you meet some discouraged immigrants ("Waiting, waiting . . . I'll die in Casablanca") . . . a woman trying to sell her jewelry ("Everyone sells diamonds") . . . an obviously Jewish man arranging a private boat with a shady type ("Remember to bring fifteen thousand dollars in cash, *in cash*") . . . some mysterious Asians . . . and more. It is a place in which subversive and illegal activities, both personal and political, are allowed to take place. It also represents America. In addition to the name, Rick's Café Americain—which you have seen twice in case you are a slow reader—you have entered to the sound of a very American song, "It Had To Be You" played by Dooley Wilson, who then changes into the more jazzy "Just because my hair is curly. . . ." An American café, American music, a southern black man, and, of course, Rick himself.

After some well-dressed women ask a waiter if Rick will sit with them (they're told no), the camera presents another waiter presenting a tab to be signed to a figure that is offscreen. This unseen character takes the tab, and a close-up shows his signature—*"OK, Rick"*—being signed. On his table are a martini glass, a full ashtray, and his pen. Only the arm of his white dinner jacket is seen. Finally you are allowed a look-see: Rick is Humphrey Bogart in a star entrance.

*"There's a town up ahead."*
*"What town is it?"*
*"I don't know, I suppose it's Hollywood."*

Dialog from *Sullivan's Travels*

Now all your pieces are in place, except for Henreid and Bergman. Your two worlds are established, your secondary characters are all present, and your hero awaits his destiny in the form of Ingrid Bergman. This is perfect, efficient moviemaking, to bring you in and hold you there, entertained and happy for 102 minutes. This is what the Hollywood movie did for a living.

I always think of the audience. I can't always think of it at the moment I'm doing it, but what is the audience going to think is always in my mind. Movie makers know that a certain angle, a certain camera move, a certain line of dialogue, a certain cut will create a certain impression emotionally and psychologically in the audience. We have to become the audience in a sense. I sit there and I react to the actors' performances as the audience. If I believe it, fine. If I don't believe it, sorry, we have to do it again. And then I have to find out why I don't believe it or, if it's not convincing, what is convincing, et cetera. That's one level. On the other hand, what device do I want to use to be able to get this idea across, or this emotion across? I think I try to find the best device, even if it's a simple device of holding the camera static and letting an actor move across the frame and not moving and not cutting. I'm aware of all of that. It's a constant battle. I mean Hitchcock *always* thought of the audience.

Martin Scorsese

**"Round up the usual suspects," directs Claude Rains at the end of 1942's *Casablanca*, while Paul Henreid, Humphrey Bogart, and Ingrid Bergman stand by in the fog—-a moment of movie time that has been played and replayed over the years.**

*"The first thing was always how the star looked."*
Lawrence Kasdan

# 2 STARDOM

"If we were a primitive society, movie stars would be gods."

Sydney Pollack

One of Hollywood's greatest devices for connecting with its audiences was that of creating stars the public loved to see, forming identifications between actors and viewers. The well-known tag line "a star is born" is really a tribute to Hollywood's great ability to manufacture movie stars as reliably and effectively as if they were toasters.

How did the system make stars? How were they "born"? In the golden age of the studios literally hundreds of talent scouts and studio employees were traveling the

United States and most of Europe looking for potential movie stars. If a young man with a good body and handsome face won a local diving contest, someone spotted him and gave him a ticket to Hollywood for a screen test. If a beautiful young woman won the "Miss Oatmeal of the Year" contest, became an Olympic ice-skating star, appeared on the cover of *Farm Journal*, modeled evening gowns at a Dallas department store, ran an elevator at Saks Fifth Avenue, or just sat on a drugstore stool at Schwab's, someone spotted her and invited her to Hollywood. Local beauty pageants, low-level modeling jobs, legitimate stage work, extra work in films, sports contests—anything and everything was a breeding ground for a potential star. More time and energy went into the search for new movie stars than anyone today can imagine because stars drew the public to films, kept them coming back, and bound them to the system and its products.

The system was set up to find the right young people and cast them in movies, and it found all types: tall and short, blonde and brunette, talented and untalented, with lisps and stutters, with crooked teeth and broken noses. All physical flaws could be fixed up or erased if the public showed interest in a newcomer. Rita Hayworth's hairline could be elevated with electrolysis, Clark Gable's protruding ears could be taped down, and Alan Ladd's short stature could be enhanced with elevator shoes. Whoever they were and wherever they were, Hollywood polished and shellacked potential stars and stuck them in movies like bait. A lot of time and money went into the "birth" of a great movie star.

Once identified and targeted or responded to by the public, the "star," or "starlet," was put through the studio's factory process. This could include anything from cosmetic surgery to pointers on how to dress, from a publicity "build-up" to serious acting lessons and a diction coach. The key to potential success was the build-up, in which

| Alexis Smith | Ann Sothern | J. Carroll Naish | Dean Stockwell | Lewis Stone | Clinton Sundberg | Robert Taylor | Audrey Totter |
| Peter Lawford | Jeanette MacDonald | Ann Miller | Ricardo Montalban | Jules Munshin | George Murphy | Reginald Owen | Walter Pidgeon |
| Katharine Hepburn | John Hodiak | Claude Jarman, Jr. | Van Johnson | Jennifer Jones | Louis Jourdan | Howard Keel | Gene Kelly |
| Gloria De Haven | Tom Drake | Jimmy Durante | Vera-Ellen | Errol Flynn | Clark Gable | Ava Gardner | Judy Garland |
| Lionel Barrymore | June Allyson | Leon Ames | Fred Astaire | Edward Arnold | Lassie | Mary Astor | Ethel Barrymore |

| | | | |
|---|---|---|---|
| Spencer Tracy | Esther Williams | Keenan Wynn | |
| Jane Powell | Ginger Rogers | Frank Sinatra | Red Skelton |
| Christopher Kent | Angela Lansbury | Mario Lanza | Janet Leigh |
| Betty Garrett | Edmund Gwenn | Kathryn Grayson | Van Heflin |
| Spring Byington | James Craig | Arlene Dahl | |

studio machinery went to work to convince audiences they should want to buy the new star. In accomplishing this, the movie studios found a useful partnership in collaborating with the movie magazines of the era. Unlike the unattractive and destructive tabloids of today, these magazines specialized in beautiful layouts, color portraits, and sumptuous ads. Although published on cheap paper, magazines such as *Photoplay, Modern Screen, Screenland, Movie Stories,* and *Screen Album,* among many others, existed to feed the public's appetite for photographs and stories on their favorites, as well as to help create new stars.

Movie magazines covered every single film released, with capsule reviews and rankings to indicate quality and with large advertisements hawking the films that were currently in the theaters. Announcements were made about coming attractions, and the magazines also contained recipes, Ann Landers–type advice columns, beauty tips, fashion, letters to the editors, and gossip of a harmless sort. The studios cooperated with the publishers of these magazines, providing them with an endless supply of stills, and the stars also posed willingly for layouts done especially for the magazines. The articles were often gushy puff pieces, but there was also, especially in the earlier years, excellent writing that defined the studio system, its directorial style, the contributions made by specific writers and designers, and such concerns of the business as censorship, patriotism, and morality.

It is possible to trace the evolution of an individual star by tracking his or her progress in these magazines. The first time an actor's name or face appears it is usually in candid snapshots in the gossip section. For instance, Betty Grable, who became the leading female box-office star of all time, is seen "dancing at Mocambo" or "cheering her favorite horse at Santa Anita" in the gossip-column section of *Modern Screen* in 1938. Grable is in the company of her then-husband, Jackie Coogan. Although beginning to be a name, she is still just a "starlet," or featured player. In the back of the magazine she is shown dancing in a still from her current film, *College Swing.* Her skirt is flying high to reveal her famous legs (an amazing number of such "cheesecake" photos of Grable would appear in the 1940s).

By the October 1940 issue Grable was obviously moving up the ladder of success. She appears on page 16, in an article entitled "Lovely To Look At." She is modeling hand-knit sweaters for a column that uses her as a hook to draw the reader's eye, since the article is really little more than an ad for knitting directions, not a story on Grable. The reader can write to *Modern Screen* and, "at no cost," be sent the knitting instructions as long as a self-addressed stamped envelope is enclosed. ("Betty Grable's Bermuda blue slip-on with diamond pattern and tucked shoulders has that elegant imported look.")

Grable is also seen on page 44, brushing her teeth, in an article called "Brighten Your Smile," which tells readers that clothes may make the man, but a beautiful smile will hold him. Grable, the story tells us, "has the gay, flashing smile that goes with her dancing talent." On page 36 she is shown at the Jitterbug Jamboree at the Hollywood

*"All my life I've been a symbol—
a symbol of immortal change.
I'm tired of being a symbol—
I long to be a human being."*

Greta Garbo in *Queen Christina*


*"Why shouldn't I be nervous?
I'm human. What can I tell you?"*

Julia Roberts

**Portraits such as this were taken as "candid" shots of the stars in everyday real life, supposed to be having a relaxed lunch. Above: Katharine Hepburn and Douglas Fairbanks, Jr., possibly during the filming of 1933's *Morning Glory*, in which they co-starred. Opposite top: Ronald Reagan and Olivia DeHavilland in the Warner Brothers commissary in the 1940s. Opposite bottom: teen stars Marshall Thompson, Elizabeth Taylor, and Janet Leigh at the MGM studios.**

Legion Stadium in the company of George Raft, her date, and Tyrone Power and his wife. On page 52 a picture of her appears in an article on "Color Your Fingertips." Grable, the caption says, "can well be proud of those pretty nails she displays in her latest hit, *Coney Island*." On page 100 her two latest films are rated: *Footlight Serenade* is given a three-star rating and *Springtime in the Rockies*, three and a half stars. On page 108 a gossip item under "Good News" tells us that "Betty Grable, who is practically Mama of the Morale Department, came into the commissary from the *Coney Island* set wearing a skin tight cerise jacket, a hip-swathing plaid skirt, a superdark suntan makeup, a perky pillbox hat and a gorgeous blue black wig."

By March 1943 Grable is featured in one of the magazine's leading pieces. Called "Miss Terrific!," it defines its title as "alias Betty Grable, the gal who out-hollers lusty Dodger fans, bowls a mighty 230 and reaps 14,000 fan letters each month." By this point, Betty Grable had been successfully built up into a real star. From then on, full-page color photographs of her appeared in several fan mags per month, and her face was on the cover at least once per year of every movie magazine published, the prime recognition of star power. She also appeared on the cover of *Time* magazine, the ultimate proof of her status.

In the 1930s fan magazines told their readers everything they might want to know about their favorite stars:

WHAT STARS EAT. "The Diet Secrets of Beauties Revealed." (Kay Francis, a leading glamour star of the times, is said to have to have her eggs cooked just so, with whites soft and yolks well done.)

WHAT THE GREAT STARS OF OUR TIME HATE. (Kay Francis hates someone else driving the car she is riding in.)

WHAT STARS SUGGEST FOR BEAUTY TIPS. (Kay Francis thinks "your perfume should always mirror your mood." If a woman wants to be like Francis, she is advised to buy perfume that would make her "sophisticated, svelte, and worldly" because that's the Kay Francis type.)

Under studio supervision (and for no extra personal dollars) stars endorsed all sorts of commercial products. This kept their faces in front of the fans and conveniently sold their latest movies at the same time. "Follow our Hollywood way," says Joan Blondell in a full-page 1933 ad for soap flakes. "We keep frocks smart looking with Lux." Blondell appears in a low-cut gown with a diamond belt and a diamond pin on her bosom. She is identified as a "smart young star appearing in *Footlight Parade*." A costume designer from Warner Brothers–First National is shown in a small photo at the bottom of the page. Accompanied by a female assistant, he is fingering a lavish gown and standing in front of a wardrobe of clothes. He is quoted as saying, "We're washing almost every fabric here in Lux—dresses, negligees, flannels, even draperies. Lux keeps stockings and costumes new looking twice as long. It cuts down cleaning bills, too. It would pay us to use Lux even if it cost $1.00 a box." In big type across the bottom of the page, running alongside a box of Lux and a reprint of the National Recovery Administration eagle, are the words "HOLLYWOOD SAYS—DON'T TRUST TO LUCK, TRUST TO LUX."

The back page of a 1942 issue of *Movie Story* shows Claudette Colbert cheerfully passing out cartons of cigarettes to soldiers. The caption reads, "Claudette Colbert is doing a grand job in the Volunteer Army Canteen Service (VACS to the boys). You should see her starring in the new Paramount picture *Palm Beach Story*." Colbert wears a VACS uniform, and the ad reminds us, "KEEP 'EM SATISFIED WITH CHESTERFIELD, milder . . . cooler . . . better tasting cigarettes."

In a 1933 issue of *Modern Screen*, Cary Grant and Randolph Scott are featured in— of all things—a recipe column called "The Modern Hostess." Scott and Grant, forks in hand, are seen staring into each other's eyes while presiding over a table loaded with food. "Cary Grant and Randolph Scott busy over a seafood luncheon" gushes the caption. The columnist tells readers all about the home the two men share, the expertise of Grant on fish, and Scott's pontificating on how it takes both brains and skill to do right by shellfish. Seafood, these men tell readers, combines economy with tastiness. This same issue offers readers "The Truth about Katharine Hepburn's Marriage" (she lied about having been married, but it was a "gallant lie") as well as photographed portraits of Will Rogers, Mae West, Robert Young, Dolores Del Rio, Lionel Barrymore, Preston Foster, Francis Dee, Joan Bennett, and Leslie Howard. The Bennett and Young photos are by famed Hollywood portraitist Hurrell, and the Francis Dee by Robert Coburn. There are many articles on individual stars and a forecast of who among the young newcomers will actually manage to become stars. (Carl Laemmle, Jr., correctly picks Margaret Sullivan, John Boles, and Lew Ayres, but he also predicts that Leila Hyams, June Knight, and Onslow Stevens will make it.) There are lavish fashion layouts, articles on health, reviews, recipes, gossip, patterns to sew dresses from, candid shots of the stars at the Los Angeles air races, and much, much more. The high point of the magazine is an ad that asks "Would You Like to Visit Joan Crawford in Hollywood?" It offers a free trip to California and a week's visit with the star. "Joan will be glad to see you," says the ad. "She is all set to entertain you . . . she's a grand hostess, you know." The

> *"They became stars because of their very difference.*
> *They don't match the crowd at all. . . . They don't even*
> *come close to it. . . . Some have it, some don't."*
>
> Sydney Guilaroff

contest will be explained in detail in the next month's issue—so, of course, you will just *have* to buy it.

Publicity, of course, could only do so much to influence stardom. The studios also had to have a series of the right movies in which to feature a potential star. First a newcomer generally played in small parts. If these worked out, a series of larger roles would be slated, some of them probably opposite an already established star of the opposite sex. The studio would then see what type of role the public most liked the young hopeful to play. How did the public imagine this young person to be in real life? Virginal or sexy? Rugged or sophisticated? How they liked to see them would become how they *did* see them, and this characterization would become associated with them. The legendary movie stars were actors who were believed to be in real life exactly like the characters they played on the screen. This phenomenon, known as "star persona," was what separated the film actor and the stage actor. When the mass of the moviegoing public accepted the image of an actor on screen as if it were that person's true self, the studios knew they had a winner.

Film acting differs from stage acting because the camera affects a performance. In film, the face of the actor can be shown in startling close-up. This allows for a subtle, small response to be seen clearly by the audience. The movie actor can "do nothing" and elicit a strong response. This is what helps to create the passionate feeling fans have for movie stars. In *Queen Christina* (1933), Greta Garbo stands on a ship as it pulls out of the harbor, her beautiful face an enigmatic mask. Seen in medium close-up, she seems to express grief, a remembered lost love, resolution, acceptance of duty—myriad emotions that the film has set up for her character. Actually, Garbo's director, Rouben Mamoulian, had asked her to keep her face as blank as possible, because he knew that part of any film performance is supplied by the audience's thoughts as they look intently on the human face. Great film acting is partly the acceptance of this relationship with the camera.

A close-up can show a tiny tear in the corner of any eye, a look of hidden malice, an emerging feeling of love, an anger repressed through force of will, an uncontrolled distaste. More than that, movies can make an actor fly through the air, disappear and dissolve, and move in slow motion. Through the wonderful device of film editing, actors

Two who definitely had it: enigmatic, glamorous, unique. Greta Garbo (opposite)—expressing one of her famously cryptic gazes—from director Rouben Mamoulian's *Queen Christina* (1933) and Marlene Dietrich in her trademark tuxedo from *Morocco* (1930; above).

*"Cary Grant was irreplaceable, because he was gorgeous, but still willing to do incredibly foolish things. Very few people today are willing to do that."*

Andrew Bergman

can also leave the bad parts of their performances on the cutting-room floor. All film acting requires a face the camera can love, an unusual voice rather than perfect diction, and a certain subtle something that cannot be defined—the elusive "star power" that makes audiences identify with what is happening on the screen. If more actors and actresses seemed to have that kind of power in the old days, it is partly due to the fact that the old studio system of Hollywood was so good at creating stars. A perfect example of this process of creation is the career of Cary Grant.

Although people today might think of the unique and elegant Cary Grant as beyond such crass manipulation, he was, in fact, very much a product of the system. In 1932, when Cary Grant began making feature films in the United States, he appeared in no less than seven movies: *This Is the Night, Sinners in the Sun, Merrily We Go to Hell, The Devil and the Deep, Blonde Venus, Hot Saturday,* and *Madame Butterfly.* Of these, only *Blonde Venus* is even remotely known today. The parts Grant played were minor and varied, everything from the rich man who loses the leading lady (*Blonde Venus,* in which he is rejected by Marlene Dietrich for Herbert Marshall, a seemingly improbable event) to a famous javelin thrower in *This Is the Night.*

In his second year in films, 1933, Grant acted in six films, and in his third year, 1934, he acted in four. In 1935 and 1936, he made a total of seven features. By early 1937, his accumulation of roles opposite such glamorous actresses as Katharine Hepburn, Sylvia Sydney, Mae West, Loretta Young, and Jean Harlow had established him as a name, if not a true movie star. A careful examination of his career allows one to say that, if it isn't possible to pinpoint the exact moment *when* it happened, it is at least possible to say that before the end of 1937, Cary Grant made the transition from well-known leading man to movie star, because during that year he made five movies, two of which are among his most famous: *Topper* and *The Awful Truth.* Immediately following, in 1938, he made two films in which not only is he unquestionably a movie star, he is also unquestionably Cary Grant as

**The making of 1940s glamour: Cary Grant in various test shots and Rita Hayworth, the "Love Goddess," in a studio portrait.**

The evolution of a star's persona was not always so predictable—and in the golden age versatility was an important commodity, as these two sides of James Cagney show: in costume for *Frisco Kid* (1935) and in modern dress for the role that won him lasting fame, the leading gangster in *Public Enemy* (1951).

we know him: *Bringing Up Baby* and *Holiday.* From then on, he is presumably "just playing himself"—the mark of the old Hollywood star—the indication of an established star persona. Yet it took five years—from 1932 through 1937—and more than twenty-five movies in which he played a variety of roles to make it happen.

In the 1930s and 1940s, actors such as Grant had a chance to develop this friendship with the audience because the studio system released so many films each year. They "manufactured" a Cary Grant, and then allowed the public to "find" him. They gave him the time to become a star. In the early films of Grant, he was not the handsome, elegant man we associate with the name. He was good-looking, but he seemed rather awkward and ill-at-ease. He had been an acrobat in the British musical halls, and he brought that sense of timing and physical awareness into his film roles, but he had no background of polish and manners. Hollywood utilized his size and dark good looks, adding to his acrobatic, energetic music hall self the costume of a tuxedo and the prop of a champagne glass. Over the years, the two halves seemed to fuse, so he turned into a film actor who was able to combine a rowdy humor with a romantic mien. He could be a hero who was both romantic and sexy, as well as hilarious and inept. The public loved both halves, and the combination—the fact that one man could be both—endeared him to both men and women alike.

Because of the intimacy of the camera, the successful film actor must base his roles or his acting style largely on the physical characteristics he is born with. Grant made a strength out of a deadpan expression, à la Jack Benny, and used it to say much by saying little. His stiff-necked body and his mobile eyebrows became his comedic stance—or his heroic one—depending on the plot. He looked solid and strong. He could pull a heroine up to safety if she were falling off the face of Mount Rushmore. He also looked handsome and graceful. He could pull her up into the upper berth of a train compartment, too. He used what he had to advantage—and hid none of it. The shifting, nervous eyes. The skeptical look, with the raised eyebrows. The unusual voice, with its Cockney cadences that made him sound like no one else in the world and that kept comic imitators employed ("Judy, Judy, Judy"). The dented chin. The moles.

Cary Grant became a special being, the man all women secretly hoped to meet, and yet he was not just a matinee idol or a sex symbol. A woman felt that if she met him, he might call for her in a Rolls Royce, bring flowers, take her to a great restaurant, converse wittily, and, above all, make her laugh. If her skirt tore up the back in the nightclub as Hepburn's did in *Bringing Up Baby,* he would nobly cover the problem with his top hat. Men liked him, too. His persona was that of an intelligent man, a class act. A man felt an evening with Cary Grant might be fun, unusual, adventurous, even dangerous in a positive way.

Part of Grant's longevity is due to an uncontradictory persona, and yet he had a doubleness. Underneath his surface of suave sophisticate seemed to lurk a naughty child. There was something in him that mocked serious situations, and many of his films cast him as a character who had to pretend to be, or who became through some comic accident, a second character. Thus, he pretended to be his own wife in *I Was a Male War Bride* (1949), and he was transformed literally into the child he once was in *Monkey Business* (1952). To such ridiculousness, he brought charm, grace, and believ-

*"Somebody can be an accidental star. A person can be a giant star in one movie or two movies, maybe, but if a star has staying power, generally speaking, they're talented. I mean anybody can get lucky once. Somebody can make an accident. Anybody could have a good round of golf, but you're not going to have twenty good rounds of golf in a row unless you're good. So I do think stars are good. I think that the contract stars in the old days were special. Those people were really good."*

Michael Eisner

**Manufacturing the look: Marlon Brando in wardrobe test shots for his portrayal of Stanley Kowalski in *A Streetcar Named Desire* (1951).**

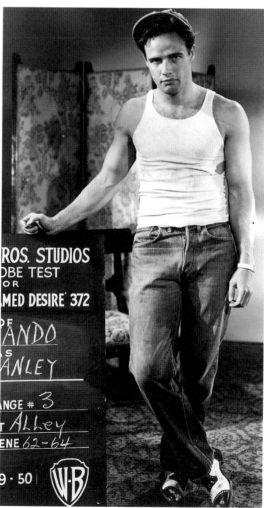

ability. Is this acting? If five generations of Americans believe in it, why not? Grant's career is a tribute to his skill, but also to the system that made him.

Star making, however programmed, is a mysterious process. All his years in films playing different kinds of parts add up to one thing: Cary Grant was "playing himself." Moviegoers like to familiarize themselves with the physical presence of a star, keep in memory the kind of roles they like to see him in, and discard the rest. What is kept becomes the "real Cary Grant presence." After the process has taken place, it becomes even more mysterious when you realize that once the persona of Cary Grant is established, the roles that follow are not exactly uniform either. Two of his films of the 1940s illustrate the point: he was a nutty drama critic in the comedy *Arsenic and Old Lace* and a frustrated Cockney gangster in the tragedy *None But the Lonely Heart*. The years that followed afforded him a different set of characters to portray: a trusted doctor in *People Will Talk* (1951), a suave jewel thief in *To Catch a Thief* (1955), a British naval officer during the Napoleonic Wars in *The Pride and the Passion* (1957). He played everything from a submarine commander, a family man, a real-life composer (Cole Porter), a suspected murderer, to the ultimate challenge—an angel (*The Bishop's Wife*, 1947). Why then is he thought to be always playing himself, always the same? Although his roles are varied, Grant brings to each the common denominator of his physical self, that self that the old Hollywood studio system could package so successfully for the moviegoer, so that Grant became a familiar friend, a trusted presence. His accumulated film roles made him known to us as CARY GRANT, the movie star. The ease and charm with which he appeared, and the number of times he appeared, made us accept him as many different people, all of whom we thought of as Cary Grant, not Mr. Lucky or Mr. Blandings. He was able to play *them* because *they* were like *him*. This is the highest form of film acting, in which the film actor makes the audience believe that the performance is not a performance at all, but a photograph of reality.

Today's actors have a different situation. Cary Grant had a lifetime to appear in movies and establish his persona. To achieve his status as Cary Grant, he had the support of a thriving studio system. Because fewer films are made today, actors have to convince audiences they are great the first time out. They play fewer roles. To make one film every year is unusual, and to make seven in one year the way Cary Grant did is impossible. The chance of becoming a familiar friend to the audience has been greatly reduced in film (although not in television). The new young actor who is trying to establish his image also competes in a world gone mad with images: TV stars, movie stars, politicians as stars, sports stars, rock stars, models as stars. Instant Superstars. Viewers, too, are more sophisticated. They want many kinds of heroes: astronauts, basketball players, authors, medical wizards, and daredevils. Competition is fierce. The world has always had multiple heroes, but today's world assimilates them and brings new ones to our living room on a daily basis. Is it any wonder that today's stars eschew the concept of Movie Star and try to establish themselves via a series of unusual and contradictory roles that are said to "stretch" their talents? "Stretching" really means always giving the voracious public something different, keeping ahead of their boredom. Audiences go to see a Robert De Niro film to see the De Niro performance, not the De Niro persona.

Today's stars try to create a roster of different roles in which to showcase the variety of their talent (clockwise from top left): Robert De Niro is a sadistic tatooed killer in *Cape Fear* . . . a jazz saxophone player in *New York, New York* . . . real life boxer Jake LaMotta in *Raging Bull* . . . and Jodie Foster's protector, Travis Bickle, in *Taxi Driver* . . . four films directed by Martin Scorsese.

*"People like stars. It's part of the charisma of the business. They like to see them. They like to think they can look like them. They like to think they could live like them."*

Michael Eisner

Yet, De Niro, like Cary Grant, lives within his physical limits on film. Although he gained a great deal of weight in order to play Jake La Motta in *Raging Bull* (1980), the camera was close enough that we could still see it's Robert De Niro (inside there somewhere). The historical truth is that there were always actors on film who submerged themselves to the roles they played. Even in the days of Cary Grant, actors Paul Muni and George Arliss undertook roles that consciously were different and that did not create a persona. And today, despite the difficulty of achieving it, we still have some "movie stars" who are recognized by audiences for a "persona" or particular type: Clint Eastwood, who has lasted nineteen years in the top box-office rankings, and, of course, Burt Reynolds and Arnold Schwarzenegger. Even Jack Nicholson, considered a fine and versatile actor, has a "Jack Nicholson role"—the antisocietal misfit. The bottom line of film acting is, false nose or not, the audience actually *does* decide whom they believe in when they see them.

The creation of a movie star still is a mysterious process. What we can say for sure is that it was more planned in the past than it is today. In the years 1930–1960, studios *invested* in creating stars, because those men and women were employees of the system and thus valuable commodities. Despite all the calculations, however, stardom was still promoted on the one hand (the studio set the young person up, developed his or her skills and gifts, and heavily promoted and advertised him or her) and serendipitous on the other (audiences discovered someone in a bit part and liked them, or bought or didn't buy the manufactured "star" product the studio put out there).

There are enough mistakes made by Hollywood in creating stars, and enough accidents in someone's becoming one, that it can only give pause. Which came first, the chicken or the egg? Did Joan Crawford become a star because MGM made her over and publicized her, or did she become a star because she seemed real, authentic to women in the audience who, like her, wanted something better in life?

The star-making system wasn't always perfect. For instance, Samuel Goldwyn brought the exceptionally beautiful and quite talented Anna Sten to the United States

In the 1950s and early 1960s audiences identified with alienated young actors such as James Dean (left), the hero of *Rebel Without a Cause*, and Steve McQueen (opposite, upper left), who got his start in television as the hero of the western *Wanted: Dead or Alive*. Method-trained actors from Broadway such as Paul Newman (opposite, below) and Sidney Poitier (opposite, right) also found stardom on the big screen, playing heroes who, for differing reasons, stood outside of society and judged its rules harshly.

Two of today's most popular actors, who are triumphs of personality in the tradition of the stars from an older Hollywood: Jack Nicholson (opposite), who can make even a cartoon character such as the Joker from *Batman* become eerily real, and the larger than life Arnold Schwarzenegger (right), who as the Terminator has brought action films to the pinnacle of box-office success.

to "become the next Garbo." Sten was a flop. Although audiences had embraced European actresses with exotic looks, such as Garbo and Dietrich, they did not take to Sten. Home she went, her name forever associated with a mistake in star making. The legend became: you can't make a star—the public makes stars. This was further borne out by the example of Gloria De Haven and June Allyson in MGM's 1944 movie *Two Girls and A Sailor*. De Haven and Allyson were cast as sisters, with the assumption being that de Haven would become the next big star and Allyson would become the next lovable sidekick. De Haven was sweetly pretty in the healthy, plump-cheeked style of the All-American girl of the era. She also had a great figure, and could sing and dance with skill. She was a cross between Betty Grable and Lana Turner, two successful box-office stars. Allyson could also sing and dance, and she was a solid actress. She was cute, not beautiful, and she had a gravelly, almost masculine voice. She was not the sort of female that men pinned up pictures of in their lockers, but De Haven was. Both were under contract to MGM and the film presented them paired for the public to enjoy. Result: Allyson became one of the biggest box-office draws of the next decade, a beloved star whose name is still well known today. De Haven had a solid career, and still works, but never attained top-drawer stardom. Here the public *did* decide, but only, of course, after MGM polished the two women and put them forward.

An example of the star-manufacturing process that worked in the 1950s was Kim Novak. Originally a shy, slightly clumsy girl from Chicago named Marilyn Novak, the actress was actively groomed for stardom by Harry Cohn of Columbia Pictures as a threat to his top female star of the day, Rita Hayworth. Novak's hair was dyed from her natural dark to platinum blonde, and she was carefully cast in a series of low-budget films to develop her skills. She was heavily promoted with a series of articles in such magazines as *Life*, and the word was put out that she wore *only* lavender. Glamorous photographs of her appeared in all the major magazines of the day. Novak, unlike Sten, caught on with the public and played leading roles for over a decade.

Quite possibly the perfect and most enduring example of Hollywood female stardom is Joan Crawford. She was born poor in Texas in 1908 and had to fight for everything she had. With a minimum of education and a maximum of good looks, she forged her way forward in life, dancing in the chorus and ending up in California with a beginner's contract in 1925. Her name was Lucille Le Sueur, but she had also been known as Billie Cassin. "Cassin" was the name of her mother's second husband, and "Billie" was Crawford's family nickname. MGM signed her to a five-year contract for seventy-five dollars per week. During that time, Crawford was totally obligated to MGM, but they had the option of cancelling their agreement with her every six months. Thus, if she did not work hard or did not catch the public's eye, they could dump her.

## *"I never learned how to spell regret."*

Joan Crawford

Crawford accepted this willingly. For her, it was more money than she had ever had, and it was a chance to make something of herself. She agreed to anything the studio told her to do: cover up her natural freckles with heavy makeup; straighten her teeth; take diction lessons, singing lessons, and lessons in manners; and, the big one, undergo a contest in which she allowed the public to choose a new name for her. Thus it was that Lucille/Billie became "Joan." The fan magazine *Movie Weekly* ran a contest with Crawford's picture, asking subscribers to think up her new name and promising them that whatever name won the contest, she would willingly adopt it. And she did. She said many times when the name "Joan Crawford" was finally settled on, she didn't even know how to pronounce it, calling herself "Jo-Ann" for several years until someone straightened her out.

The contest was real, but whether or not the studio actually went with the name it generated or secretly made up one, the fact is that Crawford willingly lost her birth name and accepted another. In fact, she accepted a whole new other self, doing everything she possibly could to obey her new bosses, MGM. Over the years Crawford became known as a "self-made" movie star, a woman who literally invented herself. Ironically, of course, the studio owned her during those years, controlling her personal life, her weekly schedule, and her career. Although she begged to be given serious roles "like Norma Shearer," she was cast in movies such as *Ice Follies of 1939* (1939) and finally dumped by MGM when the public began to tire of her. (Crawford had the last laugh, moving over to Warner Brothers, winning an Oscar, and going on for another twenty years of stardom.)

In order to keep the products coming down the assembly line, the studios had to ensure that their most famous and successful stars (and directors, too, for that matter) were readily available. The most popular stars signed elaborate contracts that gave a studio virtually total control of their careers. The studio could assign any performer they had to any film they were making without consultation of the performer, and with or without his or her consent. It could lend them out to other studios. It could suspend them for bad behavior. As a result, even as successful an actress as Bette Davis could be stuck in junk, because she was an employee drawing a salary. If there were no good parts available, she was put to work in what *was* available. Even after she was nominated for an Oscar for *Of Human Bondage* (1934), Davis was assigned such minor material as the "other woman" in *Housewife.*

In the studio system a star's working day was long and exhausting. There would inevitably be many periods of time in which a star was kept waiting to be called before the camera. These times, if known to be of a specified duration, would be used to pose the stars for stills and glamour photographs. They also had to grant interviews, answer fan mail, take lessons in acting and diction, have their hairdos and makeup retouched,

*"She had it. She really did. I met her somewhere around 1931. She was absolutely stunning, but she was very modest about herself. I was so struck by her beauty when she walked into my beauty shop, and she wasn't already made up either. I was overwhelmed by her."*

Sidney Guilaroff

The epitome of stardom, Joan Crawford, stares frankly into her old friend the camera in one of the thousands of photographs (this one of about 1930–1931) taken of her throughout her long career.

Joan Crawford . . . from 1925 to the 1970s a top star in the front ranks, adapting her image from flapper to shop girl to glamour queen to motherhood to demented older woman. Whatever it took, she did it, fifty years a star. Finally rewarded for her efforts with her ultimate goal, the Oscar, Crawford was too ill with the flu to attend the ceremony, but not too ill to pose for photos immediately after the award was secured (opposite).

*"We had a finishing school on the lot, and when you were finally good enough you were turned over to directors and put into movies."*

Arthur Wilde

practice posture, and rehearse dance numbers—all supervised and planned for maximum exploitation of their time. On days when delays occurred, and no plans could be made since at any moment the star would be needed, the actors and actresses of Hollywood had to find things to fill their idle time. They were not allowed to leave the lot. Child stars did their homework. Henry Wilcoxin carved tiny boats. John Barrymore and Gary Cooper painted. Joan Crawford knitted and Errol Flynn . . . well, he had his own hobbies.

In a studio publicity book from 1938, Myrna Loy described her workday—a typical day for any star in the studio system. She pointed out that a fan's idea of a star's life—"the lie-abed-till-noon, lily-of-the-field character"—was far removed from her life. Loy described what was required from her after being assigned to a role in a movie that would not start for three weeks:

The first week is devoted entirely to the Wardrobe Department. A dozen or more gowns, each requiring from three to four hours in the fitting room, are prepared. After they are perfectly fit to the body, each has to be tried on for endless camera tests to be made, because no matter how good it may look in the fitting room, it is the eye of the camera that must be satisfied. Does the material photograph with the desired lustre? Is the drapery effect graceful when the star is actually in motion wearing it, if, for instance, it is a ball gown? Will the hat brim cause an unexpected shadow on the face? Every detail has to be perfect in advance, so as not to hold up shooting or cause a need for reshoots. Most of this requires me to stand patiently and quietly for hours.

After her clothes were correct, Loy had to undergo hairdressing and makeup tests. For instance, if the picture was about a story taking place in the 1880s, careful research would have to be made into the exact arrangements of her curls. Several different coiffures would be devised and tested,

*"I'll give Joan Crawford very high honors. She knew what she wanted, and she went out and got it."*

Joseph Mankiewicz

perhaps three or four chosen for the actual film, with corresponding makeup. She was not allowed to eat, read, talk on the telephone, or sleep during the process. Loy would sit still for all of this, while teams of men and women pulled at her, probed her, and studied her.

Loy had to pose for the photographs required for the film and to study her script to learn the role. On the day shooting began, she had to be up by six or earlier in order to arrive at the studio by seven A.M. Since all stars were required to be dressed in costume, made up, and coiffed for a nine A.M. start, two hours were allowed to get the star ready on time.

Loy described how films are shot out of sequence and how scenes must be repeated so that they can be photographed from various angles. Loy pointed out, "If you could accompany an actress on her day's work, you would realize just how much time is spent in repetition of one kind or another. So many things happen to mar a scene, even after it has been carefully planned and rehearsed. Someone may forget a line or stumble over a word. A lamp may start 'singing,' or some inflections or sound effect may register incorrectly. Work continues past six P.M., sometimes until seven or eight if the production requirements demand it." (Stars worked six days a week in those days, and there was no overtime pay.) After arriving home at approximately ten P.M., Loy only had time to eat, take off her makeup, bathe, and study lines for the next day. It was, also, she reminded her fans, necessary to "get a good eight hours of rest in preparation for the following day."

Many stars struggled with this ownership of their lives. Once they began to be popular, and developed real box-office appeal, they attempted to use their positions as leverage against the studio. Some brave ones, cast in roles they hated or that they felt were demeaning to their careers, refused to work. Up until 1944 this got them nowhere, because studios were able to "suspend" the stars. "Suspension" of a star meant that any amount of time that a star refused to show up for work was just added to the end of their contract. In this way, an original seven-year contract could end up running for nine or ten years. This was broken in 1944 by Olivia DeHavilland, who, while most stars feared losing their livelihoods, found the courage to sue her home studio, Warner Brothers. Resulting in what became known as "the DeHavilland decision," this lawsuit freed stars from studio bondage, as the studios were forced to release stars from their contracts after no more than seven years, including suspension time. At that point, a star could either renegotiate a more favorable contract or move on to another studio.

Today's stars are not "employees" who are "owned" in the manner DeHavilland fought or Loy described. The star today can form a company to produce his or her own films, and most stars search for good scripts, good costar deals, and good directors to work with, developing and making their own careers as they go forward. Big-name stars,

Previous pages: The height of style—Audrey Hepburn (right) and Grace Kelly and Frank Sinatra in *High Society* (left; 1955).

Above: Myrna Loy's career lasted over fifty years, as she progressed from playing oriental beauties to the perfect American wife.

Opposite: Just four of Hollywood's most beautiful women from the 1940s and 1950s: Maureen O'Hara (top left), Irish redhead; Ava Gardner (top right), sultry sex symbol; Susan Hayward (bottom right), Oscar winner for *I Want to Live*; and Jane Russell, who injected humor into her status as sex symbol—and thereby attained enduring fame.

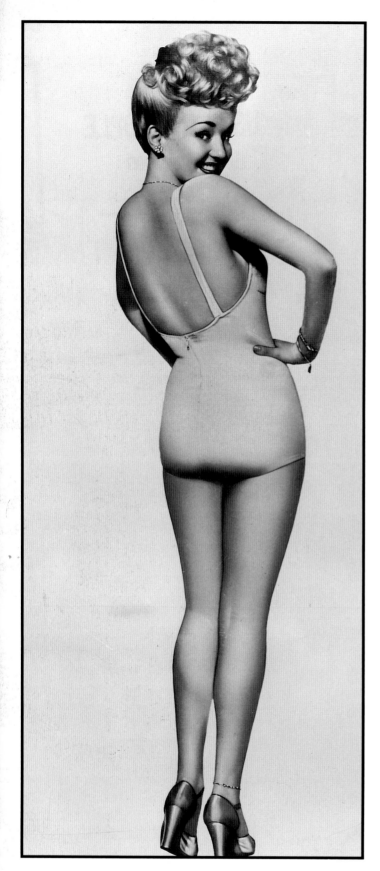

*"I wanna be loved by you. . . .*
*Just you and nobody else but you."*

Marilyn Monroe, singing in *Some Like It Hot*

such as Clint Eastwood, Goldie Hawn, or Robert Redford, have their own production companies. Madonna, Meg Ryan, or Sharon Stone have people who search out properties for them and who are hired exclusively to develop properties that suit their particular talents and interests. Although stars have publicists, these men and women are working for the star, not vice-versa, and often their job is to keep publicity away from their overhyped employers. Daily newspapers, weekly magazines, monthly magazines, TV talk shows, and specialized entertainment news programs all compete for movie stars and are hungry to interview them and cover their latest projects. No movie star today would ever make five movies a year the way the old-timers did, and star salaries are astronomical compared with the past. Furthermore, stars today often earn a percentage of the film's gross, insuring financial security if even one film becomes a hit.

Although stars are still "found," in that unknowns get leading roles and the public still discovers secondary players they want to see more of, there are serious proving grounds for beginners in college theater, regional theater, comedy clubs, and television outlets that have replaced the chorus lines and drugstore counters of the past. Stars are no longer sought out on the basis of beauty alone as much as in the past. Aspirants to stardom still flock to Hollywood, but they come more reared for what stardom will mean in their lives, and they come better equipped to protect their own financial interests. Most of the young people who enter the motion picture world now are well educated, and they hire powerful agents to represent their interests. Thus they have better control over what happens to them, but they do not have total control.

Although today's stars have more freedom over their careers than those of yesterday, they pay a heavy price for that independence. The old studio system coddled stars, nurtured them, and protected them from harm. If a star in the golden era became involved in a minor scandal, it was in the studio's interest to have it hushed up by press agents. If they needed money, the studio loaned it to them. And they seldom met the public face to face, as they were protected by studio gates, studio police, and studio policy, which kept them working full time. Today's stars are often victimized by the tabloid press and a voracious public that literally stalks them from home to restaurant to office and back.

**Left:** The most famous pin-up girl from World War II, box-office queen of the 1940s, Betty Grable. Grable's place as the blonde and sexy star of the 1940s was taken by Marilyn Monroe in the 1950s. Grable, who liked Monroe, allegedly told her: "I've had mine. Go get yours." **Opposite:** Monroe and Tom Ewell in *The Seven-Year Itch* (1955). **Following pages:** Today's blondes, Madonna (with Willem Dafoe in *Body of Evidence*, 1993) and Sharon Stone (with William Baldwin in *Sliver*; 1993), put a more overt kind of sexuality on the screen, but come from a long film tradition of blonde "bombshells."

*"You become a prisoner of your image.
It's a gold-plated cell, but it's still a cell."*

Rick Nicita

What is more or less the same about stardom today is that the public still selects who to like and who not to like. No matter how much the critics may scorn Tom Cruise, the people who go to the movies like him. No matter how much critics tried to write Sylvester Stallone's career off, when he appeared in the kind of movie people like to see him in during the summer of 1993 (*Cliffhanger*), moviegoers turned out and made the film a hit. What can finally be said about the creation of movie stars that is unequivocally true is simply this: it's a mysterious process.

"In real life, all movie stars are short and their heads are too big for their bodies. That's true. I mean, their heads are like a total eclipse sometimes at a premiere. I don't think I've ever met a movie star, almost, that her head or his head was not too big. Gives them more room for makeup. It's a bigger canvas. I mean all of them. Think about it. Look at them. Their heads are too big. A movie star is mythic. A movie star is like no one you've ever seen walking around in your daily life. I think there are movie stars today that are like old movie stars. I mean, I like new movie stars, but I like the old kind better. Does fame ruin people's lives? Well, maybe. But why did they become actors? A lot of them are so obsessed to become famous that if they were given the choice . . . you could become more famous in twenty years if you died right now . . . I am convinced that some of them would say yes. I *admire* those kind of people."

John Waters

Child stars, despite W.C. Fields's warnings against working with them, have always been sure-fire box office in American movies, from Shirley Temple (opposite) in the 1930s to Anna Pacquin (left; with Holly Hunter) in *The Piano* (1993) and Macaulay Culkin (above) in the *Home Alone* movies of the early 1990s.

# Genres

## Nine Basic Rules, Learned at the Movies:

1. Never go down to the basement or up to the attic when you are alone in the house at night, especially if it's raining. (There is something really bad there.)

2. Never lose the telephone number or address of the person of the opposite sex that you just met and truly, truly hated. (You are going to end up marrying him or her.)

3. Never say how terribly, deeply happy you are. (If you are riding in a car, it will immediately run into a tree. If you are on a plane, it will crash. If you are walking down the street, you'll be run over by a runaway bicycle. And if you follow up those words with a cough, you will die within ten minutes of an unnamed disease.)

4. Never believe that nice old couple that you met while traveling were really a nice old couple. (They are kidnappers or spies or worse.)

5. Never climb a tree in a combat zone. (Those who do are instantly shot in the head by a sniper, even in peacetime.)

6. Never wear an undershirt if you are a man. (Clark Gable didn't.)

7. Never wear a black satin shirt with a slit in the side if you are a woman. (People will think you are bad, and you will also be murdered by a madman who thinks you are his mother.)

8. Never accept a date to the prom with the best-looking, richest, most popular boy in school. (He will desert you for his own kind, and the cruel laughter of your peers will ring in your ears.)

9. Never, but never, stop at the Bates Motel.

Opposite: The modern version of the western morality tale is effectively realized by Gene Hackman and Clint Eastwood, the reluctant hero, in *Unforgiven* (1993) (top), directed by Eastwood. One of the best examples of neo-noir (and in this case noir filmed in color) is director Lawrence Kasdan's 1981 *Body Heat* (center), with William Hurt playing a Southern lawyer entrapped into crimes of passion by Kathleen Turner.

"Hits create genres. You know, everybody tries to do the same thing over and over again. And since the public creates hits, they also create genres. Movie studios have never changed. If something is successful, they will say give me five of those. It's like the dress business, or any business."

Andrew Bergman

The world of the Hollywood movie is a unique place where we hear and see all manner of things. It's a world that suggests how we live, how we pretend to live, and how we want to live. It's the world of the prairie oyster and Wilma's Waffle Shop, the place where people bark out wondrous expressions that we never hear in real life, such as "Snap out of it!" "Where am I?" and "Now you're talkin'." It's also a world that teaches us some basic lessons in life (see sidebar).

These nine rules are known to all filmgoers. Why? Because they are basic genre conventions that we have seen over and over again in countless movies. They come to us from horror movies, screwball comedies, melodramas, spy films, war movies, romantic comedies, women's films, high school movies, and the Alfred Hitchcock movie, a genre unto itself. We recognize them and laugh at them, but we don't necessarily laugh while we are watching the films that contain them. Then, they seem real, and somehow right. They are part of our national filmgoing heritage, part of the product we've been sold—and have bought—over the years that Hollywood has been making movies.

Although the motion picture has a rich international heritage of great films, most people think of movies and Hollywood as synonymous. Over the years, America has made more movies that people remember than any other country, only partly because we've just made more movies, period. The popularity and success of American cinema can be defined by many things: stars such as Cagney and Monroe and Eastwood, technical innovations such as the development of sound, or concepts such as "glamour" through which women were persuaded to pluck their eyebrows and men were inspired to ditch their undershirts. But the real reason is this: Hollywood movies know how to tell a story.

No matter what criticism might be made about Hollywood movies, there is one thing everyone can agree on: the good ones know how to tell a story, how to draw you in and hold you there till the last frame. And, like all good storytellers, the filmmakers in Hollywood have always known that once you think up one the audience really likes, it's a smart thing to repeat it. Tell it again. And again and again. This shrewd business ploy was so common in Hollywood that, during the 1930s, the writing department at Warner Brothers was known as "the echo chamber." Still today, studios are remaking sure-fire hits from the past, as movies such as *Born Yesterday* (1950), *Cape Fear* (1962), *The Ghost and Mrs. Muir* (1947), *An Affair to Remember* (1957), and *The Bad Seed* (1956) have all been remade recently. Mostly, however, the practice of telling familiar and successful stories takes the form that is known as "genre."

Genre, as related to the movies, is a tricky term to define. Although models of genre exist in literature and art, film genre as pursued by a large business system and the collaborative filmmaking process that is Hollywood becomes an ever-changing and evolving concept. Basically, genre stories were movies the audience could recognize in advance as something familiar, or known, something they had seen before with similar characters and situations and settings. This type of movie was important in a business that wanted to sell as much product as it could and that had to supply a seemingly never-ending demand on the part of the public. Hollywood put out between four hundred and six hundred movies per year during the golden age of the studio system. Where were the ideas for six hundred different movie plots? Where was the time to develop even a hundred totally original stories? Since the studios were actually efficient factories, they used assembly-line tactics. They had available familiar star faces and familiar popular stories with familiar costumes and settings. The stars each represented a certain "type" (all-American girl, flawed hero, fallen woman, red-blooded he-man), and the stories themselves were soon labeled as "types" (westerns, musicals, screwball comedies, gangster movies).

Movies were—and still are—labeled by the industry that makes them according to type. Nothing can wreck the commercial success of a movie more than for an audience to go into a cinema expecting one thing and finding something else. No matter how good the "something else" might be, viewers are inevitably disappointed, and the film fails. ("I thought it was going to be an Arnold Schwarzenegger action film," said people who hated *Last Action Hero*, a big flop in the summer of 1993. Instead, it was a bizarre comedy spoof of a Schwarzenegger film, but the audience had expected it to play straight with them.)

Film genres can be seen positively, as a chance to vary and enliven familiar tales in new ways; or negatively, as a willful conformity and dullness, a lack of originality that is potentially subversive in that it can become a propaganda tool that sells a load of clams to the unwary masses.

There are many popular genres associated with Hollywood. Most of them emerged during the era of silent films, because they were already popular forms in fiction and theater. For instance, melodramas, stories of family conflict, social realism, comedy (both slapstick and sophisticated), crime, horror, western tales, and epics were all made in the silent-movie days. Gangster movies got their beginnings then, too, but were given new life and pizzazz by Prohibition and by the coming of sound, which could not only add the rat-a-tat of gunfire to the stories, but also the "dese, dem, dose" colorful conversations of the gangsters. One popular genre had to wait for the invention of sound: the musical film. Musicals, of course, were also already popular on Broadway and in vaudeville, so all the forms of genre story that Hollywood developed were probably already present somewhere in the storytelling world. Even science fiction, which most people associate with more modern times, was popular from the very first days of movies.

What Hollywood did was visualize all these familiar stories in specific ways. It made them come alive and move, and, ultimately, talk to viewers. Westerns meant "smile when you say that, pardner," and gangsters meant "you're going for a ride." Horror populated our dreams with wolfmen, monsters manufactured in laboratories by mad doctors, vampires, and mummies out on the town. Science fiction gave us the man in the moon getting a rocket in his eyeball, and underwater submarines with huge pipe organs to be played. Musicals—one of Hollywood's most influential genres—brought us Fred Astaire and Ginger Rogers dancing on Bakelite floors in a Venice no one could possibly have thought was meant to be real . . . Gene Kelly dancing in the rain . . . Judy Garland, lips trembling, looking over the rainbow . . . and the sense that, if a man and woman truly loved one another the way that Jeanette MacDonald and Nelson Eddy did, they would step back and sing at each other with a vengeance.

# 3 THE WESTERN

"We know that people like legends. I think people like legends more than
they like truth. I think there is a fascination with the western hero, because
the West is a great myth."

Lindsay Anderson

No genre is more typically American than the western. No storytelling format is
more indigenous to Hollywood. It's our West—an awesome landscape, a dramatic history, and a colorful cast of real-life characters who settled it. Although "the
death of the western" has been announced more than once in film history, both in
the early 1940s and in the 1980s, the format never really goes away. In 1993 Clint
Eastwood was awarded an Oscar for Best Director and nominated for Best Actor for
his western film *Unforgiven*, which also won the academy's Best Picture award. In that
same year no less than eight new westerns were in the works, three of which were to

> *"Just another person adrift on the great landscape of the West. Maybe he drifted along; maybe he was asked for. He has to work his situation through ingenuity— if he doesn't, he doesn't exist."*
>
> Clint Eastwood

feature women in key roles in a kind of retelling of the usual stories from a more feminine point of view.

Just as the settlement of the West and the closing of the frontier were key to the development of nineteenth-century America's social and political identity, the creating of the western film is key to America's cultural sense of itself in the twentieth century. Every American knows what a western is. Ask anyone for a list of characters and situations that are typical of westerns, and you'll hear: "The good guy in the white hat, the bad guy in the black hat, the schoolmarm from the East, the saloon singer, the ranchers and the sheepherders, cowboys and Indians." The concept of The American West as a place in which to set a particular kind of story is basic to Hollywood's history.

What are the conventions of the American western, and how do they reflect American values and, at the same time, shape them? First, there must be the Hero. He is associated with the natural landscape from which he seems to emerge. He is strong and rugged, and he is mostly a loner. He stays outside of the settled community, allied with the wilderness, and he settles matters, if pushed, through violent confrontation.

The western heroes of American films have been portrayed by a magnificent list of male movie stars: William S. Hart, Tom Mix, Gary Cooper, John Wayne, James Stewart, Randolph Scott, Joel McCrea, Henry Fonda, Clint Eastwood. Even their musical counterparts, Gene Autry and Roy Rogers, and their comic variations, such as Bob Hope in *The Paleface* (1948), are impressive. What most western actors have in common are large physical statures, distinctive voices, a calm presence, a particular way of moving and walking, and above-average looks. In fact, all these men are beautiful, although no one would ever think to describe them that way. Gary Cooper, John Wayne, and Clint Eastwood were particularly good looking as young men.

The heroes these western actors play are what is called "strong, silent types." Although Stewart's western roles, for example, are often highly emotional and violent

**Previous pages: Modern westerns such as director and writer Lawrence Kasdan's *Silverado* (1985) revived the traditional image of the lonely rider against the sky, moving his horses across the open, rugged landscape of the American West.**

**Left: In *The Far Country* (1955), James Stewart (foreground) rides ahead of his saddle pal Walter Brennan through a landscape typical of a western directed by Anthony Mann.**

**Following pages: Producer David O. Selznick brought his epic vision of America to the drama *Duel in the Sun* (1946), directed by King Vidor, attempting to duplicate the success of *Gone with the Wind* with his enlarged vision of the western genre.**

men as compared to the more noble and quietly mythic heroes of Scott, all these men play the sort of western hero who does not discuss things. He just *acts*. Collectively, they represent America's idea of what it took to tame the West: men of action and courage.

The next requirement for the western is the Villain, an opposing personality to the Hero, so that they may meet in a final shootout, or showdown, against the last of the necessary motifs, the Landscape. In westerns, the landscape inside the frame is a real place. It's the American West: broad, open, dramatic, vast. Although there are a few exceptions, most westerns were shot on location because part of what people paid to see was the scenery, the epic space.

Landscape is all-important to a western movie. It tends to dictate the primary meaning of the story. The hero is positioned in it according to how the movie is trying to get you to see his position in the story. Men such as the heroes of the Old West need to be set against landscapes that not only provide a dramatic backdrop, but that also reflect the simple dignity and physical beauty they represent. Fortunately, the American West can more than meet the challenge. Famous westerns have been set in Monument Valley in Utah and in Arizona (director John Ford's movies), the Pacific Northwest (*The Far Country*, 1954), Texas (*The Texas Rangers*, 1936), the Dakotas (*Dances with Wolves*, 1990), Wyoming (*Wyoming Kid*, 1947), Montana (*The Missouri Breaks*, 1976), and even Florida (*Seminole*, 1953).

Three of the most famous directors of American westerns—John Ford, Raoul Walsh, and Anthony Mann—worked with their filmmaking teams to use the space in different ways. John Ford put his heroes inside a landscape that is so monumental (in the literal and figurative sense) that they can only be seen as icons against a dramatic background. When the cavalry walks its horses across Monument Valley while lightning strikes, the sky darkens, and rain threatens in *She Wore a Yellow Ribbon* (1949), the space becomes a dramatic backdrop for heroism. As Ford's characters and story are vibrant and alive, he uses the western space almost as a stage on which to parade

**Right: One of the most influential and respected westerns in the history of the genre was director John Ford's *Stagecoach* (1939). In addition to establishing John Wayne as a western landmark, the film presented this memorable image: a stagecoach full of passengers, crossing the dramatic landscape of Monument Valley.**

their heroic actions. Mann's *Bend of the River* (1952), *The Naked Spur* (1953), and *The Far Country* (1954) all starring James Stewart, show a different space. The landscape in which Stewart struggles with himself suggests his psychological state and the changes he is undergoing. In *Bend of the River*, the river represents the turning point, or change in his life, and in *The Naked Spur* he fights for his life on a precarious ledge above a roaring river. In *The Far Country*, he is a man who has turned his back on civilization, and his landscape is the frozen north of the Yukon.

Mann's western heroes live inside a changing frame, with a shifting geography. In the epic *Man of the West* (1958), the hero (Gary Cooper) begins a long and hazardous journey from a green and fertile world, in which he feels secure, across an increasingly rocky and barren landscape. His story is a journey in which the space is constantly redefined and changed as he is redefined and changed by events. He ends up fighting for his life in a ghost town, an arid, rocky, and unforgiving space. The landscape is used not just to give a simplified change from safety to danger, but also to indicate that the hero, once a cruel and violent outlaw, has left civilization and gone out to face what is inside himself.

In Walsh's *Colorado Territory* (1949), the hero (Joel McCrea) is an outlaw on the run, a man desperate for a last chance at a real life on a ranch of his own. The open space he rides across after he breaks out of jail seems never-ending. Even on his horse, he looks small and insignificant against the enormous rocks. The way McCrea is set against the landscape speaks of his ultimate chances at getting what he wants. He is in a situation that he will not be able to control because, like the space he rides through,

The many faces of the western hero (left to right): Paul Newman, the angry young outlaw; William S. Hart, the rugged frontiersman; John Wayne, the great icon of the genre; Randolph Scott, one of the most underrated and most popular with the general audience; Gary Cooper, in his Oscar-winning role as the sheriff in *High Noon* . . . and the most recent of the great American western stars, Clint Eastwood, who directed and starred in films that dramatically expanded on the traditional western morality plays.

it is bigger than he is. Although McCrea plays a rugged and capable hero, a man with great skill and brains, the space he is in will finally dominate him. (There is no happy ending to *Colorado Territory*. McCrea ends up dead.)

You might see the powerful western landscape in long shot in both *Colorado Territory* and Ford's *My Darling Clementine* (1946). It might even look the same to you. But the way the heroes live in it differs. Joel McCrea would ride alone, seen in a long-distance shot, small against the overpowering rocks. The heroes of *Clementine*, who live in Tombstone, Arizona, are mostly seen in foreground, with the rocky monuments in a distance behind them, defining their legendary status. It happens that the heroes of *Clementine* are named Wyatt Earp (Henry Fonda) and Doc Holliday (Victor Mature). They *are* legendary. The awesome land behind them seems to *be* them, to represent who and what they are. Thus, the landscape never overwhelms them as it does McCrea, even if they, too, are seen in long shot. The space inside the frame, although impressive in size and beauty, creates a suitable arena in which these truly mythic heroes live and die.

Using Hero, Villain, and Landscape as a basic configuration, many different kinds of western stories have been told over the years: cowboys versus Indians, outlaws on the run; sheepherders versus ranchers; farmers versus cattlemen; stagecoach robbery; lone gunfighter cleaning up a corrupt town; famous gunfighter unable to escape his leg-

end. All more or less still present a viewer with the basic ingredients of hero, villain, and landscape, even when a hero is an antihero, or an outlaw, and the landscape is a town (as in *High Noon*).

Over the years, the western has been used to reflect America's changing attitudes. Current historical events—World War II, the HUAC investigations, and Vietnam for instance—are often reflected by or buried in story forms, and this helped Hollywood keep the western form alive. For instance, the famous real-life outlaw, Billy the Kid, has been a popular hero of many westerns, from 1930 to 1990. Tracing the changes reflected in a series of films that all purport to tell the story of Billy the Kid shows the way that westerns make use of old legends for new concerns. The movies are authenticated by the fact that there really *was* a Billy the Kid. (Part of the appeal of westerns is that they seem to be true, since after all there *is* a West and we *did* settle it. Seeing the stories photographed against their authentic western landscapes gives a truth and credibility to the stories. Film makes them live for us. Yet as John Ford once pointed out, movies don't give us the true West, but "the West we ought to have had.")

William Bonney (Billy the Kid) in real life was a twenty-one-year-old condemned man when he shot down two deputies in a Lincoln, New Mexico, courthouse, stole a horse, and rode off to hide in the rugged Capitan Mountains. Within three months, Billy (whose birth name was actually Henry McCarty) was shot down by Sheriff Pat Garrett in a Fort Sumner ranch house. Those are the facts, but the movies (as well as books and short stories) have twisted them, turned them, decorated them, and embellished them to the point where almost no one knows for sure what is really true: more than fifty movies have been made that have Billy the Kid somewhere in the plot.

*Billy the Kid* (directed by King Vidor; 1930), *Billy the Kid* (David Miller; 1941), *The Left Handed Gun* (Arthur Penn; 1958), *Pat Garrett and Billy the Kid* (Sam Peckinpah; 1973), and *Young Guns* (Christopher Cain; 1988) span almost sixty years of movie history, each telling essentially the same story to a new decade of moviegoers. Billy progresses from a jolly free spirit of the range who works with the good guys (1930), to an aging juvenile delinquent who needs an understanding father figure to help him change from a bad guy into a good guy (1941), to a twisted juvenile (1958), to a potentially decent guy betrayed by authorities (1973), to a young punk with an inborn love of violence (1988). Billy's character is the leading role in all these movies, and he is played, in chronological order, by John Mack Brown (a former football star who was a favorite cowboy actor of the time), Robert Taylor (a handsome leading man), Paul Newman (a method actor), Kris Kristofferson (an actor associated with antiestablishment roles both on and off the screen), and Emilio Esteves (a popular young actor of the period).

The man who kills Billy, Pat Garrett, is similarly portrayed in different ways. In 1930, Wallace Beery, a great ham actor known for his appeal to audiences as a lovable bad guy, presents Garrett as a worthy rival who respects Billy's ability with a gun. The two are friendly enemies, with Garrett often tipping Billy off in advance to trouble as if they were allies. In the 1941 version, the character of Pat Garrett does not even appear. A pseudo-Garrett, a "childhood friend" of Billy's, played by Brian Donlevy, takes his place as the man who gets Billy a job working for a sympathetic rancher. By 1958 Pat Garrett (John Dehner) has become a remorseless figure who can

make his reputation by killing Billy, for whom he has no sympathy. One of the best Pat Garretts is in the 1973 version. James Coburn, who looks more like an authentic western figure than "Billy" (Kris Kristofferson), effectively creates the role. The two men are played as former close friends, violent, and even evil, but Billy is that way because he has a higher understanding of the meaninglessness and corruption of the institutions of "good." He is nobly bad. Coburn is on the side of "good" in that he is a sheriff. Yet he is portrayed as an opportunistic, selfish man who sides with the law only because times are changing. Where once the power was in the hands of outlaws who broke the law, power will now be in the hands of the law, whose enforcers will do what they want to do in an outlaw manner but with the sanctions of justice. Coburn's Garrett is cynical and represents a loss of faith with America and its institutions.

Victor Mature (foreground) as Doc Holliday is confronted by Henry Fonda as Wyatt Earp in *My Darling Clementine* (1946), the best of the many movies that tell the story of the gunfight at the OK Corral.

Opposite, top to bottom: The changing face of Billy the Kid: John Mack Brown as Billy in 1930; Robert Taylor in the role in 1941; Kris Kristofferson in 1973.

In the 1988 rendition, Patrick Wayne, the son of John Wayne, was cast as the somewhat enigmatic Pat Garrett, whose brief appearances in *Young Guns* are designed to resonate both with his father's image and with the audience's prior knowledge that it is, in fact, Pat Garrett who kills Billy the Kid in the long run. The film ends with Billy on the run, and a voice-over tells us that Pat Garrett is the one who captures Billy. (Garrett will return in the 1990 sequel, *Young Guns II*.) Garrett is used in *Young Guns* as a direct reference point to genre. He is barely explained and rarely seen, and his appearance acts as a kind of omen or harbinger of what will happen to Billy. The audience is clearly expected to know who Garrett is and what will happen.

The endings of these movies are significantly different, also. In 1930 Garrett lets Billy go free, and Billy rides to safety across the border to Mexico, his jolly laugh echoing back, matched by Garrett's equally jolly chuckle. In 1941 Billy is shot by his childhood friend, in a scene in which Billy literally asks for it, knowing that he must be punished for killing people and also knowing he has no future in the changing West. In 1958 Billy is tracked and killed by Garrett; in 1973 he is betrayed by his former friend, Garrett, who is as evil as anyone in the movie; and in 1988 he rides on, getting ready for the sequel (although the aforementioned voice-over does tell the audience his ultimate fate).

Although sixty years pass by from the first Billy to the last, audiences have continued to respond to his story. However, if there had been a consistent attitude taken toward Billy, that might not have been true. If Billy had remained the jolly, straightforward hero of the 1930 version, he would probably not have appealed to the audience of the 1970s or 1980s. What happened was that the story—a typical western format—was subtly shaded to reflect the current attitudes of the decade in which it appeared. Looking at each film, it is possible to see how easily the filmmakers, in a very overt and highly simplified way, created Billy to represent the audience of his day.

In 1930 Billy represented the joy and freedom of the American frontier life. He is energetic and gets things done. He fights with the good guys against a monopolistic "bad guy," a man trying to buy up all the land for himself. The movie celebrates the naughty, anti-authority behavior of Billy, but suggests it is not harmful or destructive to society, that it can be used to help change things for the better. Billy is on the side of those who come to settle the West, the ranchers, and his fight is for everyone to have a piece of the pie. Although the movie reflects Depression fears it still maintains a faith in the American system.

In 1941 Billy is at first an outlaw figure who uses violence to solve all problems and who joins the bad guys. When he meets up with his former childhood friend (Donlevy) and a British father figure (Ian Hunter), he learns how destructive and uncivilized his ways are. The West is changing, says the movie, and outlaws like Billy are no longer needed. The film is on the side of civilized behavior and suggests how important parental guidance is. It believes in wealthy insiders like the father figure (a wealthy rancher) who says problems can be solved by writing to the government. The movie supports the representatives of authority and the status quo. Violence cannot be used to change things, says the film. We must follow the rules of civilized behavior and trust our institutions to make decisions.

The 1958 version was based on a television play, *The Death of Billy the Kid*, by Gore Vidal, and it presents Billy as a misunderstood youth. In this case, it is a classic example of the juvenile delinquent movie of the 1950s, a *Blackboard Jungle* of the West. It is also an attempt to make a "serious" western, as if earlier westerns were not serious. As such, it becomes a pretentious examination of a confused adolescent (Billy) with a violent and self-destructive nature, one who does have good in him if only society will help him bring it out. Newman interprets the role in the classic method-acting style,

**Right: One of a trilogy of films by director John Ford about the U.S. Cavalry, *She Wore a Yellow Ribbon* (1949) beautifully glorifies the rituals of cavalry life, such as this scene at a dance in which Joanne Dru presents her bouquet to John Wayne as Mildred Natwick looks on.**

Above: The violation of the frontier white woman by "savages" was a perennial western theme never so eloquently expressed as in director John Ford's *The Searchers* (1956). In the film's climactic moment, Jeffrey Hunter tries to prevent John Wayne from killing Natalie Wood, who had "gone over to the Indians."

> *"Violence is the ultimate conflict
> and conflict is the ultimate drama."*
>
> Clint Eastwood

internalizing the character's problems so that his neurotic Billy represents the decade of the 1950s with its misunderstood young hero that is failed by the society around him. Billy is a crazy, mixed-up kid trying to avenge the murder of his benefactor.

By 1973 the story presents everything and everybody as corrupt. The concepts of "good guy" are blurred, and all faith with authority and with the system is broken. This movie, excessively violent, suggests that America has lost faith with its old legends and is now retelling the stories to show what the truth was behind legends like Billy the Kid: Billy was a killer and so was Pat Garrett. In this sense, the movie is what is known as a "Vietnam western," or a western that reflects the national despair during the era of the Vietnam War.

In 1988 *Young Guns* was released, a time when teenagers formed the majority of the moviegoing audience that actually saw movies in theaters. To appeal to these fans,

**Violent confrontation is synonymous with westerns. By 1973, after changes in censorship, an even greater level of violence was explicitly shown in the genre. Left: Director Clint Eastwood's** *High Plains Drifter* **(1973). Right: Director Sam Peckinpah's bloody** *Pat Garrett and Billy the Kid* **(1973).**

Billy the Kid and his gang are presented as good-looking, violent young males, with 1980s styles, language, looks, and attitudes. They are a surrogate force for their contemporary audience, merely set in the Old West for some glamour and pizzazz in an attempt to update the old story for modern times. The British father figure who takes the gang in tow to use their gunslinging ability to his own advantage is killed and they lose control. Billy leads them away from good behavior toward more and more violence. He is not mixed up. He is just crazy—a sort of violent street-gang punk for whom there is no real explanation or reform possible. The absence of a parental authority figure leaves these young people on the streets and available for trouble, an obvious 1980s metaphor.

Each of these movies uses the same story and the same drama to refer indirectly to a current historical concern or attitude. A simple overview indicates that the 1930s version is a Depression story and the 1940s calls for a return to normalcy. The 1950s film is worried about juvenile delinquency; the 1970s is concerned with Vietnam; and the 1980s reflects the breakdown of authority.

Westerns continue to be made in this tradition, because any vessel that contains messages with a direct connection to the audience continues in film history. In the 1990s the issues that have found direct connection to audiences through westerns are the exploitation of Native Americans and respect for the environment (*Dances with Wolves*), the issue of violence and its place in our society (*Unforgiven*), and the definition of women's place in American culture (*Outlaws*). The old stories are still told (*Wyatt Earp* and *Tombstone*) and new variations are being put in place. As of 1994, it appears that there will continue to be majestic western heroes, treacherous villains whose skills must be respected, brave and beautiful women, and—ever-present and unforgettable—the picture of the unique American western landscape on the screen. It is the issues these films will deal with that are yet undetermined.

> What would happen if John Wayne met The Man With No Name? Well, if John Wayne met The Man With No Name, The Man would just have to shoot him before he ever had a chance to think about it. Duke would just have to go. That's all. But that's the way it goes in history. He'd still have Walter Brennan to hang on to.
>
> Clint Eastwood

**Inset: In the Vietnam War era, westerns such as director Arthur Penn's *Little Big Man* (1970) reflected on the violent collision of modern America with a less-developed society. Dustin Hoffman starred as a 121-year-old frontiersman who had survived Custer's Last Stand.**

**Right: *Dances with Wolves* (1992) brought a new perspective to the western genre by attempting to present sensitively the daily lives and beliefs of Native Americans, some of whom are sharply contrasted with their wasteful and ignorant white counterparts. Kevin Costner, who starred in the movie (playing a lone frontier soldier who peaceably comes to terms with his neighbors), won the Academy Award for Best Director for this, the first film he directed, which was shot on location in South Dakota.**

# 4 SCREWBALL COMEDY

"There's a pitch in baseball called a screw ball, which was perfected by a pitcher named Carl Hubbell back in the 1930s. It's a pitch with a particular spin that sort of flutters and drops and goes in very unexpected manners. . . screwball comedy was unconventional and went in unexpected directions."

Andrew Bergman

The movie critic James Agee described the essence of Laurel and Hardy's comedy as the scene in which the two are moving a piano across a narrow suspension bridge in the Alps, and halfway across they meet a gorilla. This may be more

*"You introduce the man and the woman— and then you complicate it."*

Susan Seidelman

than the essence of Laurel and Hardy. It may be the essence of all American comedy: it's nuts, it's illogical, it's impossible—it's hilarious. It's also pregnant with endless comic variations, open to unexpected solutions, and primarily grounded in danger.

What *is* a typically American comedy? If, as Freud suggested, jokes are a form of liberation, a release from repressed feelings, then what are the things that Hollywood feels Americans repressed? There are lots of things that Hollywood makes comedies about—any subject is fair game, actually—but there is one popular topic that recurs and recurs. All topics pale beside the one peculiarly American source of hilarity: the battle of the sexes as presented in the Hollywood romantic comedy. Only in America does one find the male-female relationship depicted as a vicious but delightful war in which a man and a woman resist their feelings for one another by battling each other with a peculiarly desperate passion. And only in America is a story of destructive sexual passion told as a freewheeling slapstick event laced with acid wit. What is the subject for stark tragedy in other cultures is, in Hollywood's hands, perfect material for comedy and romance. Movies that treat the battle of the sexes as romantic comedy are also known as "screwball comedies."

As Andrew Bergman defines it through that other classical American art form, baseball, "screwball" means throwing a curve, tossing the viewer something they don't expect. The dictionary defines the term as meaning "erratic, unbalanced, irrational, unconventional." It became a popular slang word in the 1930s and was thus available to apply to movies in which everything is a juxtaposition of opposites: rich and poor, educated and uneducated, resourceful and dumb, honest and dishonest, but most of all, male and female. When two people fall in love, they don't just surrender to the feeling. They fight it out, pulling hideous tricks on one another, impersonating other people, telling lie upon lie, until they finally run out of invention and collapse in each other's arms. It's caveman comedy, physical and painful, but mixed with the highest level of wit and sophistication.

**Previous pages: Cary Grant is behind bars, and Katharine Hepburn likes having him just where she wants him in director Howard Hawks's classic screwball comedy *Bringing Up Baby* (1938).**

**Opposite: *The Awful Truth* (1937) finds the perfect way to present the audience with a couple contemplating sex, without seeming to be about a couple contemplating sex. Cary Grant and Irene Dunne were married once . . . only now they're not . . . only. . . .**

**Right: Maurice Chevalier as the ladies' man, Count Danilo, in Ernst Lubitsch's musical comedy, *The Merry Widow*, the 1934 version of the Erich von Stroheim 1925 favorite.**

These are the prime characteristics of the romantic screwball comedy genre:

- Mistaken and/or feigned identity, a concept which reaches its high point in *Bringing Up Baby*, which has a mistaken identity plot involving two leopards.

- Reverse class snobbery, in which we are given the message that to be poor is to understand life, to be rich is merely to be rich. In fact, to be rich is likely to be bored and unhappy.

- A skillful blend of sophistication and slapstick. Although screwball characters move in an elegant world, flitting through houses in which even the kitchens seem to be the center of the universe, they may still hit one another over the head. In cruder comedy, characters are struck with baseball bats. In screwball comedy, a silver chafing dish is a more likely weapon.

- A well-written script laced with barbed dialogue. Lines are tossed off in a rapid, overlapping style of delivery.

- Emphasis on beautiful clothes and furniture, and use of exotic locales.

- A hero and/or heroine living by wits alone, often balanced by a love interest who is steady and reliable. (In comedy, an unstable, out-of-work lover convinces the steady one that life is just a bowl of cherries. In forties comedy, the resolution of a love complication finds the unreliable lover reformed by the reliable one, setting off at fade-out to find respectable work).

- Supporting casts of first-rate character actors. playing eccentric types as well as a "stable" of familiar faces in leading roles (William Powell, Carole Lombard, Jean Arthur, Claudette Colbert, Fred MacMurray).

**Above: A pair who epitomized the battle of the sexes: Katharine Hepburn and Spencer Tracy in *Adam's Rib* (1949), directed by George Cukor and written by Ruth Gordon and Garson Kanin."**

**Opposite: The granddaddy of all the screwball comedies, and the only one to win a sweep of Best Director, Best Picture, Best Actress, Best Actor, and Best Screenplay Academy Awards, director Frank Capra's 1934 *It Happened One Night*, with Claudette Colbert as a runaway heiress and Clark Gable as a hardboiled newspaperman.**

A good opening for the type of screwball comedy just described might be a scene in which a late-afternoon train pulls into a rainy Paris station. Sound asleep amidst the straw in a third-class compartment might be a beautiful woman wearing a gold lamé evening gown. In fact, this very scene is the beginning of one of the best films of the genre, the 1939 *Midnight*, directed by Mitchell Leisen and written by Billy Wilder and Charles Brackett. Claudette Colbert plays the woman, and as soon as she wakes up and remembers there's nothing but a pawn ticket in her evening bag, she spends her last cent on a newspaper to keep the rain off her head and sets out to make her fortune.

Right: When Marilyn Monroe is around, men do silly things. Jack Lemmon, dressed as a woman in Billy Wilder's provocative *Some Like It Hot* (production still; 1959), climbs into an upper berth with an all-girl orchestra to get closer to Monroe. Below: Doris Day and Rock Hudson carry on the male/female squabbles à la suburbia in *Send Me No Flowers* (1964).

136   SCREWBALL COMEDY

All the characteristics of the genre are clearly present as *Midnight* unfolds. Colbert, playing a poor American girl whose "roulette system has collapsed under her," bluffs her way into a rich soiree by coolly palming her only asset—the pawn ticket—off as an engraved invitation. She introduces herself to the crowd as "Madame Czerny," having stolen the last name from a friendly cab driver who picked her up at the rainy station and bought her a meal (Don Ameche). A wealthy Parisian (John Barrymore) soon discovers her ruse and blackmails/sells her on the idea of continuing her impersonation at his summer home. Her task, in return for his money, is to steal away his wife's current lover. Just as Colbert is about to be exposed as an out-of-work chorus girl with shady morals, the taxi-cab driver turns up, announces himself as Baron Czerny and claims her as his wife. Colbert and Ameche then engage in deadly social combat, which is how we know they are perfect for one another. He tells her she's got to marry for love, and she tells him, oh no, not that, she saw how her mother suffered. He tells her to just stick with him awhile, and she says, oh no, she knows she can't trust herself not to fall for the wrong man. He tells her to relax, and she tells him, oh no, let me out of here.

Above: John Barrymore, Don Ameche, Claudette Colbert, and Mary Astor form a thoroughly confused romantic quadrangle of sorts in the witty *Midnight*.

Right: Cary Grant and Rosalind Russell demonstrated with barbed words—and more—the way to spar in Howard Hawks's 1940 version of *The Front Page: His Girl Friday*.

# Men, Women, and Love — Screwball Style

**Charles Boyer and Eugene Pallette in** *Appointment for Love* **(1941):**

"My wife eats breakfast at seven in the morning. Ham. Eggs. Oatmeal. Then walks to work. One mile. If I'm dressed, she's going to let me walk with her."

"What can I do?"

"Shoot her."

"I love her."

"Then shoot yourself."

**Fred MacMurray to Carole Lombard in** *True Confession* **(1937):**

"I'm not mad. I was just thinking I could wring your neck, that's all."

**Planning marriage, Henry Fonda and Margaret Sullavan in** *The Moon's Our Home* **(1936):**

SULLAVAN: "We'll fight every day!"

FONDA: "We'll make up every night!"

SULLAVAN: "I'll leave you over and over again."

FONDA: "I'll always find you."

William Powell to Myrna Loy in
*The Thin Man* (1934):

"How did you like Grant's tomb?"

"Lovely. I'm having it copied for you."

Barbara Stanwyck about Henry Fonda in
*The Lady Eve* (1941):

"I need him like the axe needs the turkey."

Henry Fonda to Barbara Stanwyck in
*The Mad Miss Manton* (1938):

"Listen, before I knew you I disliked you
intensely. When I met you, I disliked you
intensely. Even now I dislike you intensely.
That was the sane, sensible portion of me.
But there's an insane portion of me that gets
a little violent every time I think of you."
(Speech delivered after Stanwyck has first
pledged her love to Fonda, then flies into
rage, then stabs him in the rear with a fork.)

*When Harry Met Sally* (1989) updated the romantic comedy for
the 1990s. Meg Ryan (as Sally) and Billy Crystal (as Harry) are
devoted friends with everything in common. They just can't bring
themselves to recognize they're perfect for one another. Instead
of trying to find ways to have sex, as movies did in the old days,
this one finds ways to keep it from happening.

*Midnight* has one of the best scripts (by Brackett and Wilder) of the entire romantic screwball genre. From the heroine's first sizing up of her situation as she arrives without money and baggage ("So this, as they say, is Paris. From here it looks an awful lot like a rainy night in Kokomo, Indiana") through her philosophizing along the way ("You don't fall in a tub of butter. You jump for it") to her final gentle put-down of a rich suitor ("You mustn't ever get married. It would be so unfair to so many women"), Colbert's lines have a mean glitter. Her Eve Peabody is a character who can look a man right in the eye while she takes him ("I wouldn't have had the oysters, but I thought they were on the regular dinner"). She can put down a rival without so much as a blush ("That hat does something for your face, dear. It gives you a chin"). Yet she is honest enough to face facts when caught out in her pretenses ("From the moment I saw you, I had an idea you had an idea").

The script reaches an insane pinnacle of hilarity in a breakfast table scene at the country estate in which Ameche and Colbert vie with one another in the feigned identity sweepstakes. Ameche invents a fake child "who needs you," and Colbert, denying motherhood, explains to the assembled guests that Ameche is crazy. In fact, the entire Czerny family is mad. "I should have known something was odd when his uncle sent us an engagement present of one roller skate covered with Thousand Island dressing." Confronted with this, Ameche can do nothing but fall back on the truth, thus sealing his doom. If there's one thing that no one believes in a screwball comedy, it's the truth. The awful truth.

*Midnight* is greatly strengthened by its supporting cast: John Barrymore as the man who hires Colbert to rid him of his wife's lover, pretending to be a small child on the telephone (his "Da-Da" has to be seen), deliciously humming an evil and self-satisfied little "Cheery-beery-bin, cheery-boo," delicately advising his employee that all is not well ("We've fallen into something—and it's not butter"); the effeminate Rex O'Malley as a professional socializer ("When I was a child, I used to swallow things. They didn't dare leave me alone in the room with an armchair") who tells about the day his father fell off the yacht while they were having crepes suzette ("*Well*, it makes *all* the difference"); Elaine Barrie as a hat-shop owner who ruthlessly sells dreadful hats to eager customers and has nothing good to say about her best friend ("It always rains when Stephanie gives one of her dull parties. Even nature weeps"); Francis Lederer, a prime candidate in the 1930s disposable lover contest, whose un-American ripples in his hair mean he won't get the girl; Mary Astor as Barrymore's appropriately bitchy wife; Monty Woolly as a pompous judge in a divorce court; and Hedda Hopper as a brainless society snob ("Stephanie would have an admission card at her own funeral, just to keep it chic").

When Colbert accepts the proposition Barrymore offers, she enters the world of real Hollywood 1930s glamour. This gives the audience a chance to enjoy some beauti-

Changes in censorship restrictions and social attitudes toward sex and nudity added new dimensions to the old battles between the sexes, but the comedy—and embarrassment—still prevailed in a few films: Anne Bancroft and Dustin Hoffman in *The Graduate* (above; 1967) and John Cleese in the British import *A Fish Called Wanda* (opposite; 1988).

ful clothes, some luxurious furs, and some awesome jewels, along with a lot of lavish sets and furniture. Colbert, a down-and-out "Cinderella" meets her fairy godfather in the form of John Barrymore, who buys her a high-class wardrobe, a fancy hotel room, a car and chauffeur—and not for the usual reasons. Barrymore wants only one thing in return from Colbert: seduce the young count his wife has fallen for and get him out of town.

To accomplish this, Colbert changes her clothes every time she appears on camera. She wears crazy hats, furs, and beautiful evening gowns. Her hotel room is big enough to house a battleship, and her chauffeured limousine takes her to Barrymore's country estate, where there's a ballroom, a bridge leading to a breakfast area, and suites for guests with closets the size of football fields.

One of the most decorative scenes in *Midnight* is that in which Colbert crashes the musical soiree. In a scene richly played out, detailed, and with elegant pace, Colbert is at her best. Not a world of dialogue is heard as she enters the plush room. The background noise of arriving guests is replaced by the hushed, respectful silence of the crowd listening to the aforementioned opera singer. As Colbert picks her way into the room, trying to be unobtrusive, we are treated to a view of a roomful of grotesques who might have been assembled by Fellini: rich fat ladies with small dogs, dozing old men, glaring matrons, and finally, the obviously bored (but alert for the unusual) Barrymore. As Colbert settles into an overstuffed chair (allowing the faintest smile of smug satisfaction to flit across her face) and begins to remove her rain-soaked shoes, we observe Barrymore spotting her as an intruder, just as the doorman discovers the pawn ticket and begins to search the room. This scene establishes the milieu of the world Colbert has crashed with superb aplomb. An audience not only follows a character through an important plot event, but also gets to enjoy a gorgeous setting with many beautiful clothes and specially designed chairs, wallpaper, and lighting.

Besides *Midnight*, there are many other good examples of these hilarious American romantic battles: *The Moon's Our Home* (1936; starring Margaret Sullavan and Henry Fonda), *Bringing Up Baby* (1938; Katharine Hepburn and Cary Grant), *My Man Godfrey* (1936; Carole Lombard and William Powell), to name a few. All follow the described list of characteristics that define the genre. In many cases, just describing the action makes the movie sound as if it's anything but funny, because the male/female battles in them are for real. For instance, in *His Girl Friday* (1940) Cary Grant plays a man who tricks his ex-wife, performed by Rosalind Russell, into postponing her marriage so she can cover a story for his newspaper. He lies to her, has her fiancé arrested, argues with her, pushes her around, and wrecks her engagement. For her part, she gets the story, but not without berating him along the way. It's a classic battle between two professionals for whom love is competition, but real.

Trickery and deception formed the basis for many of the laughs in screwball comedy. In *The Awful Truth* (1937), Irene Dunne plays a woman who divorces her philandering husband, played by Cary Grant. She tricks him out of custody of their dog and sabotages his engagement to a society belle by showing up disguised as his no-account, low-class sister who's a stripper that does a routine to "Gone with the Wind." Grant makes fun of Dunne's new fiancé (a hick from Omaha played by Ralph Bellamy), disgraces her in front of her future mother-in-law, and ruins her vocal recital by bursting

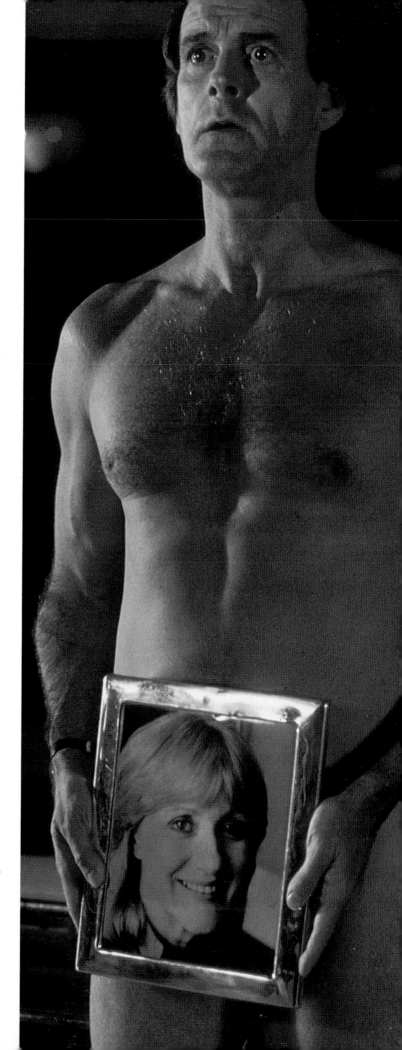

in thinking she's having an affair with the music teacher. (They will remarry, of course.) Greta Garbo pretends to be her own sister in order to see if her husband (Melvyn Douglas) can be seduced in *Two-Faced Woman* (1941). Barbara Stanwyck claims she's "the Lady Eve" and marries Henry Fonda only to punish and humiliate him in the 1941 film of the same title.

Three famous directors of the "golden era" of Hollywood were Frank Capra, Howard Hawks, and Ernst Lubitsch. All three directed classic examples of the romantic screwball comedy, following the basic rules of the genre. Yet each found ways to personalize his version of it, partly through casting particular actors and actresses that became a sort of stock company for him and partly through the selection of talented collaborators whose work he used to complete his own vision of the genre.

Capra's *It Happened One Night* (1934; the foundation of the genre), Hawks's *Bringing Up Baby* (one of the most popular examples), and Lubitsch's exquisite *The Merry Widow* (1934; a musical variation) show how varied and original the genre could be while still maintaining the basics. Capra almost always set his story in the allegedly realistic world of the United States. Lubitsch, a sophisticated European, usually set his in Paris or Budapest or some imaginary Balkan country. Hawks set his anywhere, anyplace, because his stories are disconnected from anything other than a world of his own design, even if, as in *Bringing Up Baby*, the characters were supposed to be in Connecticut.

The romantic couple in all three films, whether set in Depression America (the Capra film), a strange Connecticut full of wandering leopards (Hawks), or the imaginary "Marshovia," (Lubitsch), start out in conflict. Clark Gable and Claudette Colbert, lovers in *It Happened One Night*, meet on a night bus from Florida to New York. They hate each other on first sight. Gable finds her snooty and out of touch with real people. She finds him common and coarse. When he realizes she's really a runaway heiress, his newspaperman instincts tell him to tag along on her trip and exploit her.

Katharine Hepburn and Cary Grant star in *Bringing Up Baby*. She plays a spoiled rich girl with a ditzy manner and he is a sober paleontologist. He's engaged to a woman of his own ilk, and she's got a leopard she wants to take to her wealthy aunt. When their lives become entangled, Grant has to restrain himself from strangling Hepburn. She wrecks his car, loses his valuable dinosaur bone, drives off his fiancé, and nearly ruins his career. In the Lubitsch film, the lovers of the musical begin with a basic conflict about how to live life. Maurice Chevalier feels a woman ought to kick up her heels, especially with him, but Jeanette MacDonald believes correct behavior is called for, especially for a wealthy widow like herself.

All these couples have their relationships grounded in trouble. As their stories progress, crazy events and crazy characters enter their worlds. They argue with and misunderstand each other. They tell lies to one another and get each other into predicaments. In the end, however, they wind up in love.

What is interesting about these three directors and their three examples of the genre, is that considering them demonstrates how strong the genre definition quickly became. Capra, Hawks, and Lubitsch were artists, each with a distinctive directorial style, a specific attitude toward the audience. Capra asks you to be a happy viewer, enjoying his characters and their love. You are set to participate in his story as a member of an audience—one of his little people—and feel good about what happens. You're supposed to laugh and enjoy the victory of love when his leading man and leading lady finally get together at the end.

Hawks, on the other hand, asks you to get right into the action of his comedy. You're supposed to feel as if you're a part of the action, a member of whatever is happening right up on the screen. You are in the middle of his comic chaos. You're supposed to participate as if you are one of the two people in the warring couple. Lubitsch's style is even more unique. He asks you, as the viewer, to step back and look at his sophisticated world and at how much that is happening to his couple is actually taking place behind doors. You're supposed to participate fully, but by realizing how much you yourself are left out of! Lubitsch's invitation to you is to be sophisticated yourself—let yourself imagine what is happening offscreen. You laugh and enjoy the movie by figuring out the secret desires and thoughts of the couple and by anticipating what is going to happen to them—only to get a big surprise, because Lubitsch, the director, can outthink you. In short, Capra asks you to be a feeling member of the audience, Lubitsch asks you to be a thinking member of the audience, and Hawks asks you to enter the frame and get into the battle of the sexes. All three, however, are effective because they carry out basic genre rules and guidelines.

Most film historians feel that romantic screwball comedy hit its peak in the 1930s. There was, however, a brief revival of the format in the postwar years with such films as *The Mating of Millie* (1948), *Confidentially Connie* (1953), and *Please Believe Me* (1950). None of these movies made a particular splash, nor are they well remembered today. Although some of them were charming, they failed to connect to the changes taking place in America. The screwball format no longer had the same zany appeal because in the 1930s the crazy male-female battles were also partly about being rich versus being poor, and the elegant clothes and settings provided Depression-era audi-

**Men and women are forever trying to figure it out in screwball: Woody Allen and Louise Lasser in the 1972** *Everything You Always Wanted to Know About Sex (But Were Afraid To Ask)* **and, opposite, Robin Williams in the 1993** *Mrs. Doubtfire.*

Neuroses replace the class war—but men and women still combat each other to define their roles: Holly Hunter and William Hurt play professionals doing it with words in director James Brooks's *Broadcast News* (above; 1987); homemaker Kathleen Turner and lawyer Michael Douglas fight to the death with no-holds-barred in Danny DeVito's *The War of the Roses* (right; 1989).

ences with an escape. The genre more or less disappeared until the 1960s, when another peak period of the romantic comedy emerged. These movies might better be called sex comedies, since they treated the fights between men and women as being basically about going to bed or not going to bed.

In a series of movies starring Doris Day, paired with such actors as Cary Grant, Rod Taylor, and, in particular, Rock Hudson (with whom she made three movies), Day portrayed the wise career girl without a sex life. Here the battle of the sexes was overtly about the man trying to seduce and thereby transform or "reform" the woman rather than trying to marry her.

An offshoot of the 1960s sex comedy questioned the definition of sexuality itself. Movies such as *Some Like It Hot* (1959) and later *Tootsie* (1982) and *Victor/Victoria* (1982) made fun of the conventional roles men and women play in life, using cross-dressing as a comedy motif.

However, these movies continue the old genre traditions. In her comedies, Doris Day wears an astonishing number of coats, dresses, evening gowns, furs, and jewels, changing her clothes every time she appears. Her living quarters are posh. No longer in the Art Deco tradition, they are prime examples of the Scandinavian influence on home furnishings in the 1960s. Day and her various would-be lovers visit resorts, ski lodges, nightclubs, country houses, fancy restaurants—all designed in the great escapist tradition of the earlier comedies.

Many feel that these unique American romantic comedies, which other countries seem unable to make, died out because of the sexual revolution of the 1960s. The feminist movement liberated women from thinking a romantic marriage was their only goal in life, and the arrival of the pill created a new sexual attitude. When it was no longer necessary to keep the couple out of bed, the "battle" became unnecessary. The elaborate masquerades couples took to fool each other, punish each other, and stay out of the bedroom were useless. Today, the return of the romantic comedy, in such movies as *When Harry Met Sally* (1989) and *Sleepless in Seattle* (1993), presents courtship as a gentler, more cerebral effort; with both parties' agendas well-represented. Movies such as *Housesitter* (1992), *Soapdish* (1991), *Honeymoon in Vegas* (1992), and *A Fish Called Wanda* (1988) keep up the old fight on new terms. Although romantic comedies continue to be popular with audiences, Hollywood has found it increasingly difficult to create new ones. A new freedom in society regarding sex removed the basis of many of the old plots, which involved seduction, remarriage, or couples forced to spend the night together because they were pretending to be married. What has remained constant is the battle of the sexes in comedy terms, as in *The War of the Roses* (1989), in which a married couple (Kathleen Turner and Michael Douglas) literally destroy their entire home in a battle to the finish over a divorce settlement. Today, romantic screwball comedy finds its best outlet in television in such series as *Mad About You*, *Love and War*, *Seinfeld*, and *Moonlighting*, in which writers are allowed to develop sparring relationships between equally strong male and female leads surrounded by casts of colorful characters.

# 5 FILM NOIR

"I feel as if I'm being backed up in a dark corner. Someone is punching me, but I don't know who," says the hero of the 1946 film noir *Dark Corner*. This is as good a definition of film noir as you can find. A hero is saying that he feels trapped, alienated, and confused about what is happening to him. The situation fills him with despair and there's not much—short of violent action—he can do about it. That's what film noir stands for: movies in which such a hero in such a situation hangs on as best he can until he finally, most likely, ends up dead in the gutter. Raymond Chandler, writing in 1950, described the world his fictional heroes were living in, and his words are an often-cited definition of the world of film noir: "A world gone wrong, a world in which long before the atom bomb, civilization had created the machinery for its own destruction and was learning to use it with all the moronic

Left: Francis L. Sullivan as an oily night club owner in *Night and the City* (1950), framed by a prison-like windowsill.

*The Film Noir Hero:*
"I think I'm in a frame, and I can't get out of it."
Robert Mitchum in *Out of the Past* (1947)

*The Film Noir Heroine:*
"She can't be all bad. No one is."
"She comes closest."
— *Out of the Past*

*The Film Noir Approach to Religion:*
"I don't go to Church. Kneeling bags my nylons."
—*The Big Carnival* (1951)

*The Film Noir Values:*
"First is first, and second is nobody."
—*The Big Combo* (1955)

*The Film Noir Perspective on Life:*
"Someday fate or some mysterious force can put the finger on you or me for no reason at all."
—*Detour* (1945)

*The Film Noir Final Statement:*
"Everybody's in trouble."
—*His Kind of Woman* (1951)

Previous pages: A definitive turning point in *Out of the Past* (1947) takes place when the hero (Robert Mitchum) finally realizes the woman he loves (Jane Greer) has entangled him in a web of murder and deceit he can never get out of.

Both men and women faced the dark, mean streets of the film noir world. Alone in the unfriendly night, not knowing whether darkness is shelter or danger, or whether light is safety or exposure, are Osa Massen (opposite) in *Deadline at Dawn* (1946) and Robert Ryan (following pages), one of noir's most prolific heroes.

delight of a gangster trying out his first machine gun. The law was something to be manipulated for profit and power. The streets were dark with something more than night."

Actually no two critics quite agree on exactly what film noir is. Some define it as a genre, and it is certainly true that a typical attitude or mood prevails and that the stories are generally those in which there is not a happy ending or easy solution to be found. There are typical characters—the femme fatale, the lone wolf hero, the corrupt politician, the insane killer—and typical settings—broken-down beaneries, low-rent apartments, rain-slick urban streets, posh nightclubs, boxing arenas, sleazy massage parlors. The stories are about greed, corruption, lust, violence, and horror. While it is also certainly true that these generic patterns exist, there's a problem with defining film noir simply as a genre because "noir" versions of other genres exist. For instance, there are noir westerns (*Pursued* [1947], *The Halliday Brand* [1956]), noir women's

"The city is really the arena for most of the noir action, isn't it? Dramatic conflicts on any kind of a large scale have to take place in some kind of urban environment. The city becomes the seething caldron for all the tensions and the malaise and the anxieties that are reflected in the human nature. So it's natural that dramatically and thematically, filmmakers would gravitate to the city as the focal point for all of that. Visually, I think the city offers the potential for a very raw and rough, extremely textured and coarsened background.

There isn't anything very foreboding necessarily or intimidating about a natural outdoor landscape. It tends to be horizontal and softly contoured and rolling. The city is quite the antithesis of that. It's angular. It's jutting. It's vertical, threatening, ominous. It diminishes the scale of man, which is a tremendous theme, both dramatically and visually, in noir films. There's a depersonalization and diminution of man's sense of place in the urban universe.

The architecture of the city is very threatening, depending upon how it's presented. And of course, the film noir filmmakers consciously exploited every element they could find with their tools to make that environment seem even more foreboding and ominous and threatening.

In 'night for night' photography they often wet down the streets. Reflections create a tremendous sense of mood.

One of the visual dramatic progressions in a lot of film noir is escape from the city. The characters are under threat or they're on the run. If it's an emotional distress they have, they look for solace or recovery or healing outside of the city in nature or in the woods or in the mountains a lot of times."

**John Bailey**

German Expressionism influenced both the look and the attitude of American film noir: The architectural entrapment and bizarre backgrounds of *M* (bottom) and *The Cabinet of Dr. Caligari* (top) can be seen in the presentation of Charlton Heston in Orson Welles's *Touch of Evil* (above).

films (*Mildred Pierce* [1945], *The File on Thelma Jordan* [1949]), and noir musicals (*Young Man with a Horn* [1950]). When films as different as *The House on 92nd Street* (1945), *Beyond the Forest* (1949), and *Key Largo* (1948) are all labeled "film noir," it becomes apparent that "film noir" is something in addition to genre.

Another way of defining film noir is by linking it to a historical era, primarily the postwar period. The majority of "noir" movies began to appear following World War II, and the obvious point is to call them a response to the war, to a loss of innocence and faith after fighting a second great world war within twenty years. The usual definition of the period of time for film noir is approximately 1940–1960, although many gangster films of the early Depression period also contain a similar look and a similar downbeat attitude toward life. To consider film noir as a period in film, like German Expressionism or the French New Wave, is an alternative way of looking at the body of work. By any standards, it can be seen as an immensely creative period in film in terms of style and unusual cinematic experiments.

The best way to define noir, however, is the most interesting way: to claim it as a visual style. It is really the look of the films that identify them and link them. They are recognized by a shared cinematic language: low-key lighting, which creates an image of high contrast with rich, deep, dark shadows; depth-of-field photography, which gives background objects the same sharp focus as those in the foreground; unbalanced, unusual com-positions; claustrophobic, entrapping framing; night-for-night photography; unusual lighting patterns, such as areas of total darkness, strange highlights, and silhouettes; cutting patterns, which jar viewers, jumping them from one viewpoint or position to another; the use of the wide-angle lens to distort. By this defin-ition, only black-and-white films are truly films noir. Their later siblings, the dark and moody films of the 1960s and 1970s that are shot in color, have to be identified as "post-noir" movies or perhaps a better term would be "neo-noir."

A typical noir sequence is found in *Border Incident* (1949). An audience first sees a tiny pinpoint of light in a far distance on a dark and shadowy night. A sudden cut shifts the perspective to one in which the audience is suddenly up-close to the light, blinded by white hot-glare, with only a shadow of the former blackness around the outer frame. Such sudden changes in camera angle, perspective, and screen size typify the look of noir. The effect on viewing audiences is dramatic, as they are jarred both by light and sudden shifts in perspective. The effect is akin to what is going to happen to the characters in the story: they'll be jerked around in a situation out of their control.

In its time, noir was addressing a sense of despair in society. Alienation, loneli-ness, the loss of individual worth, the inability to take decisive action, the increasing use of violence to solve social problems, the lack of justice in our social systems, the fear of the atom bomb, and the missing sense of purpose in the industrialized life

Vince Barnett as a small-time hood backs up Paul Muni in the title role of *Scarface* (1932), one of the most brutal and violent of the early gangster films. Originally made in 1931, *Scarface*'s release date was delayed a year due to its troubles with the censors.

Two femmes fatales of the film noir universe, circa 1946: Rita Hayworth (opposite) plays the title role in Charles Vidor's noir *Gilda*, who says if she were a ranch, she'd be the Bar Nothing . . . and Lana Turner (right), who warns a would-be lover in *The Postman Always Rings Twice*, "You won't find anything cheap around here."

characterize noir. As America seemed to lose its optimistic outlook, these films addressed the loss in narrative terms. Noir stories were direct, even brutal. They told a kind of truth, in that they seldom had happy endings. They fed the appetites of movie-goers who had not only fought a war, but who were looking at more and more movies of a different type from Europe. New ideas, new attitudes, and a new sense of aesthetics emerged. Noir films still provided the old Hollywood excitement and glamour, but they showed a new darkness, and a new and terrible kind of beauty in the frame.

But whether noir is defined as a genre, a visual style, a mood, a relationship to audiences, a period of film history, or all of the above, one thing is certain: It is totally different from any other genre definition for Hollywood films in that it was not defined within the business itself. Unlike such designations as "western," "screwball comedy," "women's film," or "musical," film noir was not a type of film that anyone in Hollywood consciously set out to make. As far as Hollywood was concerned, film noir did not exist.

Where did the terminology come from? It is a designation coined by French crit-ics, who were inundated by American movies in the immediate postwar period. From mid-July to August 1946, a series of downbeat films opened in Paris: *The Maltese Falcon, Laura, Murder My Sweet, Double Indemnity,* and *Woman in the Window.* These films, all of which were about murder, treacherous (or seemingly treacherous) women, and the dark forces of life, were observed by French critics as having something in common: a dark malaise, a downbeat attitude. They were similar in their visual style as well. Compared to many of the films from America from before the war—the energetic, more upbeat films of the late 1930s—these movies were seen to be very dark. The term "film noir" was coined to describe them, and they were linked together as a group. When universities began offering film studies at the end of the 1960s and movies became a source of academic examination, the term became familiar as a designation that united movies across other genres. Film noir was born. And thanks to students going to work in the film business, the term ultimately became a label, like "western," "musical," or "comedy."

"Noir," or dark plots and stories, did not originate with the movies, of course. In America, there is a solid tradition of gothic literature and mystery tales, as well as hor-ror stories and detective novels. As a film tradition, what is now called "noir" has been identified as having three main cinematic origins: German Expressionism of the 1920s, French films of the 1930s, such as *Pépé Le Moko* (1936), and America's own mystery, detective, gangster, and horror films of the early years. Many of noir's best directors were refugees from Nazi Germany, men who brought to Hollywood the finest traditions of European filmmaking: Robert Siodmak, Douglas Sirk, Otto Preminger, Billy Wilder,

> *"There's an element in film noir, the way light and shadow are used in such extreme contrast, that is almost religious or spiritual or philosophic, if you will. You know, the age-old notion, or the Manichaeist dialectic of light against dark. Good against evil. And when you look at the film noir film, you're dealing almost with a very simple, fundamental notion of morality, of what is good and evil. I mean, there's really no gray scale of behavior; things stand in very bold relief."*
>
> John Bailey

Fritz Lang, and others. Jean Renoir from France, André DeToth from Hungary, and others added their visions to those of Americans such as Howard Hawks and Raoul Walsh to create a synthesis of the best of several different cultures.

The storytelling mode of film noir is one that does not stress clarity, but rather stresses mood and atmosphere. In noir, one does not find the straight linear progression that is commonly associated with Hollywood filmmaking. Instead, there are ellipses and trickery. Key facts are held back. Information is omitted until the audience has made a false assumption on which the plot will turn. And the flashback is king.

A classic example of film noir is the 1947 *Out of the Past*, based on a novel by Geoffrey Homes called *Build My Gallows High*. It was directed by Jacques Tourneur, and it stars Robert Mitchum, Kirk Douglas, Jane Greer, Rhonda Fleming, and Dickie Moore. At the time of its original release, it was just another movie. It was given no special attention by critics, and it certainly won no awards. Over the years, however, especially after its discovery as a prime example of sophisticated visual storytelling, *Out of the Past* has become so popular that the story was remade in 1984 (entitled *Against All Odds*).

*Out of the Past* perfectly illustrates the phenomenon known as "film noir." Its key characters include an ex-private eye, now working in a small-town gas station (Robert Mitchum); a femme fatale (Jane

Modern films try to re-create the ambiance, the implied sexuality, and the tangled plot of the 1940s films noir. Two attempts are *Basic Instinct* (opposite; 1992, with Michael Douglas and Sharon Stone) and *Dead Again* (right; 1992, directed by and starring Kenneth Branagh, with Emma Thompson).

Greer); a "Mr. Big" villain (Kirk Douglas); a trustworthy friend who cannot speak or hear (Dickie Moore); a second femme fatale, a look-alike to Greer (Rhonda Fleming); an innocent blonde (Virginia Houston); and a tough-guy body guard/henchman (Paul Valentine).

The settings for *Out of the Past* are a pastoral small town, with a gas station, a church, and a diner seen in sunlight; a dark, dangerous big city with rain-slick streets, expensive apartments, and ritzy nightclubs, seen only at night (the opposite of the small town); a race track; a movie theater; an Acapulco bar; a Harlem jazz joint; a deserted cabin in the woods; Mr. Big's posh retreat on Lake Tahoe.

The story is told partly through a long flashback, and the narrative has enough red herrings, plot twists, and unexplained events to leave any average audience confused. The problems of the story concern the theft of forty thousand dollars, income-tax evasion, two dead bodies, a false murder rap, a set-up for framing the hero, an "affidavit in a safe," and more.

The flashback is narrated by the super-cool, low-key voice of Robert Mitchum, who talks in the kind of tough-guy dialogue associated with such films. "There she was, coming along like a girl out of school," he says of the murderous leading lady when she gets her hooks in him. He sits around waiting for her "to walk in out of the moonlight."

The physical look of *Out of the Past* is black-and-white cinematography at its most dramatic. When Robert Mitchum and Jane Greer embrace on the Mexican beach, trapped in a spider's web of fishing nets, the lighting patterns play with shadows and silhouettes. When Jane Greer tries to talk Mitchum back into her clutches later in a San Francisco apartment, the light bounces off one of her eyes like a warning beacon. When Mitchum fights for his life with a would-be killer in a remote cabin in the woods, Greer watches in fascination, the lighting casting the struggler's shadows on the wall and a dark, oppressive, and dangerous shadow across her face. This is the true essence of film noir: a visual style, a shadowed look, a convoluted plot, a no-win situation. Perhaps the best definition of noir is the one I use: noir is a kind of virus that attacks a healthy genre and makes it sick.

*Out of the Past* is uncompromisingly heartless in killing its hero off at the end. It tells a complex story that keeps a viewer always aware of the pressure of Mitchum's past mistakes on his present chance for any real happiness in life. At the beginning of the movie, Mitchum lives a pastoral life in a small town. He has a true and loyal friend (Moore) and a beautiful, sweet, blonde girlfriend whom he loves (Houston). He owns his own business, the well-positioned gas station, and he has time to go fishing and picnicking with his sweetheart. And then, from out of his past, driving a large white convertible, arrives a dark figure: the henchman who summons him back to his old life and his ultimate death.

*Out of the Past* skillfully mixes location shooting and studio sets. By doing so, it makes its story seem real, but at the same time, its visual look is almost hallucinatory in its romantic entrapment of Mitchum. It is his fate to die, to never come "out of his past."

**Director Steven Soderbergh's *Kafka* carries on the traditional look of noir, but in color, bringing it into the 1990s.**

Today, noir movies from the years between 1940 and 1960 are among the most popular and most often-revived of Hollywood's product of the era. In their own time, they were often treated much more casually, and the majority of them did not win Oscars or receive top reviews. The tendency to value "serious content" in a movie over visual style often relegated noir movies to genre categories that were not respected. *Kiss Me Deadly* (1955), an outstanding film noir directed by Robert Aldrich and based on a Mickey Spillane novel, was "just another tough guy gangster movie." Today it is seen as an outstanding example of a tradition that offered moviemakers an opportunity for experimentation in the medium. In some cases, such as the low-budget *Detour* (1945), directed by Edgar G. Ulmer, the filmmaking team overcame the restrictions of no money and no time through creative solutions involving lighting, sound manipulation, and narration.

Many of Hollywood's greatest writers, directors, and stars were involved in noir movies. Alfred Hitchcock made *Strangers on a Train* (1951) and *The Wrong Man* (1957); John Huston made *The Asphalt Jungle* (1950) and *Key Largo;* Fritz Lang directed *The Big Heat* (1953), *Scarlet Street* (1945), and *The Woman in the Window* (1944); Otto Preminger contributed *Laura* (1944), *Angel Face* (1952), *Fallen Angel* (1945), and *Where the Sidewalk Ends* (1950); Orson Welles was responsible for *The Lady from Shanghai* (1948), *The Stranger* (1946), and *Touch of Evil* (1958); Stanley Kubrick as a young filmmaker directed *The Killing* (1956) and *Killer's Kiss* (1955). Other directors have worked almost exclusively associated with this type of movie: Joseph M. Lewis, Samuel Fuller, John Brahm, Nicholas Ray, and many, many more. Their names are not as well known generally to the public as those of Hitchcock and Billy Wilder, but they made major contributions. No matter what type of movie a director might be associated with, it was unlikely he finished the decades of the 1940s and 1950s without making at least one film noir. For instance, Robert Wise, famous for *The Sound of Music* (1965), directed *The Set-Up* (1949) and *Born to Kill* (1947), and Joseph L. Mankiewicz, who won Oscars for the sophisticated comedies *All About Eve* (1950) and *A Letter to Three Wives* (1949), directed *House of Strangers* (1949) and *Somewhere in the Night* (1946).

Today, noir is perhaps the most popular of the old types of Hollywood films with new moviemakers. Although today's variations are shot mostly in color, the attitudes they suggest seem to shape the old aesthetics to fit today's sense of reality. *The Grifters* (1990), *After Dark, My Sweet* (1990), *Goodfellas* (1990), *Basic Instinct* (1992), *Dead Again* (1992)—these are "neo-noirs." A new series of films called *Fallen Angels* was presented on cable television in late 1993 with each title shot and written as an homage to the old noir tradition. Although today's audiences find such movies more romantic than realistic, noir still appeals to American moviegoers.

*"Light in film noir is just barely there, and flares up when somebody lights a cigarette, or a light source kind of sweeps across the frame. It's just eruptive and quick, and then it falls back into darkness. . . . Light is a difficult thing to maintain itself, to find definition, because the world is dark. Film noir has to be done at night. Otherwise it's not film noir."*

John Bailey

One of the signature images from the world of film noir is this silhouette in the fog from *The Big Combo* (1955). Jean Wallace and Cornel Wilde wait for the danger that will come. The cinematography was directed by the masterful John Alton.

*"Tell me the story of the foot soldier
and I will tell you the story of all wars."*

**Men in War (1950)**

# 6 COMBAT

"I want to see the war," says a character in the 1945 combat film *A Walk in the Sun*. "I want to see what it really looks like." He takes a little walk over the hill to have a look, and gets killed for his troubles. The implication is obvious: you can't "see" war, really see it, without paying a heavy price. However, the average American audience has been able to "see" war without being there ever since the invention of the motion picture. The question is, what is the war it sees? Does it star John Wayne and glamorize combat? Is it a newsreel that was staged just for the cameraman? Is it a careful reenactment of an actual battle, re-created visually down to the last detail? Samuel Fuller, producer-writer-director of *The Big Red One* (1980), summarized this quandary:

> ## *"This war and glory racket is kind of like a religion."*
>
> Flagg (James Cagney) in *What Price Glory?*

**Previous pages:** *Hamburger Hill* (1987). **Left:** *All Quiet on the Western Front* (1930) is one of the most eloquent antiwar movies. Adapted from Erich Maria Remarque's novel about German schoolboys who, caught up in the glamour of war as glorified in the classroom, enlist to find in reality only death. The film won Best Picture and Best Director Oscars for Louis Milestone. **Right:** *Wings*, a 1927 silent film, was the first movie to win the Oscar as Best Picture of the Year. Audiences were quite impressed by its stunning aerial combat sequences. Directed by William Wellman and starring Clara Bow, Richard Arlen, and Charles "Buddy" Rogers, the World War I story is about two American boys and the girl they both love.

A war movie is just like a man doing an autopsy on his own body. It's impossible. You cannot make a real war movie. You can make a real love story. You can make a real mystery. You can make a real dramatic story about unemployment. Socialism. Optimism. Communism. You can make a story about anything like that, but you cannot, absolutely cannot, make a real war movie. The closest I can think of making a real war movie is to have a couple of riflemen behind the screen and during a fire fight in the movie, people in the audience are shot at. Not killed, but wounded. Seeing that picture, going to it, you might get shot. That's about the only way I can see you make a legitimate movie about war.

The war film is a special case. It appears to be more realistic than other genres because it is supposed to be re-creating actual historical events. However, war movies are linked to stories of individuals in combat, and these stories, however inspired by true cases they might have been, are still fictionalized accounts. Although the war movie is influenced by real images from newsreels and combat photos, and, most recently, from television coverage, it still provides created and designed images. These images inevitably "sell" Americans ideas about war. In the 1940s war seemed necessary and thus might be sold as "good," but in Vietnam in the 1960s it seemed to many unnecessary, and the movies more or less avoided the subject until after the war ended. Movies about war shape our sense of historical reality in much the same way that the western genre does. There is, however, one significant difference. Unlike the romanti-

*"I can't murder anyone."*

*"We don't murder, we kill."*

*The Big Red One*

cized West of the 1800s, the wars of the twentieth century—World Wars I and II, the Korean conflict, and Vietnam—are wars that the American moviegoer was "seeing" on a daily basis through some visual medium other than Hollywood stories. Newsreel and television coverage, as well as the photographs that appeared in daily newspapers and magazines, provided Americans with another sort of look at the events. This influenced the genre of the American combat film.

Two films about World War II, both made by men who had experienced the events being depicted, illustrate different ways in which combat was turned into a movie experience: *The Longest Day* is an epic CinemaScope box-office success from 1962, *The Big Red One* is a smaller, more personal movie from 1980. *The Longest Day* was directed by Ken Annakin, Andrew Morton, and Bernhard Wicki and produced by Darryl F. Zanuck, whose brainchild it was. Zanuck was present for the invasion of Normandy, the subject of the movie. He was in the Signal Corps covering the war, and he saw it happen, but with a journalist/photographer's eye rather than a foot soldier's. Samuel Fuller was a foot soldier who landed in the third wave at Omaha Beach on the morning of June 6, 1944—D-Day. His experience was up-close, fighting to survive.

*The Longest Day*, under the guidance of Zanuck, presents the events of the invasion in a careful historical re-creation. The idea behind the movie is to make it look like a newsreel, albeit a *big* newsreel. It was shot in black-and-white to use the look associated with actual news coverage of war, and also with the documentary movies of the period. *The Longest Day*, in fact, presents itself as a document of the event. Every character introduced into the story is first seen with his name and identification under their image, in the documentary tradition. Everyone speaks in his native language, with appropriate translations provided, and the cast is international. Every major event is presented with a timeline, so that the audience knows exactly where they are in the day's events.

*The Longest Day* is, in fact, the story of one long day in American history. It begins with the moment when General Eisenhower has to make the decision to order the invasion. When the decision is a "go," the film covers all the events on land, sea, and air on both sides of the conflict.

Samuel Fuller wrote and directed his magnum opus, *The Big Red One* (1980), in which he told the story of one unit of the First Infantry (which wore the identification patch of a large, red numeral on its uniforms). Lee Marvin played an experienced sergeant who keeps his troops alive as best he can because "survivin' . . . that's the glory of war." The film is largely an autobiographical memory of war.

> ***"Only the actual invasion was possibly
> more complicated than this re-creation."***
>
> Darryl F. Zanuck, speaking of *The Longest Day*

To prevent this from being a dull documentary, the movie skillfully weaves famous real-life leaders—Lieutenant Colonel Ben Vandervoot (John Wayne), Teddy Roosevelt, Jr. (Henry Fonda), Brigadier General Norman Cota (Robert Mitchum)—together with the fictional stories of the common foot soldiers of the war, depicted by actors such as Jeffrey Hunter. The result is a stirring epic event, celebrating the American victory and the American way of life, but not without paying tribute to our allies in the combat. The finished product is very much what members of the Signal Corps might have been able to see and certainly offers a sense of what the event meant to someone sent there to observe the filmed event. It is an excellent semi-documentary creation of real events.

Zanuck, by his own description, said *The Longest Day* is "the most ambitious undertaking since *Gone with the Wind* and *Birth of a Nation*." No stock footage was used. It involved restaging the D-Day invasion. (One of the ironies of the project was that the Production Code office objected to "an excessive amount of slaughter" in the movie.) Zanuck had to assemble an army and enough equipment to win World War III in order to shoot his picture. "My job was tougher than Ike's," said Zanuck. "He had the men and he had the equipment. I had to find both."

For Fuller, the war was not an epic event, seen from a distance, but a bloody and chaotic scramble to keep from dying. A viewer does not have an overview, or a series of identification tags as to characters, time, and place. Rather, a viewer has the experience of the energy and abstraction of danger. Watching it happen is like being in a car accident: some odd things are clearly seen, but the overall event is not coherent. Fuller has explained his intentions:

> In the real war, there are no signs to tell you where you are. You never know when you're going into Belgium, when you're going into Germany, when you're going into Czechoslovakia. It's all the same, and there's no welcome sign. That's how a war is fought from a G.I.'s point of view. Everything is the same. In war, all terrain is the same. The most important thing that we wanted to know was how many enemies were out there and not the name of the damned country.

Yet, of the two movies, which is more truly documentary? Fuller re-created his memory of what it was like, as a young man, to be in combat. Zanuck and his directors created a filmed experience of an event from start to finish. It is the difference between something experienced directly and something watched from a distance. Fuller's movie has

**In 1962 producer Darryl Zanuck released *The Longest Day*, a movie that details the story of D-Day. Photographed on a grand scale, starring a roster of international actors, and bolstered by Oscar-winning special effects, this is one of the most successful of the epic re-creations of World War II battles, a sub-genre that includes *Midway*, *Tora! Tora! Tora!*, and *A Bridge Too Far*.**

no start or finish in the traditional sense—one plunges in and out, and then it's over. Fuller identified this desire to overwhelm the viewer with war's noise and confusion:

> I didn't want to make a big, massive production, because the war I had was about thirty-five, maybe seventy-five, yards around me. Me and the men around me. We didn't know what the hell was going on, and I wanted to catch that on the screen. War is very personal. Death is so personal that you can't show it with mass production because each man is an entity. Instead of making war about heroes and people who gave their lives for their country . . . men never gave their lives . . . their lives were taken . . . I wanted to tell the story of survivors, a few representative dogfaces to encompass the whole war, from Africa to Czechoslovakia, three years of combat, highly personal. I wanted to get under the skin of each man because he is a representative of all the wonderful, lucky guys that made it.

The definition of genre is something recognized, a familiar story with conventions and characters known to a particular cultural group. When it comes to the combat film, satirists know exactly what to do to get a laugh. Set up a democratic group of American ethnic types and put them down in the jungle with no maps, no salt tablets, and plenty of Japanese. The basic unit of the American combat has always been a democratic mix known as "the group." America was, after all, a democratic mix, and the possibility that any one combat patrol would have people from different ethnic backgrounds was perfectly valid. It was just that it became, over the years, a cliché that seemed amusing. "Okay," barks the company commander, "let's have some volunteers. O'Hara, Kowalski, Rinaldi, Schmidt, Adams, and Nillson, get over here. And you, the old guy, Pop, and you, too, what's your name? Thomas Jefferson Brown? You get over here, too." Thus we get a group with an Irishman, a Pole, an Italian, a German, a WASP, a Scandinavian, an old man (which was a World War II type for some reason), and some other minority representation, in this case a black man, although it could be a Mexican, a Jew, or an Asian. Generally, these people also had to come from different geographic areas: the mountains or hills, a farm, an urban city, a small midwestern town.

The combat film found audience identification through this democratic process. After this format was established just after World War II, a peak period for combat movies, it more or less became the format for all movies about combat. Even films about Vietnam that were designed to be realistic in a way the more propagandistic films of earlier periods were not, followed this format to a certain degree. This is because a mix of men from different backgrounds had a basis in reality.

Two renowned directors who turned their personal vision to the Vietnam combat experience are Stanley Kubrick in *Full Metal Jacket* (opposite; 1987) and Francis Ford Coppola in *Apocalypse Now* (above; 1979).

*"Everything in the army is simple. You live or you die."*

*A Walk in the Sun*

**Sylvester Stallone's *Rambo* films have adapted a different genre, the action movie, to the traditional combat settings.**

Combat stories, as is true for all genres, can be used both to celebrate and to denigrate the war. In days of patriotism and pride, combat movies are like recruiting posters. In days of shame and fear of further national involvements, they are powerful antiwar messages. One of their primary purposes is to show those who stay behind and do not fight what it is like to be involved in war, and this purpose remains valid for moviegoers generation after generation.

Of course, as television has gone onto the battlefields to cover the war directly as it happens—which was the case in Vietnam—the need for an audience to have story films that provide information has lessened. During the Vietnam War itself, there were very few combat films made about the subject, as the American population could turn on their TV sets every evening and see the war happening, hear the voices of its soldiers being interviewed. The first big-budget, big-star movie about the Vietnam War was John Wayne's *Green Berets* in 1968. From its release until 1982, only approximately four significant films were made about Vietnam combat: *The Boys in Company C* (1978), *Go Tell the Spartans* (1978), *The Deer Hunter* (1978), and *Apocalypse Now* (1979). This situation changed with the release of Oliver Stone's award-winning *Platoon* in 1986, after which more films were made, such as Stanley Kubrick's *Full Metal Jacket* and *Hamburger Hill*, both in 1987.

For many years, filmmakers avoided the subject of Vietnam combat in popular movies. Although a few films appeared, such as *The Boys in Company C* (1978), *The Green Berets* (1968), and *Go Tell the Spartans* (1979), it was Oliver Stone's 1987 Oscar-winning *Platoon* that broke through the barriers to make the day-to-day combat experience of Vietnam into a successful, mainstream movie.

# Remakes

Hollywood had another form of telling familiar stories besides the creation of genres. It was a simple form. It just retold the same story with new people in it and a new person directing it. Sometimes filmmakers didn't even bother with new people, as when Clark Gable starred both in the 1932 *Red Dust* and in its remake, *Mogambo* in 1953, or when Frank Capra directed both *Lady for a Day* in 1933 and its 1961 remake, *Pocketful of Miracles,* or *Broadway Bill* in 1934 and the new version, *Riding High* in 1950. (Leo McCarey did the same with *Love Affair* in 1939 and its remake, *An Affair to Remember,* in 1957). Remakes are still going on today. *The Ghost and Mrs. Muir* (1947) has been remade, and two successful foreign films, *The Vanishing* (1988) and *La Femme Nikita* (1990), have both been remade with American settings. The hugely successful *Three Men and a Baby* (1987) was a remake of a 1985 French film called *Three Men and a Cradle.*

Recent examples of this phenomenon are the two versions of *Cape Fear,* 1962 and 1992, and the two versions of *Born Yesterday,* 1950 and 1993. In searching for stories that have wide appeal, and that are not too dated to be remade thirty or forty years after the original, film producers have these considerations: Was the film a hit originally? Is there a way the story can be "updated" to reach modern audiences more directly? In the cases of *Cape Fear* and *Born Yesterday,* both original films were successful, with the latter winning a Best Actress Oscar for Judy Holliday in the lead role of Billie Dawn. *Cape Fear* is a universally compelling story of a family menaced by a deranged killer, presumably a scary premise in any decade. *Born Yesterday* is the story of a kept woman who is basically uneducated, but not stupid, and who finds out she has brains. Oddly enough, this story has more potential relevance and audience appeal today than it did even in the 1950s. Updated, it can be changed from a story about a dumb, used blonde finding a man who loves her more for herself and who encourages her to read and learn into a story about a woman who becomes liberated in the modern sense of that term. *Cape Fear* was updated through an increased sense of evil, the addition of a biblical obsession on the part of the killer, and the changing of the family from an innocent, happy, and solid group into a family cut apart by infidelity, frustration, and their teenage daughter's loss of innocence.

Remakes take two forms: straight retelling with updated settings and attitudes, or the variation, in which the film is changed in some significant way. For instance, *The Front Page* was remade as *His Girl Friday,* with the sex of the lead character changed from male to female. The French film *Le Courbeau* was remade as *The Thirteenth Letter* (1951), with the setting moved from a small French village to Canada. *High Sierra,* a 1941 crime film, was remade as a 1949 western, *Colorado Territory.*

Many movies were remade into musicals, which shows how carefully Hollywood considered its audiences. They had already seen the story. Presumably, they had liked it, because why remake a movie everyone hated? If it was a particularly successful film, remaking it directly might not succeed because people still loved the old film. Why not change its genre, make it into a musical? This would please those who loved the original— they get to see the same story again—and create a whole new set of viewers who would experience the story in a different format. The list of movies remade as musicals is quite long. Some of the most famous are *The Philadelphia Story* (1940) and *High Society* (1956); *The Matchmaker* (1958) and *Hello, Dolly!* (1969); *Nights of Cabiria* (1957) and *Sweet*

Statistics indicate the ten characters most frequently depicted on the screen include four real people: Lincoln, Napoleon, Jesus, and Hitler. Among the imaginary favorites are Hopalong Cassidy, Zorro, Dracula, Frankenstein's monster, Sherlock Holmes, and Tarzan. Tarzan's appeal has lasted from some of the earliest motion pictures (1918) to *Greystoke* in 1984. The most popular was Johnny Weissmuller (with Maureen O'Sullivan as Jane; above) in the 1930s.

*Charity* (1969); *Ninotchka* (1939) and *Silk Stockings* (1957); *The Shop Around the Corner* (1940) and *In the Good Old Summertime* (1949); *Ah, Wilderness* (1935) and *Summer Holiday* (1948).

A subcategory of remakes is the sequel picture. Sylvester Stallone kept a cottage industry going with his *Rocky* pictures, and there has been more than one sequel to *Star Wars, Lethal Weapon, Star Trek, Raiders of the Lost Ark*, and *The Godfather*, to name a few. In the old Hollywood, though in a somewhat different manner, they were called "series" films, and such popular characters as Andy Hardy, Tarzan, Dr. Kildare, Henry Aldrich, Torchy Blane, and Maisie all were presented in series of small hits. Serials, too, were ways to provide audiences with characters and situations they had responded to and might want to see again.

What Hollywood was doing was "telling familiar stories." In every case—western, war, screwball comedy or film noir, remakes or sequels—the American film business was fulfilling its obligations as an audience-driven machine. The faces of the actors might change. The clothing might change, with hemlines going up and then down, with hats and gloves disappearing, with shoulders being padded and left natural. The attitudes might change a character from a hero to a villain and back again. But if an audience liked it, it reappeared. What you wanted was what you got, and what you wanted was determined by what you were willing to pay for.

Hollywood's ability to retell the same stories often takes the form of a direct remake, as in *Cape Fear* (1962 and 1992), but a very different approach to representing violence reflects a new public's mores and expectations. Gregory Peck and Robert Mitchum played hero and villain in the original version (above), and Robert De Niro and Nick Nolte (left) played villain and hero in the remake. In the first, the issues of good and evil are black and white, but in the latter, the lines are blurred, as Nolte plays a flawed hero.

*"The trouble with movies as a business is that they're an art; the trouble with movies as an art is that they're a business."*

Charlton Heston (quoting an old Hollywood adage)

# 7 THE HOLLYWOOD STUDIO SYSTEM THEN AND NOW

When people talk about Hollywood, they have something specific in mind, but it may not be what is, or was, ever really there. Hollywood stands for glamour or glitz to some people, ethical digression to others. For some it's Mecca and to others it's roughly equivalent to Hell. Hollywood gets blamed for everything from the collapse of morality to the death of the undershirt business. While many Americans look down on Hollywood ("Oh, I like those serious, artistic foreign films much better"), foreign filmmakers most often cite Hollywood filmmaking as their inspiration.

"*It was a manufacturing business, and the parts were the actors and actresses.*"

Richard Brandt

Glamour in the golden age of Hollywood was designed to appeal to both sexes. Left: Singer Dick Powell surrounded by an admiring chorus in a typical Busby Berkeley musical. Below: Lana Turner, at the peak of her personal glamour, as a woman who commanded the attention and admiration of a group of tuxedoed males in *The Bad and the Beautiful* (1952).

Previous pages: The visual power of the Hollywood studio system of the 1930s is well illustrated by the production values of the lavish MGM production of *Romeo and Juliet*, starring Leslie Howard as Romeo. With sets designed by Cedric Gibbons and Oliver Messel, costumes by Messel and Adrian, dances choreographed by Agnes DeMille, and a cast that included Norma Shearer, John Barrymore, Edna May Oliver, Basil Rathbone, Violet Kemble Cooper, and C. Aubrey Smith under the direction of George Cukor and produced by Irving Thalberg, *Romeo and Juliet* went nearly one million dollars over budget, an unheard of sum for its day. It remains one of Hollywood's most beautiful and carefully produced films, a classic example of what the industry could create as popular entertainment for mass audiences.

In formulating its stars, Hollywood has adjusted its role models and identification figures, some of whom challenge stereotypical viewpoints, such as the pair from *Thelma and Louise* (1991), Geena Davis and Susan Sarandon, two runaway women looking for freedom and meaning for their lives.

What Hollywood is, of course, is a business system. From the mid-1920s until approximately 1960, it was a powerful factory that just happened to manufacture what Bogart in *The Maltese Falcon* calls "the stuff dreams are made of." Hollywood can't function any other way. It is, after all, not subsidized by the government like many of the foreign film industries.

Hollywood in 1994 is not much different from Hollywood in 1934. That is, it still is a commercial system that produces movies to sell to the widest possible audience for the highest profit possible. Studios existed then, and they still exist. Stars and stories are still what draw the paying customer inside the door. Agents are still around, and movies still cost a lot of money to make. And most important of all: nobody knows for sure in advance what will become a hit and what won't. It's still the same colorful, fascinating, infuriating, and irresistibly glamorous business it always was.

To understand Hollywood fully, it is important to know what remained the same over the years (the desire to be profitable, to tell great stories, to create stars, and to produce hits) and what is different (the day-to-day business organization). There is, as always, a star and an audience. The production system, however, had to transform itself to accommodate changing laws and changing times, and this resulted in some fundamental changes in the choice and style of films Hollywood has produced. As a result, the Hollywood movie production system can be separated into these basic overlapping periods: The "golden age" of the studio system (approximately 1925–1960), the years of transition, or the television era (1960–1975), and Hollywood of the film school generation (1975–1990).

## The Golden Age (1925–1960)

By 1935, what has come to be known as the golden age of the studio system was in full bloom. The "Big Five" studio corporations—Paramount, Loew's MGM, Twentieth Century-Fox, Warner Brothers, and RKO—as well as the "Little Three"—Universal, Columbia, and United Artists (UA)—dominated the industry. In addition, there were independent production companies (such as Chaplin and Goldwyn) and much smaller studios (such as Republic and Monogram; Disney did not enter the live-action feature film market until the 1940s.)

"Big," as in the "Big Five," implied certain standards of measurement—profitability, number of movies made, list of Oscar winners, personnel under contract, or sometimes just sheer physical size. Each of these studios made a great deal of money, turned out fifty or so features a year, won lots of awards, and occupied a great deal of real estate. The Twentieth Century-Fox lot, situated on more than 108 acres of prime Los Angeles land in the 1920s, was half a mile wide and nearly a mile long. MGM was staffed by almost four thousand people. At their peak, the five studios combined turned out as many as five hundred features in a year. (In 1950, there were 19,048 movie houses in the United States, with a total of 11,977,081 seats to be filled—and filled they were, to capacity.)

Attention to detail is still a mark of the best Hollywood period films. MGM's lavish costume drama *Marie Antoinette* (1938) was a sumptuous historical spectacle that re-created the world of Versailles. Norma Shearer (above left) played the doomed queen, and hundreds of extras (above) were hired for such scenes as this ball, in which every costume was carefully made from a different design.

Opposite: Director Martin Scorsese had his stars, Daniel Day-Lewis and Michelle Pfeiffer, study the manners and mores of the times for his magnificently reproduced world of Edith Wharton's *The Age of Innocence* (1993).

As times changed, so did censorship requirements: William Powell and Carole Lombard made screwball comedy history as the elegant butler and madcap heiress in *My Man Godfrey* (1936), but they revealed their sensual emotions with a discretion guided by the MPPDA.

## The Original List of "Don'ts" and "Be Carefuls"

[This list of "Don'ts" and "Be Carefuls" was adopted by the major film studios in 1927. Later, in March 1930, it was adopted and expanded into the Production Code.]

Resolved, that those things which are included in the following list shall not appear in pictures produced by members of this Association, irrespective of the manner in which they are treated:

1. Pointed profanity—by either title or lip—this includes words "God," "Lord," "Jesus," "Christ" (unless used reverently in connection with proper religious ceremonies), "hell," "damn," "Gawd," and every other profane and vulgar expression, however it may be spelled.
2. Any licentious or suggestive nudity—in fact or in silhouette; and any lecherous or licentious notice thereof by other characters in the picture.
3. The illegal traffic in drugs.
4. Any inference of sex perversion.
5. White slavery.
6. Miscegenation (sex relationships between the white and black races).
7. Sex hygiene and venereal diseases.
8. Scenes of actual childbirth—in fact or in silhouette.
9. Children's sex organs.
10. Ridicule of the clergy.
11. Willful offense to any nation, race or creed.

The Big Five were big because they were all things to all moviegoers. Each had its own big-time legendary mogul boss, its own roster of beautiful stars and hopeful starlets, its own sturdy technicians who could design a gown, build and light a set, cement false eyelashes on everything from a leading lady to a canine star, and create a hurricane by next Thursday.

Like everything else about Hollywood, the five studios were contradictory: they were the same, only they were different. They were the same in that they were all businesses, economically and tightly run by shrewd businessmen. They all operated on a daily basis in roughly the same way. First, the studios made movies to be sold. Then they sold them. Then they distributed them to the people they sold them to. Then they showed the movies they made and sold and distributed in the theaters they owned. In other words, they controlled production, distribution, and exhibition—and had a virtual monopoly on the market. Although they were in dead-heat competition with one another for good stories, good stars, and good reviews, they still cooperated with one another to support a business system that allowed them collectively to maintain control of 95 percent of the revenues from the country's movie screens.

Hollywood in the old days is always referred to as *the* studio system—implying *one*—when there were really five separate big studios, three smaller ones, and several independents. But their power lay in the oneness, the ways in which they were the same.

## Production

To make a movie, a studio needed to have financing, equipment and space, a story or plan, above-the-line talent (a highly paid "creative" team of producers, directors, stars, and writers), and backstage talent. During the golden era, every studio had all these essential assets on staff. Furthermore, an internal specialization of labor, much as in any large American corporation, was designed to make maximum use of these resources for the lowest possible cost, although every corner by no means was cut.

The bulk of the companies' financing came from theater admissions and investment capital, although they drew and used profits from film rentals, sale of film accessories, and affiliated companies, too. Each year, in the New York offices, company executives, uninvolved in the day-to-day hands-on process of filmmaking, would decide how many films to make (generally between forty and sixty) and what the budget for each one would be. Although these decisions were not final (the West Coast studio boss could renegotiate with the eastern business office), ultimately the decision, based on the profit motive, was made in New York.

There was a complicated system of production designed to produce both "B" films (less expensive, short features used to fill out the second half of a double feature), and quality "A" films. The studios' primary aim was to produce these A features, despite the fact that they cost a great deal of money to make. The definition of quality was tied both to economic success and to high standards of storytelling realism, accessibility, clarity, and spectacle. Movies with famous stars and directors, elaborate costumes, sets, and camera set-ups or movies that required specialized equipment and personnel (such as musicals and westerns) or a lavish adaptation of best-selling novels, proved that they could draw large crowds to offset the large production budgets. Studios were prepared to spend exorbitant sums to get such a film's quality just right. For instance, in the late 1920s and early 1930s MGM's production boss, Irving Thalberg, instituted a system of previewing his studio's films. Once he felt that an edited version was complete, he would test it with a preview audience. Based on the audience's specific reactions to particular scenes, he would often recut or even reshoot various parts of the film, even if the preview audience had judged the film to be an overall success. (In fact, not only is Thalberg credited with establishing this as fairly standard practice at MGM, but other studios began to use similar systems.) This practice clearly illustrates Hollywood's high opinion of the audience in those days; the viewer was king, and money should be spent to make pictures the right way.

When making either A or B pictures, each studio used some version of a producer-unit system. In general, a number of producers were employed by the studios, and they were responsible only to the studio boss, a man who had varying amounts of involvement in the actual moviemaking process depending on the particular studio. Each unit producer would cover one or two genres, with a number of directors working under him, and one of the producers would generally be responsible for all B productions. While directors and stars often did move between genres and producers, sometimes particularly successful combinations of people would be organized into units to work together. For example, teams at MGM in the golden age produced the Thin Man series (1934–1947), featuring Myrna Loy and William Powell; the Tarzan series (1932–1942, but continued into the 1950s by RKO), with Johnny Weissmuller and Maureen O'Sullivan; the Andy Hardy series (1931–1958) with Mickey Rooney; and the Dr. Kildare series (1938–1947) with Lew Ayres and Lionel Barrymore; as well as the celebrated Arthur Freed unit that primarily made musicals. At Warner Brothers, Paul Muni starred in, William Dieterle directed, and Henry Blanke produced a number of biographical pictures, or "biopics," such as *The Life of Emile Zola* (1937), *Juarez* (1939), and *The Story of Louis Pasteur* (1936).

In choosing stories to be produced, studios had to consider, at least at some level, issues of censorship and government approval of content and style used to represent "sensitive topics." In an effort to avoid explicit outside control of their productions, the major studios financed and supported a censorship code and a self-regulating office. Through this office they achieved self-censorship—and, by extension, self-approval—that deterred government censorship or damaging public outcry.

The self-censorship code was established in the 1920s, largely because by the end of 1921 as many as thirty-six states were considering introducing censorship legislation. Until the 1910s there was no censorship process, as film grew rapidly as an entertainment medium during this period. In response the film business formed the Motion Picture Producers and Distributors of America (MPPDA) in 1922 in order to respond to many issues filmmakers were facing, among them censorship. (The MPPDA created a public relations department, a foreign relations office, programs to attempt to regularize trade practices, and committees that arbitrated labor

**The liberated *Bob and Carol and Ted and Alice* (1969) made cinema history with a modern story about sexual freedom in which an ultra-sophisticated couple (Natalie Wood and Robert Culp) try to involve their best friends (Dyan Cannon and Elliott Gould) in the danger and excitement of wife-swapping.**

And be it further resolved that special care be exercised in the manner in which the following subjects are treated, to the end that vulgarity and suggestiveness may be eliminated and that good taste may be emphasized:

1. The use of the flag.
2. International relations (avoiding picturization in an unfavorable light another country's religion, history, institutions, prominent people, and citizenry).
3. Arson.
4. The use of firearms.
5. Theft, robbery, safecracking, and dynamiting of trains, mines, buildings, etc. (having in mind the effect which a too-detailed description of these may have upon the moron).
6. Brutality and possible gruesomeness.
7. Technique of committing murder by whatever method.
8. Methods of smuggling.
9. Third-degree methods.
10. Actual hangings or electrocutions as legal punishment for crime.
11. Sympathy for criminals.
12. Attitude toward public characters and institutions.
13. Sedition.
14. Apparent cruelty to children and animals.
15. Branding of people or animals.
16. The sale of women, or of a woman selling her virtue.
17. Rape or attempted rape.
18. First-night scenes.
19. Man and woman in bed together.
20. Deliberate seduction of girls.
21. The institution of marriage.
22. Surgical operations.
23. The use of drugs.
24. Titles or scenes having to do with law enforcement or law-enforcing officers.
25. Excessive or lustful kissing, particularly when one character or the other is a "heavy."

Resolved, that the execution of the purpose of this resolution is a fair trade practice.

matters and internal disputes.) A subgroup of the MPPDA was the Studio Relations Committee, which was specifically formed to be responsible for censorship.

In 1927 the MPPDA drew up a list of guidelines literally called the list of "Don'ts and Be Carefuls," which was useful in avoiding trouble with state censorship boards and reform groups. Obviously, the list's purpose was not morality, but money. There was no enforcement system nor any internal review process connected with it. However, by 1928, the MPPDA had begun monitoring scripts in advance for potential censorship sensitivity, and on March 30, 1930, the membership formally adopted its famous "Production Code."

The Production Code was described by the MPPDA as a "moral document," and it was not mandatory for producers to follow it. In the beginning, many did not. Broadly described, the code put forth three main concepts: (1) No picture shall be produced that will lower the moral standards of those who see it. Hence the sympathy of the audience shall never be thrown to the side of crime, wrongdoing, evil, or sin; (2) Correct, conformist standards of life, subject only to the requirements of drama and entertainment, shall be presented; (3) Law, natural or human, shall not be ridiculed, nor shall sympathy be created for its violation. Obviously, the Production Code left considerable room for maneuvering.

Although the code was documented in 1930, it was at first loosely interpreted by the film studios according to their own designs. This period is often called the "pre-code era." (Technically, it is not pre-code, but pre–code enforcement.) Thus from 1930 to 1934, American movies were freer and sexier than they would be in the later studio years. Barbara Stanwyck, for instance, is frankly shown sleeping her way to the top in *Baby Face* (1932), and Jean Harlow, who is clearly the heroine of *Red-Headed Woman* (1932), is equally clearly a tramp. Mae West, the force that most people think single-handedly brought on censorship, can be seen vamping in *She Done Him Wrong* (1933), inviting Cary Grant to come up and see her and leaving no doubt about what she has in mind for the visit.

Movies with frank sex, loose women, violent gangsters, and unwed mothers attracted the attention of religious leaders. Such movies, combined with the industry's obviously self-serving regulation of its self-defined code, finally incited action. In April 1934 a committee of Catholic bishops formed the Legion of Decency, an organization that would instruct Catholics as to which movies they should avoid seeing. The Catholic hierarchy was supported in this move both by Protestant and Jewish leaders.

As a result, the code was revised and expanded, and Joseph Breen was put in charge of administering the code. Throughout the 1930s and 1940s the studios usually followed the Production Code Administration's recommendations, and as a result, boycotts were prevented. Very few theaters would exhibit a film that did not have the "Code Certificate," thus every studio film went through Breen's office as a matter of course during production. If the office required changes before it could grant approval, the alterations would be made. For instance, the 1935 version of *Anna Karenina*, starring Greta Garbo, was put into negotiation over scenes in which the married Anna (Garbo) passionately kissed her lover, Vronsky (Fredric March). Although the basic story by Leo Tolstoy of a woman ruined by this love remains intact, these scenes were moderated and much of the action eliminated by the Breen office. The producing studio, MGM, cooperated fully.

Left: The delightful and elegant Audrey Hepburn perfectly portrayed Holly Golightly in Truman Capote's *Breakfast at Tiffany's* (1961), written by George Axelrod and directed by Blake Edwards. The movie was enlivened by Henry Mancini's Oscar-winning score.

Below: One of the most popular musicals in the history of the genre, *Singin' in the Rain* (1952), featured Gene Kelly, Debbie Reynolds, and Donald O'Connor in a story set in Hollywood during the era of the transition to sound movies.

## Distribution

The distribution practices of the major studios effectively guaranteed the Big Five 75 percent of the nation's box-office revenues. Although this figure is quite high, the majors did not require ownership of 75 percent of the theaters in order to maintain control. Instead, they directly controlled only 16 percent of the theaters and 25 percent of the seats in the country. Through their powerful distribution networks, they exploited extensive blind bidding, block booking, admission price discrimination, and run-zone-clearance systems to guarantee maximum income. These marketing strategies had been established in the 1920s, and although there were frequent charges brought for antitrust violations, particularly in relation to block booking, the 1933 National Industry Recovery Act (NIRA) authorized the practices. By the time the NIRA was declared unconstitutional in 1935, the distribution networks and practices were firmly entrenched and continued to operate throughout the 1930s and 1940s. Films were rented to particular theaters for one, two, three, or more runs. If a theater had a first run, it would be guaranteed that the same film would not play within a particular geographic zone for a certain time period; generally the clearance was for seven to thirty days. In this way admission price discrimination was established. If customers were willing to pay more for a film, they could see it right away. If not, they had to wait a specified amount of time for a subsequent run to begin. A particularly successful film might have eleven full runs over an entire year. Furthermore, few theaters would rent a film that had not initially played in a first-run theater; they depended on the free advance advertising a first run provided, as well as on the drawing power of the big stars who appeared in first-run films. Because the majors controlled all but thirty-seven of the nation's first-run theaters, they virtually guaranteed that subsequent theaters would rent only their films. With few shifts in the demographics of the American population during the 1930s and 1940s, and with admission prices written into contracts, the run-zone-clearance system assured the film companies maximum financial returns from their films. In addition, block booking and blind bidding guaranteed every studio film a chance to be shown. Nonaffiliated theaters (and, of course, the theaters affiliated with each company) would have to show a bulk of a company's films. In other words, if exhibitors wanted to get the most successful MGM films, they would have to agree to rent an entire block (a set number) of MGM films even before they had been produced. In this way, even if a film did poorly at the box office, the film companies were guaranteed a rental fee.

The security that these distributions systems offered facilitated cooperation rather than competition among the eight major studios. Paramount controlled theaters in the South, New England, and the upper Midwest; Fox controlled the West Coast; RKO and Loew's shared New York, New Jersey, and Ohio; and Warner Brothers controlled the Mid-Atlantic states. Thus they did not have to worry about competition within a particular area. However, first-run theaters needed approximately a hundred features a year to fill their seats regularly. As a result, each company rented a controlled number of the most successful films from the others, and they did not require block booking from each other. Instead, they all benefited by playing their most profitable films around the entire country and filling their first-run theaters with big money-makers.

## Exhibition

The Big Five—MGM, Twentieth Century-Fox, Warner Brothers, Paramount, and RKO—owned their own theaters. The Little Three—Universal, Columbia, and United Artists (technically not a "studio" in the same way as the others because it did not operate production facilities)—owned no theater chains.

Despite the fact that the studios' distribution networks exerted powerful control during the 1930s and 1940s over U.S. movie screens, the profit from distributing films itself represented only 1 percent of a film company's income. Most money (94 percent) came from exhibition. Thus, the importance of owning theaters was obvious. The distribution system was important only in ensuring access to ticket sales, not in collecting money from rentals. Of course, the exhibition end of the business also worked to achieve box-office success. In general, the Big Five were using typical strategies gleaned from observing chain-store management, coupled with shrewd advertising and programming double features to boost ticket sales.

In a pioneering analysis of the film industry, historian Douglas Gomery has argued that Sam Katz, as the manager of the Publix (owned by Paramount) theater chain, brought the chain-store strategy to the U.S. movie industry. Katz had first used this system with his Balaban & Katz theaters in Chicago during the 1910s. Having come into the cinema market late, he discovered that as an independent distributor, he had to spread his cost across a number of theaters to keep his prices down. Furthermore, he had to differentiate his product in order to obtain customers. In this way he copied the chain-store strategy pioneered across the country by A&P and Woolworth.

When Katz moved into the majors by joining with Paramount, he brought with him these marketing strategies, as well as his efficient organization. Part of the success of the chain-store strategy was its emphasis on centralized and highly controlled management. The resultant specialization of labor mirrored the film companies' production process. All booking was done in New York. Local managers could sometimes pick from among a few films based on their particular environments, but for the most part they had no control over what they showed.

Furthermore, along with the films came detailed instructions and suggestions for advertising in press kits and in-house manuals. (Generally a film would be sold through its star or its genre or a combination of the two, since most audiences chose their movies by star or story.) Even pieces of gossip about the leading stars were included in press kits. In addition, spectacle and immediacy would be emphasized in order to draw the crowds to the first-run theaters as quickly as possible. All the managers had to do was to choose from a small pantry of choices how they wished to market the film locally.

Perhaps the most important change in exhibition created by the Depression was the double feature. As economic distress led to declining attendances in the early 1930s, theaters began to compete for crowds by offering giveaways, games, and double features for the same price. However, the same NIRA legislation that legalized block booking outlawed the giveaways and games as unfair competition, allowing only the double feature to continue. Like the distribution practices, the exhibition practices remained the same even after the NIRA was declared unconstitutional.

Double features are important to an understanding of the brilliance of the old studio system, illustrating how beautifully the business connected its systems of exhibition, distribution, and production. Warner Brothers might make a big-budget picture with big-name stars. This movie would be rented out as an A feature for a percentage of the profits it made. During the period of time it took to make that feature, the studio would also make two or possibly three B pictures, with running times under seventy minutes, lesser- or no-name actors, and a very small production budget. These three features would be offered for rental at a flat rate. Because the theaters not doing first-run features needed about three hundred movies a year to fill up their double-feature schedule, there was an increased market for B features, which were much less risky financially because they cost less to make. They were like hamburgers and hot dogs on the dinner menu—sure-fire, low-cost fare in case the day's ritzy special was a bomb.

Double features helped not only the Big Five studios, but also the Little Three, who did not own their own theaters. Double features also insured the success of such "B studios" as Monogram and Republic. Universal, Columbia, and UA had enough money to produce some A features for first-run release, and then Universal and Columbia produced serials and cheap features to fill out. The so-called poverty row studios produced only B features for the second-run theaters. This system evolved in the 1920s and was more or less fully in place by 1935. The studios, efficient in their business and adept at marketing and advertising, maintained these practices of production, exhibition, and distribution.

In using this system, the studios maintained cordial relationships and shared information. They stood together if threatened from the outside. They were, in that sense, "the industry," or "one system." In their art, however, they were fierce competitors, vying to sign up-and-coming stars, stealing story ideas from one another, and always racing to be the studio that had the movies the audiences most wanted to see. All movie studios made all kinds of movies in those days. They were after every dollar. They all had their comedies, their dramas, and their romances, which tended to standardize the product.

However, each studio also tried to develop specialties based on the roster of talent under contract. If you had Mae West under contract, you weren't going to be able to use her to play the mother in a family drama. You had to develop a Mae West type of movie, and that influenced the genres you emphasized, the directors you put under contract, and the set and clothing designers you needed on payroll. A studio that had spent money to develop a star wanted to hold on to its "property." They spent more money to create an audience that wanted that star's pictures. These policies also helped studios to create their own special styles. An RKO musical with Astaire and Rogers, for instance, was very different from a musical from Warner Brothers with Ruby Keeler and Dick Powell. Studios also were clever at marketing their own stars as eternally the same ("Fred and Ginger are back again") *and* as brand new and different ("Fred and Ginger are better than ever in a new kind of musical.") As a result, each studio had its own history, its own stories, its own style.

Studios and production houses had impressive buildings linked to sound stages, standing outdoor sets, and facilities of all kinds in the golden age of the Hollywood system. **Opposite:** Each studio displayed a distinctive architecture such as the Mediterranean look of Fox (top); the David O. Selznick buildings, with their Southern colonial style (middle); and RKO, with its futuristic logo and Art Deco look (bottom).

**Below:** The very distinctive Metro-Goldwyn-Mayer studio entrance (greeting Bing Crosby) was the ultimate in 1930s streamlined design and elegance.

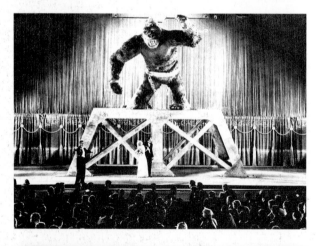

## The Studios: Big Five and Little Three

"RKO" is an acronym for "Radio-Keith-Orpheum." The studio's birth allegedly took place in an oyster bar in New York City during October 1928 when Joseph P. Kennedy, father of the country's future president, and David Sarnoff, president of the Radio Corporation of America (RCA), sat down to talk a bit of business. The result was one of the largest mergers in the history of the film industry, the wedding of Kennedy's FBO (Film Booking Office, Inc.), which had already been absorbed by RCA, to the Keith-Albee-Orpheum circuit of seven hundred vaudeville theaters. The merger was officially completed on October 23, 1928, with the three companies being renamed the Radio-Keith-Orpheum Corporation, or RKO.

RKO, born with the coming of sound, managed to delay the effects of the Depression—as did all the other studios—through the public's attraction to the new innovation. However, throughout its twenty-seven years of history, RKO became famous for being the studio with the least stability, going from one regime to another, changing its creative roster, and redefining its production policies until it finally collapsed under the bizarre management of Howard Hughes. This lack of stability was both a strength and a weakness. On the one hand, the chaos kept RKO from having a readily identifiable lasting style of its own, but it allowed dynamic individuals to make highly personal, and thus, unique, motion pictures, some of which, such as *Citizen Kane* (1941), are landmarks. Ironically, RKO's famous instability is probably what guaranteed its place in the creative hierarchy.

No one type of film dominated RKO's production roster. During the 1930s, for instance, it was famous for the elegant, sophisticated musicals starring Fred Astaire and Ginger Rogers (*Top Hat* [1935], *Swing Time* [1936], *Follow the Fleet* [1936]), but it also won its first Oscar for Best Picture for the epic western *Cimarron* (1930). And perhaps its most remembered film of the decade was the horror movie *King Kong* (1933).

Over the years RKO produced everything from Hitchcock's *Notorious* (1946) to the nourishing *Out of the Past* (1947) to the socially conscious *Crossfire* (1947) to the beloved comedy *It's a Wonderful Life* (1946). Artists who made their film names in Hollywood at RKO include Katharine Hepburn, George Cukor, Ginger Rogers, Fred Astaire, Irene Dunne, George Stevens, Orson Welles, and many others. Perhaps it is best to say that in the factory town called Hollywood, RKO was a success because it never quite became efficient enough or stable enough to really be a factory. It was the exception that proved the rule.

Warner Brothers was the opposite: famous not only for its stability, but for its efficient, cost-cutting, hard-nosed business tactics that focused on its mission of making

Left: *King Kong* (1933), one of RKO's most famous and successful movies, thrilled audiences with its dramatic sets and photography. The beauty-and-the-beast theme spawned a host of spoofs and remakes.

Right: For Frank Capra's beloved Christmas favorite *It's a Wonderful Life* (1946), with Donna Reed and James Stewart, RKO built an entire small-town main street on its ranch in order to represent "Bedford Falls," the place Stewart longs to escape from but which ends up as his warmhearted paradise.

Left: *The Adventures of Robin Hood* (1938) stars Errol Flynn in the title role and Basil Rathbone as Robin's arch enemy and was one of Warner Brothers' most lavish productions of the 1930s. Filmed in a rich Technicolor, emphasizing greens and golds, the movie presents an outstanding cast (including Olivia DeHavilland, Claude Rains, and Alan Hale) against backgrounds of jousting tournaments, gigantic castle sets, and handsomely decorated settings.

Right: Errol Flynn's first big hit for Warner Brothers cast him as Dr. Peter Blood in a swashbuckling tale of sea battles, sword fights, cutthroat pirates, and passionate romance. Directed by Michael Curtiz and co-starring Flynn for the first time with Olivia DeHavilland, who would become his most frequent leading lady, *Captain Blood* is based on a novel by Rafael Sabatini and includes a magnificent musical score by the Austrian composer Erich Wolfgang Korngold (1935).

lots of movies (high volume) for the least amount of money (low cost) following popular storytelling patterns (genre).

Warners was the only studio run by one family. Although the famous four brothers—Sam, Harry, Jack, and Albert Warner—were in the film business as early as 1913, the entity known as "Warner Brothers" is—like RKO—famous for its entrance into the major leagues with the innovation of sound. *The Jazz Singer*, starring Al Jolson, and released in 1927, is commonly and erroneously remembered as "the beginning of sound," although various successful experiments with sound had already occurred. Warners actually released forty-two other movies in 1927 and one year later solidified its position in the business by buying out the Stanley Corporation of America (a large theater chain with over 250 theaters in seventy-five cities and seven states), and by taking control of First National Pictures, so that the two companies could work in tandem.

Warner Brothers became famous for its tough, gritty gangster pictures starring such distinctive leading men as James Cagney, Edward G. Robinson, and Humphrey Bogart, and for its innovative musicals directed by Busby Berkeley. It also gained recognition for the Paul Muni biopics and for delightful, beautifully mounted costume dramas starring Olivia DeHavilland and Errol Flynn (*Captain Blood* [1935], *The Adventures of Robin Hood* [1938]). In the 1940s Warners developed "women's films" to showcase such famous female stars as Bette Davis, Joan Crawford, and Barbara Stanwyck (*Now Voyager* [1942], *Mildred Pierce* [1945], and *My Reputation* [1946], respectively) and continued its tough male film tradition in such detective classics as

*The Maltese Falcon* (1941) and *The Big Sleep* (1946) with Humphrey Bogart. It also became associated with controversial political films, such as *Mission to Moscow* (1943).

Twentieth Century-Fox was founded in 1935 by the merger of Fox Films, William Fox's pioneering company that had developed the Movietone sound system, and Darryl F. Zanuck's Twentieth Century Films, which had been founded in 1932. Twentieth's output varied over the years as tastes and times changed; for instance, in the late 1930s, profits came from such simple entertainments as Shirley Temple movies (*Captain January* [1936], *Stowaway* [1936]), lavish costume dramas such as *Suez* (1938) and *Lloyd's of London* (1936), and ice-skating musicals starring Sonja Henie (*One in a Million* [1936], *Happy Landing* [1938]). The studio also made respected prestige films like *The Prisoner of Shark Island* (1936), about Dr. Samuel Mudd who treated John Wilkes Booth as he fled from the law after assassinating Lincoln. This eclectic practice continued into the 1940s, where variety was represented by prestige films such as *The Grapes of Wrath* (1940) and *How Green Was My Valley* (1941), light entertainment by Betty Grable, Technicolor musicals such as *Sweet Rosie O'Grady* (1943) and *Mother Wore Tights* (1947), and costume dramas like *Forever Amber* (1947). Sequels and remakes were encouraged under the direction of studio head Zanuck, who also developed a series of very blonde, variously talented musical-comedy female stars who were closely associated with the studio: Alice Faye, June Haver, and Marilyn Monroe, as well as Henie and Grable.

The Rolls-Royce of the studio system was undoubtedly Loew's-MGM, the biggest of the Big Five. MGM was formed in 1924 with the merger of Loew's-Metro (a company formed in 1920), Goldwyn (a small independent company owned by Samuel Goldwyn), and Louis B. Mayer Productions. Because the resulting company owned so few theaters, it had to rely on the other four members of the Big Five for distribution. As a result, MGM tended to produce glamorous, expensive, star-filled, first-run films that just *had* to be seen. Although less expensive films were also made at MGM, the designation "B" was not used. MGM counted on star names, variety, and perfection in production to draw customers to the box office. MGM became known as the studio that had "more stars than there are in the heavens." At different times between the years 1930 and 1955, the studio had under contract such star names as Clark Gable, Joan Crawford, Norma Shearer, Greta Garbo, Jean Harlow, James Stewart, Robert Taylor, Lana Turner, Judy Garland, Greer Garson, Esther Williams, Van Johnson, Mickey Rooney, Spencer Tracy, Elizabeth Taylor, Ava Gardner, Janet Leigh, Jane Powell, Debbie Reynolds, Gene Kelly, Fred Astaire, Deborah Kerr, Stewart Granger, and Cyd Charisse.

> *"I just think a picture should say a little something."*
>
> *"Oh, a message kid. You'd have turned down* Gone with the Wind. *"*
>
> *"No, that was me. I said, 'Who wants to see a Civil War picture?'"*
>
> Dialog from *Sullivan's Travels*

MGM numbers many films among the lists of those best remembered by the moviegoing public. There are the famous MGM musicals, many of which were produced by the celebrated Arthur Freed unit: *Singin' in the Rain* (1952), *An American in Paris* (1951), *Bandwagon,* and *Gigi* (1958). There were lavish costume dramas (*That Forsyte Woman* [1949], *Quo Vadis* [1951], *Ben Hur* [1959]), literary adaptations (*David Copperfield* [1934], *The Good Earth* [1937]), play reproductions (*Romeo and Juliet* [1936], *Strange Interlude* [1932]), and all-star casts (*Grand Hotel* [1932], *Dinner at Eight* [1933], *Executive Suite* [1954], and *The Women* [1939]). There were famous pairings of big-name stars, such as Nelson Eddy and Jeanette MacDonald; Joan Crawford and Clark Gable; Mickey Rooney and Judy Garland; Katharine Hepburn and Spencer Tracy. There were biographical movies like *Madame Curie* (1943) and *The Great Ziegfeld* (1936), heartwarming stories for families (*Lassie Come Home* [1943], *The Yearling* [1946]), comedies (*Father of the Bride* [1950], *A Night at the Opera* [1935]), and films that connected exactly to what was on people's minds at the time, such as *Mrs. Miniver* (1942) during World War II. There were also such beloved classics as *The Wizard of Oz* (1939) and *Gone with the Wind* (1939), although the latter was produced by Selznick International; MGM only released it.

Paramount, the last of the Big Five, was known as the most European of the studios. In fact, so many foreigners worked there that its commissary was called "the tower of Babel," since the sound of many different languages could always be heard at lunchtime. Paramount began with Adolph Zukor's development of the Famous Players in the film industry of the 1910s. As Zukor's company came to dominate the presound era because its theater holdings exceeded those of any other company, that power allowed the company to feel the need to exert only a loose control over production.

**Some single images represent the American cinema in an instant. Here the young, pig-tailed Judy Garland is leaving Kansas behind to fly over the rainbow and enters the Technicolored world of Munchkin Land and Oz in *The Wizard of Oz* (1939).**

Therefore, the emergence of Paramount allowed directors a great deal of creative control. Continual shifts in production management kept the company fairly disorganized during the early 1930s until a 1936 investigation finally revealed that the freedom was resulting in inefficient use of stars and personnel, waste of money, and random shooting schedules. This resulted in a three-tier set-up being devised: one half of the company began to make B movies, and the other half was subdivided into two units—one that was closely supervised and another that allowed prestigious directors to have their own producing-directing units and thus more artistic freedom. Throughout this period, Paramount also released films for independent filmmakers.

Paramount was known as a studio that relied on "spillover" fame. That is, stars like Marlene Dietrich and Maurice Chevalier came to Hollywood, bringing their European-earned fame and spilling it over into America. The Marx Brothers arrived, bringing their reputations from Broadway; and the pairing of Bing Crosby and Bob Hope relied partly on their reputation from radio. Paramount followed a policy of making fewer films, but with very big stars and directors, to attract more box-office income with less investment.

**Bing Crosby and Bob Hope made a series of outrageous comedies for Paramount Pictures in which they played two likeable con artists surviving by their wits and musical talents in exotic locales. Known as "the Road pictures," the movies took the comedy team to Morocco (below; 1942), Singapore, Zanzibar, Rio, Bali, Utopia, and Hong Kong, in what press agents termed "a laff riot."**

**Opposite: A high point in American comedy, MGM's *A Night at the Opera* (1935); Kitty Carlisle and Allan Jones (left) play lovers, while Chico, Groucho, and Harpo Marx (center) confront forces of order in Sig Rumann and Margaret Dumont. Naturally, the brothers win, and it's not even close as they take on the world of opera. *Il Trovatore* has never been the same since Groucho leaned out of his box and cried out to the singing gypsy, "Boogie, boogie, boogie," or since he asked a Pagliacci clown, "Can you sleep on your stomach with such big buttons on your pajamas?"**

Paramount was called "the sophisticated studio." Its personnel were the chic European stars like Dietrich and Claudette Colbert, or American women of great personal style such as Paulette Goddard and Veronica Lake. Its male stars were suave types like Ray Milland, Alan Ladd, and John Lund. Its list of top directors and writers included Ernst Lubitsch, Joseph von Sternberg, Billy Wilder, and Preston Sturges. Of course, it also made unsophisticated musical comedies starring Betty Hutton and the widely appealing Road comedies with Hope and Crosby.

The Little Three held a slightly different position within the studio system than the Big Five. Since they did not own their own theaters, these companies had to rely on the Big Five for exhibition. The relationship worked symbiotically, however; the Big Five needed the Little Three's films to fill out their cinemas' schedules.

Thus, the studio era was marked by cooperation and friendly competition among the film companies. People frequently moved from one company to the next and then sometimes into successful independent production. Stars and directors were loaned back and forth, although always with appropriate compensation to their owners. Along with loan-outs and variations on the same genres, each studio cooperated with the others to keep the system running smoothly. The variations in production styles and products served to differentiate, but did not threaten, standardization.

Of the Little Three, United Artists alone did not have a studio. Instead, it relied on a network of the stars, having initially been formed by Mary Pickford, Douglas Fairbanks, Sr., D. W. Griffith, and Charles Chaplin, to help obtain talent. However, the company did not remain a distribution outlet for producer-stars only. As the original founders struggled to produce enough films and started to reach the end of their careers, the company began to distribute for other independent producers and other studios (such as Disney).

Opposite: Charlton Heston found lasting movie fame playing Moses in Cecil B. DeMille's epic remake of his own 1923 film, Paramount's The Ten Commandments (1956). DeMille, famous for his biblical epics, vividly presented the story of the life of Moses from birth through manhood in the Pharaoh's home into slavery and his leading the Jews out of Egypt via the parting of the Red Sea.

Below: Fairbanks, Chaplin, and Pickford, three of the legendary founders of United Artists.

United Artists struggled financially but did survive, proving there was enough space within the studio system to allow for a certain amount of independent production to be distributed by a large, centralized company and exhibited in major theaters.

Universal, unlike United Artists, *did* have studio space, and thus an internal production system. Having started back in 1909 at IMP, Carl Laemmle, Universal's boss, kept the studio on the edge of the majors, satisfied with filling out subsequent-run schedules, while making only a few A films per year, depending on the draw of its B pictures. The company's emphasis was put on placing such stars as Lon Chaney and Bela Lugosi in low-cost horror films or on popular musicals starring the young singer Deanna Durbin. By 1946 Universal merged with International, an independent company formed by William Goetz and Leo Spitz in 1943. During the war the market for

Horror was a staple for many Hollywood studios. Inset: Lon Chaney, the man of a thousand faces, dons one of them in his famous role as *The Phantom of the Opera* (1925), while Mary Philbin cowers in fear in the catacombs under the Paris Opera House. This silent production of the famous story of the composer who kidnaps a young singer presented one scene (the Bal Masque) in beautiful two-color Technicolor. The story has proved so popular with audiences that it has been remade several times for movies and television (including 1943, 1962, 1983, 1989, and 1990 versions). Left: Boris Karloff, like Chaney one of Hollywood's most beloved movie monsters, found his greatest fame playing Dr. Frankenstein's monster in the 1931 movie *Frankenstein*.

prestige pictures had increased, and Universal met the challenge by buying prepackaged deals and providing space for independent productions. For example, in 1945 Universal and the independent Diana Productions (formed by Walter Wanger, Joan Bennett, and Fritz Lang) set up a half inside–half outside deal to produce *Scarlet Street*.

Over the years, Universal was characterized predominantly by B product. Action films, westerns, and horror pictures were staples. During the 1930s, Deanna Durbin was the studio's only big-name movie star. In the 1940s Bud Abbott and Lou Costello improved Universal's financial situation by moving from B films to become Hollywood's top box-office attractions. In general, success at the studio was turned into formula, as with Abbott and Costello.

Like Universal, Columbia was involved in production and distribution, while relying on the majors and subsequent-run houses for exhibition. The firm began operations in 1919 when Joseph Brand and Jack and Harry Cohn left Universal to form a private production company, CBC. In 1924 they re-formed as Columbia with Harry Cohn as head of production. By 1926 they had established a distribution network; in 1928 they continued their growth by absorbing a number of smaller companies. Columbia was the least centralized film company, and the first to move to a producer-unit system. Columbia focused on cheap, B westerns, serials, and shorts, so the profits from these films could be used to create a few small-budget A pictures each year. The name most commonly associated with Columbia's A pictures is that of the great director Frank Capra, whose credits as director include *It Happened One Night* (1934), *Mr. Deeds Goes to Town* (1936), *Mr. Smith Goes to Washington* (1939), and *Lost Horizon* (1937).

### Independent Filmmaking During the Studio Era

Many visible and financially successful independent companies existed, Selznick's and Goldwyn's chief among them. Although they were independent from the direct control of the studio and production bosses, in the end they needed the majors to get their films to the screens. As was true with the Little Three, the relationship between the Big Five and the independents was symbiotic. The career of David O. Selznick serves as a good example of this. He learned his job by working in the studios, moving through MGM, Paramount, and RKO before he established Selznick International Pictures in 1935, and later David O. Selznick Productions in 1940. Once independent, he frequently borrowed from and loaned to the majors, and the studios were happy to work with him.

The 1939 *Motion Picture Almanac* lists seventy-three independent production companies in Hollywood. However, only eighteen of these companies actually produced any films during the 1938–1939 season. Independent companies had trouble surviving, partly because the talent was tied up in the majors. Between 1933 and 1939, 2,005 creative personnel were loaned back and forth among the majors, while only 180 were loaned to anyone outside the majors. Thus, the Big Five and the Little Three had enough economic power to control what finally got on the screens. If films not from major studios made it, it was usually because a major stood to benefit in some way from it.

Frank Capra's films for Columbia went to great lengths to establish effective screen worlds. Below: He shot this scene in an icehouse for *Lost Horizon*, his 1937 haunting movie based on the James Hilton novel about a group of five people who find themselves taken to a strange Tibetan land in which people evidently never age. John Howard (below left) and hero Ronald Colman (below right) face the truth as their plane has crashed in the forgotten wasteland of the north. Right: *Mr. Smith Goes to Washington* (1939) in the guise of James Stewart, the All-American hero who represents the decency of the common man. He is put to the test in the world of corrupt politicians and slick money-oriented politics, but he rises to the occasion in an Oscar-nominated performance. One of Frank Capra's most famous and beloved movies.

Walt Disney's *Fantasia* (1940), in which a real man, maestro
Leopold Stokowski, can meet a mouse, the famous Mickey; ele-
phants can dance on their back feet like a corps of beautiful balle-
rinas; and Mickey, playing the Sorcerer's Apprentice, has to hang on
for dear life in a maelstrom of kitchen chaos. *Fantasia* set famous
pieces of music to animated life through Disney's drawings.
Opposite: Today, long after Walt is gone, the old Disney magic still
works, as the 1993 hit film, *Aladdin*, has shown.

### *The Walt Disney Company*

Walt Disney was born in Chicago in 1901, and he began drawing figures on paper at a
very early age. When he was fourteen, he enrolled in the Kansas City Art Institute, and
after serving in World War I, he took a job with a commercial art studio in Kansas City.
While working there, he met another young artist, Ub Iwerks, and the two men soon
formed their own commercial art company. After creating animated commercials, the
two began making animated cartoons called Laugh-O-Grams, and by 1927 they were
making a popular series about a character named Oswald the Rabbit. Disney and
Iwerks joined a popular rush to Hollywood at the end of the 1920s, and by 1928 had
created an animated cartoon called *Steamboat Willie*, and introduced his famous trademark character, Mickey Mouse. For the 1930s and 1940s, however, Disney was not
like the other studios, because until the 1950s it made only animated cartoons, both
shorts and feature-length. During the 1950s, the emphasis changed from animation to
live-action movies, and in 1955 Disney also entered television.

Such successful shows as *The Mickey Mouse Club*, the *Zorro* series, and *Walt
Disney Presents* were popular with young audiences in particular. On September 24,
1961, *Walt Disney's Wonderful World of Color* debuted on NBC, providing an excellent
showcase for all of Disney's products: live-action subjects, two- and three-part films,
animation both old and new, short versions of features that functioned as advertisements for the real thing, and original creations such as "Disneyland after Dark," starring Annette Funicello, which promoted tourism and attendance at the Disneyland
theme park in Anaheim, California. This park, a dream of Walt Disney's since he first
established Disneyland Incorporated in 1951, had opened on July 17, 1955. By early
September of that same year, less than seven weeks after its opening, Disneyland welcomed its one-millionth visitor. "Disneyland," as the park is known, was a shrewd mixture of souvenir shops, educational exhibits, amusement park rides based on Disney

films, restaurants, theatrical presentations, and a series of specialized areas called such things as "Tomorrowland" and "Adventureland." A visiting family could tour the "House of Tomorrow," ride a steamboat through a Mark Twain–like Mississippi world, see "The Pirates of the Caribbean," ride the scary Matterhorn ride (two bobsleds hurtling down from a fourteen-story high "Matterhorn"), and have a hamburger or lunch in the Polynesian Tea Room.

## Studio Style

"It was an apprentice system, which you don't have now."

Henry Bumstead

In the past decade, scholars have increasingly become aware of how important "the system," in counterpoint to individual vision, was in creating the typical Hollywood film. When the first wave of scholars began seriously studying American movies as an art form, focus was given to the five most prominent individual artists who worked on any movie: producer, director, star, cinematographer, and writer. Second, the editors and art directors were discussed, with emphasis finally turning to the overall system itself, the total effort of all the movie's employees working in collaboration with one another.

In a large studio such as Paramount, MGM, or Warner Brothers, there were approximately forty department units in the business structure. Any attempt to sort out who-did-what or who-thought-up-what, is confused by the overlapping of functions, the day-to-day sharing of ideas, and the flexibility of a large staff. Although it was true that individuals could assert their ideas and style on the collaborative proc ess—a John Ford film is a John Ford film, a Von Sternberg film is a Von Sternberg film—it was also true that they did so often by choosing to use ideas submitted and created by others.

Every movie from the Hollywood system of the golden age reflects a mixture of inputs from many areas. Since each studio had a roster of employees under contract, it was inevitable that its films would frequently have a certain look, a familiar set of leads and supporting players, and a typical story form. Despite loan-outs across studio barriers and despite attempts to emulate each other's successful pictures, each studio developed its own look, its own set of genres

**Clark Gable and Joan Crawford patiently waiting for production to continue, in a publicity still (above); although Gable and Crawford wear these costumes briefly on a shipboard set at the end of _Forsaking All Others_ (1934), a scene such as this does does not actually appear in the movie.**

that it did best, its own stable of directors and stars that it catered to in projects. Audiences were not drawn to movies because of the studio that made them, however. Although certain connoisseurs might look for the new "MGM star vehicle," or latest "Fox Technicolor musical," or current "tough little Warner Brothers crime film," most people went out to see a star they liked in the kind of story they wanted to see.

Studio style, like everything about Hollywood, is directly linked to the audience. Each studio was trying to carve out the largest part of each audience for itself for every film it made. At the same time, however, it was also developing stars that were more popular with one part of the audience than another. Movies were not specifically targeted to small parts of the audience—such as the teen market—in the same way they are today, but films were made that were expected to draw wives to make their husbands accompany them or that parents would take their children to. As business progressed, each studio more or less developed a particular type of film

The studios could not only assemble armies of extras for any film, they could assemble armies of uniformed women who could both do an army rifle drill and a tap dance number, as illustrated by this set-up for a World War II movie (*Pin-Up*, with Betty Grable).

they were especially good at making, or a way that they wanted to speak to their audiences. In truth, all the studios could and did make films that were unexpected, as when MGM made the film noir *Gaslight* (1944), Warners released the musical *Yankee Doodle Dandy* (1942), and Paramount created the raucous comedy *Hail the Conquering Hero* (1944). Yet each studio *did* have its specialty, and its house style.

There is a simple overview of the studio system, a clichéd rule-of-thumb, that says Warners made films about the working class, MGM about the middle class, and Paramount about the upper class. To a certain extent this is true, as Warners did make gritty crime films about people from the tenements struggling for success; Metro fed middle-class dreams of love, glamour, and security; and Paramount often produced witty, sophisticated comedies with sexual innuendo. Each studio had a hallmark of some sort, like Fox's blonde stars or MGM's innovative musicals. However, Warner Brothers also made the sophisticated movie *Jewel Robbery* (1932), with William Powell and Kay Francis, a film that is more typical of the sophisticated Paramount. Paramount made the cornball comedy *Murder He Says* (1945), about hillbillies, and MGM made the gritty, dark crime film *The Last Gangster* (1937), which might typically be associated with Warners' style.

Studio style was a matter of emphasis, personnel assignments, and individual talents collectively pointed in the same direction. To understand this, it is instructive to compare two films based on stories by Dashiell Hammett: *The Thin Man*, made by MGM in 1934, and *The Maltese Falcon*, made by Warner Brothers in 1931 and remade in 1936 and 1941. (The 1936 version was called *Satan Met a Lady*. Since the 1941 version of *The Maltese Falcon* is the most familiar, it is the basis for this comparison. The 1931 version is extremely close to the 1941 in its entire format, and both the 1931 and 1936 versions support the points being made about Warner Brothers.) *The Thin Man* was so successful that it kicked off a series, starring William Powell and Myrna Loy as Nick and Nora Charles, and *The Maltese Falcon* was made three times within less than a decade. Both properties thus represent perfect studio projects: films that were so successful that they had rapid repeat successes, one in a series format and one in a direct remake situation. Since both are based on similar novels by Dashiell Hammett, it might be assumed that they would be made into similar films.

However, this was not the case, and the fundamental difference can be attributed to the differences between the two studios that made them: Warner Brothers was adept at crime films and MGM was skilled at elegant presentations of a glamorous world of well-dressed people. The first, and perhaps most striking difference between the two films based on Hammett's books, is that MGM stressed comedy and Warner Brothers did not. *The Thin Man* is a screwball comedy more than it is a murder mystery, and *The Maltese Falcon* stresses murder and mystery more than it makes us laugh. This does not mean that there is not a serious murder and a mystery to be solved in *The Thin Man*. There is. And it does not mean that there is not a great deal of comedy in *The Maltese Falcon*. There is. But the emphasis—the attitude toward the material, and thus toward the viewer—is different. It's simply this: comedy is laid over the narrative line of *The Thin Man*, so that you perceive all events through it; but comedy is assimilated and absorbed into the murder plot of *The Maltese Falcon*. Humor is not presented directly as comedy in *The Maltese Falcon*—going for a laugh—but rather as irony: a bitter and tough humor that does not expand the plot, or change it in any way, but that shoves it along, affirming its hard-boiled mood. Comedy is used to remind the audience just how mean a world Bogart is really living in.

Consider the introductions to the audiences of Nick Charles in *The Thin Man* and Sam Spade in the 1941 *The Maltese Falcon*. When you first see Nick, he is dancing with a cocktail shaker, having a high old time in his favorite bar. Nora, his wife, soon makes an energetic entrance being pulled through the hotel lobby by her dog. Her hat is askew and she's loaded with packages from ritzy stores. She does a belly flop onto the barroom floor, a pure comedy pratfall, recovering herself in time to exchange snappy banter with Nick as he orders his sixth martini and she demands five extras to go with the one she orders. ("Line them up right here," she demands. "She wants to catch up," he explains to the waiter.)

Sam Spade is introduced very differently in *The Maltese Falcon*. After a swift montage of San Francisco landmarks and skylines, the viewer is shown a window from the inside of an office, on which can be read, backwards, SPADE AND ARCHER. The camera moves down to reveal Spade behind his desk, wearing a dark suit with a white tie. He is rolling his own cigarette, paper in one hand, tobacco pouch in the other. He closes the tobacco bag with his teeth, while deftly wetting and closing the cigarette. He's a tough guy. He rolls his own. The two heroes are established as completely different men in completely different worlds. Spade alone behind the desk, ready for action, not laughs. Nick in a cocktail bar, with nothing but jokes and drink recipes on his mind.

The supporting casts of the two movies clearly reinforced this tendency toward emphasizing comedy or violence. *The Thin Man* presents a lovable set of almost

William Powell and Myrna Loy embodied the "perfectly married couple," Nick and Nora Charles, in the elegant MGM series of *Thin Man* movies. From the top, they toast their friends while Asta, the star dog, looks on; Loy models her new Christmas fur while Powell plays with his favorite Christmas gift, an air rifle, which he uses to destroy the Christmas tree; and together they ponder yet another clue. The expensive accoutrements illustrate MGM's presentation of the series as an elegant world of posh people who just happened also to solve murders.

Warner Brothers' *The Maltese Falcon* (1941) utilized a plain office, an ordinary hotel room, and a practical hotel lobby to describe a world of men in hats and pinstripes focused on commerce and transactions—with ensuing tension among the participants.

Runyonesque low-life "pals" of Nick Charles who attend the couple's Christmas cocktail party. Bookies, ex-cons, cops, reporters, and prizefighters fill up their elegant hotel suite, sopping up martinis and catered sandwiches. The scene is played out as pure screwball comedy, mixing the serious portion of the plot (in which the ingenue arrives to "confess" to the murder her father is accused of) into the scene of a party that grows increasingly riotous and drunken. After moving the story forward regarding a missing father, an unsolved murder, and a family of weird suspects, the scene ends with a montage of hilarious portraits of the guests: one maudlin fat man who calls his mom in San Francisco long-distance, and weeps, "Mom, it's me"; a couple who compete to see who can pop the balloons on the Christmas tree fastest; an ex-pugilist picking a fight with a shrimp in glasses; and a trio of drunks gathered around the piano singing "O Tannenbaum," while in the bedroom Asta the dog covers her ears.

*The Maltese Falcon*, on the other hand, has no peer for its bizarre parade of villains. Sydney Greenstreet is smoothly menacing, a ruthless fatso whose obsession with obtaining a prized statuette drives the plot. Greenstreet is often photographed from underneath his belly, a figure of grotesque proportion. His laughs rolls out of him in a rhythm with his double chins, and everything he says seems to be at two levels, simultaneously sane and insane ("I tell you right out that I'm a man who likes talking to a man who likes to talk."). His cohorts include Peter Lorre as the epicene Joel Cairo, who arrives at Spade's office smelling of gardenias, wearing kid gloves, and carrying a silver-headed walking cane that he apparently has a crush on. Elisha Cook, Jr., plays Wilmer the "gunsel." His character is a cheap and humorless hood who will easily kill anyone who annoys him. Bogart plays off this, by treating Cook with total contempt and lack of respect. Out of their potentially violent relationship comes a source for the type of black comedy the film does provide for viewers. When Bogart strips Cook of two big guns, later calmly handing them to Greenstreet, he says insolently, "A crippled newsie took 'em off him, but I made him give 'em back."

No scene in *The Thin Man* exists for comedy alone, as all sequences drive the murder-mystery plot forward one way or another. However, scenes such as the cocktail party neatly intercut the serious story with comedy by cleverly setting the revelation of sober plot details inside an ongoing and unfolding humorous situation. The day after the party, Nora arises with a hangover, wearing an ice pack on her head, while Nick lies on the couch, trying different bizarre poses from which to shoot at the balloons on the Christmas tree with his new present, a BB gun. Nora wears her new fur coat inside the house, and Asta admires her own holiday gift: a personalized miniature fire hydrant. (When a dog gets a fire hydrant for Christmas, we in the audience know we are not in for much danger.) The arrival of a potential suspect takes place during this sequence, and the plot is further developed accordingly.

Nick, Nora, and a police captain walk down the street, discussing the murder. Nick maneuvers Nora into a taxi in a comic turn, in order to get rid of her so the two men can investigate further. Comedy and mystery again mix when yet another suspect invades Nick and Nora's bedroom during the night, drawing a gun on them and shooting at Nick. This is serious danger, but played out with witty repartee from the couple and by showing Asta, the guard dog, running to hide under the bed.

Almost every major sequence in *The Thin Man* presents Nick and Nora Charles as lighthearted, free of fear, and capable of meeting any threat to their security through a funny remark, a daring maneuver, or some comic improvisation—such as a little song, a funny face, or a graceful pratfall. At the same time, the murder mystery itself is treated with respect and established as a strong plot line. Potential killers are identified and given clearly defined motives for the killings. We even see the dead body of a woman and watch one suspect getting gunned down outside a door. However, *The Thin Man* is presented to the audience as a screwball comedy about a delightful couple who wear great clothes, give great parties, make great love to one another—and who also solve great mysteries. This is the way MGM presented the majority of its films to audiences: through its own style, which included beautiful stars in beautiful clothes sitting on beautiful furniture. Love and comedy were stressed over violence and danger. *The Thin Man* represents a Dashiell Hammett novel turned into an MGM property. *The Maltese Falcon* shows a different world. The emphasis is more on the danger, treachery, and violence of the world.

Three people are killed in *The Thin Man*: one is murdered offscreen and never witnessed in any form; the second dies offscreen and viewers are allowed to see the dead body afterwards; and one killing takes place on screen. The latter victim—a minor character called Nunnheim—is shot as he is seen walking down the street, climbing the stairs, and going to open a door. As the door is opened, he is shot from within by an unseen assailant. This character has had no close relationship to any of the leading, sympathetic characters in the film, and he has been established as a "bad person," a gangster, from the beginning. His death elicits no sympathy. It is seen from enough distance that it is not personal, and no close-ups of his face or reaction are included.

In *The Maltese Falcon*, the viewer is shown blood on the face of Joel Cairo, and Elisha Cook, Jr., is seen kicking Bogart in the head. Bogart is himself shown viciously slapping Cook around. Within minutes after the film begins, the audience witnesses a murder in an intense and personalized way. The beginning of the movie has introduced not only Bogart as Sam Spade, but also Jerome Cowan as his partner, Miles Archer. The two men both interview Mary Astor when she first comes to them for help, and it is established that they are friends as well as partners. (Later we learn that Bogart was having an affair with his friend's wife, but that confirms the more serious attitude of this film.) The opening of the movie links the two men, establishes their friendship and partnership, and sets Cowan up as a real, somewhat likable character. He is then murdered. Viewers see his feet walking up a dark alley at night. He turns, smiles, and welcomes someone. Suddenly, his face crumples and his trusting look turns to one of horror as he cries out, "No, No!" A gun held by a gloved hand enters the frame, and he is shot at close range. He falls and rolls over and over again down an embankment. Although the scene is brief, it contains the details of the murder, including a personalized reaction to it from the victim. This is how Warner Brothers created its own style— a world of serious violence, no matter how snappy the dialogue delivered by Bogart might be ("Mrs. Spade didn't raise no kids dippy enough to make guesses in front of a D.A., an assistant D.A., and a stenographer.").

The production values of the two studios are clearly demonstrated by comparing the two movies. *The Thin Man* runs about ninety-three minutes. It has twenty-eight different scenes using multiple sets, including Nick and Nora's swanky hotel apartment, an elegant hotel bar, an inventor's laboratory, a gunman's cheap digs, a city street, the

Following his success as Sam Spade in *The Maltese Falcon*, Bogart
was cast as another detective, Philip Marlowe, in *The Big Sleep*
(1946); he was paired for the second time in his career with the
glamorous newcomer who became his wife. The excitement of
their off-screen relationship transferred to the screen; they were
one of the most dynamic film screen duos of the 1940s.

apartment of the inventor's mistress, and the apartment of his ex-wife and two children. *The Maltese Falcon* runs about ninety minutes, or approximately the same length, but it has only fifteen major scenes with fewer settings, most of which are used more than once: Spade's office and his apartment, for instance.

The set decoration for *The Thin Man* is in the Art Deco style. There are satin bedspreads and framed artworks on the walls. MGM took care to make everything associated with the principal players look elegant. Audiences are treated to a view of the world they probably don't live in—lots of expensive-looking goods to envy. In *The Maltese Falcon*, with the exception of the burning of the ship *La Paloma*, on which the statuette is brought to San Francisco, not much is seen that is visually dramatic. Sydney Greenstreet's suite is supposed to reflect his wealth, but it does not have the style and polish of the Charles's. Nick and Nora are, of course, supposed to be rich, and Spade is supposed to be an ordinary detective trying to make a living. This is part of what attracted MGM to *The Thin Man* and Warners to *The Maltese Falcon*. The former story affords an opportunity to make the mystery into a comedy of manners, juxtaposing rich and poor, high life and low life, in a joking manner. *The Maltese Falcon* is a detective movie, placing its hero squarely in the smarmy side of life, associating as he does largely with criminals, thieves, or greedy people willing to do whatever it takes to get their hands on money.

Costuming for the two films shows studio style and emphasis clearly. In *The Maltese Falcon*, everyone pretty much has a standard outfit that defines his character: Bogart in a dark suit, Cook in a long coat, Greenstreet in a big dark suit, Peter Lorre in a flamboyant dark suit and wearing a pinkie ring. Does anyone ever change his clothes? Not really. William Powell, on the other hand, sports one dapper suit after another in *The Thin Man*. He has elegant ties, pocket handkerchiefs, matching hats, a cashmere coat, a tuxedo, an elegant silk dressing gown, and a great set of 1930s men's pajamas. Even the men in MGM movies are dressed!

*The Maltese Falcon* stresses drama, and the adult relationship between two very, very tough characters: Bogart and Astor. The setting is secondary, and the women's clothes also illustrate the different house styles. Astor is well dressed in *The Maltese Falcon*, but her clothes are not what her role is about. She does not wear a single evening gown. Although she wears a hat and a fur stole the first time we see her, her every entrance is not to show off her outfit before she speaks. The only other two women in *The Maltese Falcon* are the loyal secretary Effie (Lee Patrick) and Archer's faithless widow (Gladys George). Their roles are small, and they have wardrobes to match. (Both are, however, very naked emotionally.)

The opposite is true for *The Thin Man*. First of all, there are simply more women characters in the MGM film: Myrna Loy as Nora, Maureen O'Sullivan as the ingenue daughter of the chief suspect, and four others: a mistress, an ex-wife, a moll, and a woman who turns out at the last minute to be married to the ex-wife! All these women, except for the moll and Romero's wife, change their clothes often. Each entrance establishes an outfit, and viewers are treated to furs, hats, jewels—the works. As the star of the piece, Myrna Loy is given a lavish wardrobe, including fur-trimmed sleepwear, a full-length fur coat, and two spectacular evening gowns, one of which upstages everything and everyone at the Christmas cocktail party.

In a murder mystery, there is a traditional final sequence in which "all is revealed." In *The Thin Man* and *The Maltese Falcon* these wrap-ups are presented on screen in ways that carry out the differences in studio house style between MGM and Warner Brothers. In *The Thin Man*, William Powell announces, "I'm gonna give a party and invite all the suspects." Thus, all the possible murderers arrive at his place for a lavish dinner. While Powell, in a tuxedo, gives instructions to the policemen in waiters' uniforms, Nora rushes around in a low-cut black evening gown putting place cards on her table. The table itself is loaded with crystal, china, fine linen, elaborate candelabra, and enough flowers to open a shop. The revelation of the murder is played out with everyone sitting in place while an elaborate meal is served. In *The Maltese Falcon*, an extended finale takes place in Spade's apartment, an unglamorous suite with photos of horses on the wall. It is a grim encounter in which the main characters admit to treachery, arson, murder, and greed. Hard terms are laid down. When Bogart suggests to Greenstreet that they make Cook the fall guy, Greenstreet at first says that Cook is like a son to him, but later suggests, "If you lose a son it's possible to get another, but there's only one falcon."

No one is beautifully dressed, and no deliberate comedy lightens the moments. The setting itself is no more than a suitable background—a leather chair, some curtained windows, and an ordinary apartment. As the night wears on, the space becomes littered with cigarette butts on the floor and dirty coffee cups on the tables. There is no beauty, no romance, and no perfect happy ending. In fact, the final moments—in which Sam Spade sends the lying heroine to her fate in the hands of the police—are another marked contrast to *The Thin Man*, in which the lovers end up in bed together on a train, with Asta thrown into the top bunk alone where she discreetly covers her eyes with her paw, so as not to disturb the happy couple below.

MGM and Warner Brothers both had the ability to make well-directed, tightly constructed entertainment movies. Both films are directed with pace and economy, and both have strong scripts. *The Thin Man* was directed by W. S. Van Dyke and its adaptation was done by a famous writing team, Albert Hackett and Francis Goodrich, who also wrote such comedies as *Father of the Bride*. The 1941 *The Maltese Falcon* was written and directed by John Huston. *The Thin Man*'s cinematographer was one of Hollywood's most inventive cameramen, James Wong Howe, while *The Maltese Falcon* was shot by Arthur Edeson. Both movies contain scenes of atmospheric lighting and darkness, but in *The Thin Man* these scenes are intercut with others in which the mood and lighting tone are the exact opposite.

These opposites are reflected in the two heroes, as brought to life by the two very different approaches of the actors, William Powell and Humphrey Bogart. Both were versatile and played many kinds of roles in the long run of their careers, but both were associated with a particular kind of role. Powell was usually dapper, a deft comedian who wore clothes well and was matinee-idol handsome. Bogart portrayed hard-boiled men who were romantic at the core, but whose view of the world was cynical. This casting is important, because the leading character of any movie is the person through whom the audience experiences events. Powell and Bogart organize the film for the viewer. Their reactions to problems, their ways of talking and behaving, their treatment of women, sets the tone the audience has to accept.

As Nick Charles, William Powell reacts to his wife's catching him with a young brunette in his arms with a shrug and a funny face. Nothing is serious to him. He's not worried, so why should you be if you're watching the movie? Everything strikes him as funny, so you might as well take it the same way. Bogart, on the other hand, plays Sam Spade as a hard-working detective. He gets drugged and kicked in the head and threatened with arrest. Although he laughs quietly to himself about things and throws a mean wisecrack around, he gets mad when his partner is killed. Death comes close to him, and his attitude toward it is tough, hard. He takes it seriously, so the viewer has to do that, too.

Since many Hollywood movies were about love, the leading lady is key to the definition of the hero. Powell is a married man, and Nick and Nora have what has been called "the perfect marriage" on film. (This means she lets him do anything he wants to do, and they are pals.) They are harmonious, a team, with a real domestic life that includes a dog and that will later include a child. Bogart plays the classic lone-wolf detective. The woman in his film, and thus in his life, is a lying, thieving, murderous femme fatale brilliantly portrayed by Mary Astor. No romance for Bogart. No companionship. No trust and no equality, and definitely no dog. All these factors add up together to show how MGM shaped material for viewers toward comedy, romance, and glamour, while Warner Brothers, working from the same writing source, shaped things toward grim danger, murder, and treachery. These things define studio style, but, as discussed, this "style" applied to the majority of any studio's output, not all of it.

## The Studio Working World

"It was very difficult to explain to people what it was like living in the studio. You had lunch there. You had dinner there. You ran movies after dinner. It never stopped. Everything functioned twenty-four hours a day. You didn't have to leave the studio to register to vote, because they came in and got your voter registration. You didn't have to leave the studio to renew your auto driving license. They came to you. The barber shop was open twenty-four hours a day if you needed it. They had a dentist on the lot. They had a doctor full time on the lot. They were like duchies, these studios."

Joseph L. Mankiewicz

On any ordinary day of the working week, a studio was not just making feature films. It was also creating cartoons, short subjects, newsreels, and previews. In the golden age most films were shot on the studio lot, instead of on location, so everything needed for all these films was being made or remade on the premises. The art department might be designing and building the main streets of Paris, Peoria, and outer space; the costume department might be creating clothes for cavemen, modern sophisticates, and pioneers moving West. In order to do all this, studios employed stars, directors, producers, writers, publicists, technical advisers, costumers, musicians, art directors, cinematographers, editors, carpenters, office boys, choreographers, electricians, set decorators, makeup artists, literary consultants, stenographers, file clerks, agents, cooks, dietitians, masseuses and masseurs, trainers, researchers, policemen, doctors, lawyers, dentists, teachers, and much more, including my personal favorite: the script timer. This was a person who sat in a room, reading aloud the script and recording the amount of time everything took. This information was needed by the budget department in advance. Script timers read the dialogue aloud, but had to allow for any physical action that would take place, any pauses in the acting pace, any variance in tempo between a comedy and a drama. This complicated process, requiring a deep knowledge of how movies work, was done by specially trained people. It is a function that clearly expresses the attention to detail, the fine tuning, and the careful work done behind the scenes on any movie during these years.

What was it like to work in a Hollywood studio in the golden age? For many people, it was like working anywhere else, except you might see Marlene Dietrich in your lunchroom. If you ate outside on the grounds, six Foreign Legionnaires, two apes, one Cossack, and a bathing beauty might walk by, taking their own break from filming. Whatever your specialty—lights, makeup, costumes, construction work, cooking or typing—that was your job and you did it, nine to five, unless you were on the night shift. Glamour was only what you were helping to sell.

. . .

"I came to Paramount in 1937, fifty-five years ago as Adolph Zukor's office boy. That year we made fifty-five features, and we released fifty-three. We had a contract list of about 125 or 130 stars either under direct contract or picture agreement. They were people like Marlene Dietrich. We had Cary Grant. We had Bing Crosby. We had Bob Hope. We had so many stars that we could make fifty-eight features a year without going off the lot to find talent. We had a full orchestra of fifty-five people who came in every day and worked. Maybe one day they would be prerecording, say, Bing Crosby in the prerecording stages, or maybe they'd be recording music for a movie or something of that sort. We had so many child stars under contract that we had our own school on the lot, with a principal, Rachel Smith, and three teachers. We had our own fire department. Our own wardrobe department was enormous. Edith Head was making costumes every single day. Cecil B. DeMille had a man that just made jewelry, all by hand, for his pictures like *The Ten Commandments*. We had what was called a "test stage" where each day they would bring young actors and actresses in to test them. Every single day. James Hogan was the test director. We had a voice coach. We had a dance teacher. We had a man that taught fencing. And, of course, we had Wally Westmore in the makeup department and Nellie Manley to do their hair. We were a complete city within ourselves here. Those days will never come back again because today we don't make that many pictures. We don't make fifty-five and sixty pictures a year. Maybe we will make twelve pictures a year."

A. C. Lyles

The main gate of Paramount Pictures was one of the great symbols of the glamorous, unattainable world behind the fences of Hollywood movie studios. Stills like this were shot to tell the world the situation: grace and elegance abound behind these lacy gates, where lies a world forbidden to the likes of you—and things are so ritzy that even a woman kept outside wears fur and high fashion.

Every studio was a walled fortress, not open for casual drop-ins. From the outside it looked unimpressive but formidable. Inside, it was a busy, relatively happy working environment in which everyone had a job to do. To approach a studio gate and attempt to gain entrance, however, was not an easy task. Part of Hollywood's glamour and mystique came from this heavy security system, which was, of course, a practical requirement that kept out hysterical fans. Many movies of the 1930s and 1940s have scenes in which ordinary people try to sneak by these security gates, such as *Star Spangled Rhythm* (1942) and *Anchors Aweigh* (1945).

The workaday world was highly structured. It was, after all, a kind of factory. It's possible to think of "the product"—a movie—as an object being made and trace its evolution through the studio. First, the movie would be conceived in the office of the executive producer, the man who determined and scheduled the studio's list of movies for the coming year. His job was to coordinate the stories or subjects (called "properties") already bought or planned, with the star personnel on the studio payroll. (Mae West couldn't be in two films at once.) Once a star was assigned, these projected productions also had to be assigned in groups to the associate producers, who would oversee them on a daily basis. Once an associate producer was given a film, he was responsible only to the executive producer for it.

Let's create a fake movie and follow it through production in the year 1938. Let's say it starts out as a best-selling novel by a famous woman writer, "Maybelle Davis Wilkins." It has been bought by Paramount studios to be turned into a movie starring Claudette Colbert. The movie will be called *The Royal Road to Romance*, a romantic screwball comedy set in Europe. It will tell the story of an on-the-make con girl (Colbert)

**An aerial view of Paramount Pictures from the golden age shows the considerable size of the studio, a veritable walled city of parks and walkways, huge sound stages, office buildings, and standing sets.**

who meets a naive Balkan prince. In attempting to fleece him, she actually falls for him, with the result that he gives up his throne for her. The property has been bought by Paramount because the author's previous two books have both been made into successful movies starring Carole Lombard. Since this new novel is a best-seller, it has a ready-made market. It has been snapped up by the studio, which is constantly on the lookout for short stories, novels, novellas, and magazine articles it can turn into movies.

Let's pretend the executive producer at Paramount selects Mitchell Leisen to direct. Because of his prestige and former successes, Leisen will be allowed to fulfill the role of his own associate producer, so that the film will ultimately carry the credit "Produced and Directed by Mitchell Leisen." A lesser-level, more functionary associate producer is assigned to help Leisen with daily chores and also to keep an eye on him on behalf of the studio purse strings. Leisen will have full authority over the set, however.

Initially, Leisen, the executive producer, and the associate producer all first meet to determine a working budget for the movie and then to select a writer or team of writers. We'll pretend they choose Billy Wilder and Charles Brackett, who were under contract at Paramount, just before their 1939 hit *Ninotchka*. This results in a "story conference": Leisen, acting as both producer and director, along with his associate producer and the two writers, meet to discuss transforming the novel into the movie. All aspects of the novel are discussed until basic problems are solved, and an overall approach to the screenplay is agreed upon. Brackett and Wilder want to stress the comedy, but Leisen warns them that he wants plenty of glamour. Colbert, he instructs them, is to look gorgeous and change her clothes often. They *must* write him a costume-ball scene. Furthermore, the hero is to be played by a newcomer with a pretty face and not much comic talent. They must give the good lines to Colbert, and keep his part as small as possible, considering he'll be the romantic lead and Paramount hopes to make him a star. He looks good in a tuxedo so make certain there's a scene in which he wears one.

While the two writers go off to prepare the script, Leisen begins a series of activities that move the film forward toward production. Before the final script is written, and before every plot twist is fully developed, the director-producer knows what will generally be required from every department of the studio for this production. He moves ahead accordingly, and this ability is one of the key aspects to the old studio system: its efficiency, its ability to prepare sets and costumes in advance, and its "assembly-line" characteristics. All departments are notified that *The Royal Road to Romance*, starring Claudette Colbert, is coming soon to be prepared for a December release, and a general sense of what will be needed is dictated. When a rough script is available, it is sent simultaneously around to all major departments, even though it is not a final shooting script. This rough script is the signal to department heads to submit detailed budgets, based on the money they have been allotted for this movie, and then to begin work.

Getting the art director started is one of the most important aspects of efficient production, as it is his team that will create the sets, or "world," that the film will be photographed in. It is the work of the brilliant Hollywood art directors that so many remember when they think of old American movies: the Art Deco furniture and shiny black Bakelite floors created by Van Nest Polglase and Carroll Clark for the Astaire-Rogers musicals; the detailed realism of the sets designed by Richard Day for *Dodsworth* (1936) and *How Green Was My Valley* (1941); the highly elegant rooms and sets of Hans Dreier for movies such as *Shanghai Express* (1932), *The Scarlett Empress* (1934), and *The Devil Is a Woman* (1935); the Baroque style of William Cameron Menzies for *Gone with the Wind* and *Duel in the Sun* (1946); the all-white rooms of Cedric Gibbons for MGM's Jean Harlow films and his Emerald City in *The Wizard of Oz*. The art director has working under him a large staff that includes artists, architects, draftsmen, painters, plasterers, furniture makers, and practically any trade that is needed for building. Under him, depending on the studio, may also fall set decorators and set designers, and he may have his own budget person for rough costs to be

An example of the size and scope of the Hollywood studio system is represented by this photo of a lavish new sound stage constructed at Warner Brothers for its biggest productions of the 1940s. *The Sea Hawk* (note galleon structure at right) was filmed here in 1940, and *This Is the Army* (1943) is shown in production above.

George Stevens's famous production of *Giant* (1956) built this house on location to represent the world to which Rock Hudson takes his new bride, Elizabeth Taylor. The vintage cars and catering set-ups were all shipped to the wide-open spaces of Texas for authenticity.

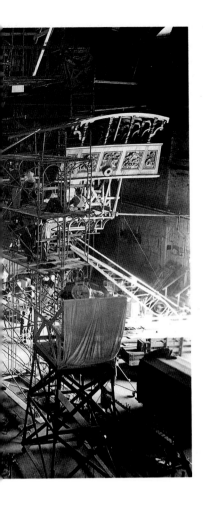

sent to the larger budget office. Henry Bumstead, art director at Paramount who designed *The Fury* (1950) and *Vertigo* (1958), has described the day-to-day work:

As an art director in Hollywood, you had everything to work with. Cedric Gibbons at MGM would take pictures before you were assigned of examples of what he wanted. Then maybe they had about fifteen illustrators—marvelous illustrators—and about forty draftsmen in the room. Gibby would lay out the whole picture. . . . At Paramount because of the German contingent, the realism of the sets was stunning. They were absolutely beautiful. They had marvelous hardware, and did lots of detail on the sets.

We got wonderful training, because we got not only to do drafting, but also to make models. We also did sketching. We drew, and we made our drawings at half-inch scale. Regular scale for architects and for everything is a quarter inch to a foot, but we doubled ours to a half inch. We went right from half inch to full-size detail. We were the only studio in town that did that.

We had about thirty or so stages. Of course, we did a lot of pictures, nearly sixty a year, and a lot of big ones. So they had an assembly stage where we built the sets. Today they sometimes build a set and maybe shoot the opening sequence there, let it set for a month, and then come back to it later to do another scene. In those days, that never happened. you could have a beautiful set there, while some other art director was building something else alongside it in the assembly stage. The minute you finished using yours, it was struck, moved out, and the other one was moved in. They had three shifts. Three eight-hour shifts, day and night. Of course, around 1952 we started going on location, but up until then we did almost everything on the lot.

The art director breaks the script down into the number of actual physical settings the film will require. It will be the job of his staff to turn these written descriptions into reality. He and his staff turn the ideas on the pages into sketches and models. If the film is set in a foreign country, or needs a period setting, he must call the research department for help. The art director needs to be a good businessman because everything in the studio system is dictated by costs. He cannot, for instance, plan to spend lavishly on every set for *Royal Road to Romance*. He must concentrate on a lavish palace set for the prince's domain, a superbly decorated hotel in which the lovers will meet, and a simple casino where the prince will be fleeced. For the latter set, the art director gets a cost break. Going through Paramount's set storage, he finds a perfect casino—furniture, draperies, and exteriors—which was last used in a Monte Carlo film from 1929. It can be repainted and slightly modernized for a reasonable sum.

The art director consults with the director of photography who has been assigned to the film, because any buildings, rooms, or streets that are created must be made with an understanding of how they are to be photographed. A beautiful setting is a waste of money if it cannot be photographed in the way that is appropriate for the movie.

When the art director is ready with ideas and sketches, Leisen calls a meeting. In attendance is the art director, and any other technicians that should be involved. Discussions of the proposed sets occur. After one or two more meetings, the final designs are approved and the director hears no more about these settings until he

moves his company into them for the shooting. In the meeting the director continues work on the script, preparing to shoot the film. Naturally, the first thing is to visualize clearly the story and each character in it. Using a miniature stage—a tiny edition of the regular set—and coins for the actors, Leisen works out each stage movement in detail. This means saving precious minutes when actual filming begins. When the script is ready, it is sent to the players, and this must be done well before the actual production begins. Leisen plans camera angles, in consultation with the director of photography. He goes over the script with the script clerk who is responsible for seeing

that no mistakes are made in the lines, and that each player is dressed correctly, that they arrive to work on time, and that the hundreds of important details are properly taken care of. He meets with his assistant director, who will carry out his orders on the set, supervising the placing of actors in new scenes, giving commands to the company, and acting as chief contact between the rest of the company and the director.

While Leisen is doing all this, and the art director is readying the sets, the dress designer is also busy. Where the art director is concerned with decorating rooms and buildings, the dress designer is concerned with decorating the stars in the movies. Most important for *The Royal Road to Romance* is the fact that its star, Claudette Colbert, is famous for being one of the best-dressed women on film. Furthermore, she is equally fashionable in private life and is keenly aware of what looks good on her and what does not. Colbert will have twenty-one costume changes, among them an elaborate ball gown, a wedding dress, a masquerade costume in which she impersonates Marie Antoinette, a riding habit, an ice-skating costume, six evening gowns with matching wraps, two fur coats, two nightgowns, and six daytime outfits, three of which are fur-trimmed suits. All of these outfits must have jewelry, hats, purses, gloves, and shoes to match. Each outfit must be sketched and sent to the person who will be doing Colbert's hair, so her hats and dresses will compliment her coiffures. Here the film gets a cost savings. Whereas most actresses cannot wear the same hairdo all through the film—four or five different coiffeurs must be created and each must be coordinated with the outfit for look, design, and appropriateness—Colbert is famous for only wearing her hair one way. Therefore, although hats and hair ornaments are still a problem, no one has to create six new hairdos for *The Royal Road to Romance*.

Colbert's status and personal desire demand her gowns be created separately and especially for her. She will be allowed to purchase the clothes at cost for her personal wardrobe at the end of the picture, if she so desires. The studio's dress designer oversees the large dressmaking department: cutters, seamstresses, embroiderers, fitters.

Tests were made of all principal players prior to shooting. Photographs were taken for comparisons and for a record of the choices and ultimate decisions. Deborah Kerr (above left) models the alternate choice for Nero's banquet in the 1951 *Quo Vadis*, and Rosalind Russell (above) offers two choices regarding makeup and hairstyles for her 1961 role in *Gypsy*.

The dress department also includes a large storage area where costumes are kept and many fitting rooms for actors and actresses to try on their costumes. The dress designer frequently needs research, also, for knowledge of period costuming and fabrics. It goes without saying that Hollywood designers had to keep up with the latest fashions from New York and Paris, although they were also trendsetters. These designers had to work with the cinematographer, as pure white would not photograph as such in black and white, and sparkles that picked up light incorrectly could become a problem. Also, if the star was to run away from danger and hang off a building until rescued, her dress had to be as up to the task as she was.

Lana Turner, the ultimate movie star, played the role of an ultimate movie star in the 1952 *The Bad and the Beautiful*. In the scene above, she is fitted for her wardrobe in a costume picture as part of the movie's action. Behind the scenes, of course, she had to be fitted for the costume for which she is being fitted! Art imitates life.

While this is all going on, the casting director is busy, along with his or her staff, going through cards and files and indexes to fill all the parts needed for the film. Some suitable character actors are under contract, but what is their availability? For how many days would they be needed? A large crowd could be formed by calling the Central Casting Corporation for a group of extras who would be paid day wages and told how to dress for their work: come as guests at a royal ball, or dress as gamblers at a European casino. (The CCC had been established in 1925 by a group of Hollywood producers to provide extras for their films. No "bit" players were provided, only extras, who were ordered into four types: dress, character, specialized, and atmosphere. In 1976 CCC ceased operations.) *The Royal Road to Romance* presents no particular problem here except for one—when the prince is shown reviewing his troops, two thousand men in dress uniforms with swords and caps are needed. The dress designer must be equally aware of this problem.

The makeup department knows how to prepare Colbert, as she is a star under contract to Paramount and she plays a woman of her own age and type in the film. Her hair does not need to be dyed or her skin darkened. Her leading man, however, the newcomer, will have to undergo elaborate makeup tests. He is found to have a nose that does not photograph well, and a special plastic is used to reshape it. Later he will have surgery to correct it. Because the new nose throws some of the lines and shadows of his face off balance, his cheekbones are also built up by the use of the same plastic. A sculptured mask of Colbert's face has been made previously, and it is used to create makeup and test new ideas so the star herself does not have to submit to this. Colbert spends her hours in wardrobe instead, for complicated fittings for her elaborate wardrobe. Since the prince's father is to be played by an actor who is not really old enough to undertake such a role, the makeup artists are working on aging him, using a wig, a nose putty, eye shapings, and other modifications.

Leisen has, in the meantime, been working with the director of photography, discussing plans for lighting and camera movement. Leisen's director of photography is

actually shooting another film, so Leisen allows him to schedule the meeting for a time when second unit photography on the other movie is being done at the Paramount ranch by his second unit director of photography. This careful coordination of the expensive time of Leisen, his director of photography, and the second-unit cameraman and crew is planned in advance by Paramount. All studios worked their personnel full time on several different projects simultaneously for maximum cost and scheduling efficiency.

Once the sets are built, both director and cinematographer visit them to discuss the overall lighting patterns. On the sets, electricians are on the overhead catwalks, setting lights as instructed. The cameraman's first assistant is peering through the camera lens to see how it all looks. His elaborate crew, controlled strictly by union rules, is ready to load, pull focus, and follow his directions. Stand-ins are walking through the movements the stars will make in the scene so that the cameraman and director can approve the lighting schedule. The stars themselves are off to the side, rehearsing their lines with the script clerk, who corrects them and prompts them as necessary.

When the first scene is to be shot, everyone that is needed is assembled. The assistant director is responsible for making sure everyone who is in the scene is present. He is also the person who carries out the instructions of the director, yelling or blowing a whistle when silence is required for a rehearsal or a take. The recording expert sits at a switchboard with his headphones on. He is in direct communication with the sound department where the sound will be carried. Boom operators are ready to move the microphones hanging above the sets as needed. Sound in the studio system went directly from these microphones into the sound department, where it was received and recorded.

After the scene is shot, all takes are sent to be printed. After the printing, the footage is sent to the cutting room in the editing department. Every take of every scene is identified and matched to the shooting script, which the film editor has right at hand. The film director, sometimes accompanied by his staff, the producer, and/or the stars, looks at these first prints, which are known as the "dailies" or the "rushes" since the prints were rushed by messen-

In a movie about movies and the moviemaking world, *Sunset Boulevard* (1950), Gloria Swanson, a silent film superstar, portrays a silent film superstar, Norma Desmond. In a grand finale, Desmond confuses her current tragic life with a scene in a movie, as she is motivated out of her house and downstairs by her butler, who used to be her director. "I'm ready for my close-up now, Mr. DeMille," is her immortal line as she descends.

ger to the studio for viewing on a daily basis. The director indicates which of the "takes" he feels are best and should be used in the assembly of the "first cut" of the scene, which will be added to other previous scenes to create the complete final film. The film editor does this assembly, turning the best material into one final, coherent filmed story for release, following the directions he or she is given. Leisen supervises this final editing, in which the film's story is shaped for the all-important viewing audience. (In 1939, the Director's Guild of America won the right to make decisions on "first cut" of the film, which meant that any director of any film had the right to present his or her version of the movie to its producer, or, if he himself was that producer, to the studio's executive producer. This meant that any director had the right to assemble the film as he wished it to be seen and released to the public. Because the producer or studio head outranked the director in the studio business hierarchy, the director's first cut *could* be rejected and changed later. This happened to Orson Welles with *The Magnificent Ambersons*.)

After the film is cut, the perforated strip carrying the sound is "married" to it. Before the sound strip is finished, the studio's music department becomes involved. A composer is given a print of *Royal Road to Romance*, so that a score can be written especially for it, with all the music timed and adapted to the length and mood of each scene. After the score is written, it is performed, recorded, and added to the sound-track by a full orchestra of musicians who are under contract to the studio and available on demand. (Orchestras heard on the screen usually recorded music separately after the scene was photographed.)

After the film is finished, the publicity department takes over. There are posters, stills, lobby cards, and press books to photograph, write, and design. There are "plants" to be foisted on the public, in which an item is planted in the news that would help promote the picture. ("Claudette Colbert fainted from wearing the heavily jewel-studded ball gown that audiences will see in *Royal Road to Romance*" . . . or "An authentic gown of Marie Antoinette's was perfectly re-created at a cost of $250,000 for *Royal Road to Romance*" . . . or "The brand-new star of *Royal Road to Romance*, Rex Richards, loves his mom's apple pie and reads Shakespeare in his spare time." His "date card is open" although "he's rumored to be dating Deanna Durbin.")

In 1938, when our fictional movie was created, the film might be taken out to be previewed with a "real" audience, which was given a sneak peak of the film prior to release. Moviegoers were given cards on which to write their opinion of the movie, and sometimes the film was taken back and reedited, based on these comments. When the film went into general release, the studio would continue to promote it according to the level of response it was receiving. After all this was finished, and the film was in the theaters right on schedule in December, was it anything special? Possibly not. It was "the product," another assembly-line object manufactured by the great Paramount Pictures in the golden era of the Hollywood studio system. Efficient, capable, creative, and magnificent, the system just cranked the pictures out one after another, bringing them to a public who saw them as magic, special, and thoroughly entertaining, the stuff, indeed, "that dreams are made of."

"It was like one big family. It was marvelous, a small city. You knew everybody and everybody cared about you. They cared about your kids and this and that. I know now it's the factory, because you meet with a group of people and you work with them for maybe sixty or eighty or eighty-three days, and then you disperse. Maybe you won't ever see them again. It's very sad."

Henry Bumstead

Following page: When the Hollywood studio system was functioning at its best, it produced stories like *It Happened One Night* (1934) with such overwhelming success that single images as the one above were instantly recognized and the scene represented remembered with a chuckle. Claudette Colbert, above in her famous striped-jacket suit, prepares to teach Clark Gable that "the power of the limb is greater than the power of the thumb" in stopping a car.

# The Academy Award

One of the most important men in Hollywood is only 13½ inches tall. He's the famous "Oscar," the gold-plated statuette that is awarded every spring by the Academy of Motion Picture Arts and Sciences (AMPAS) to outstanding movie achievement in a number of specified categories.

In January 1927 Louis B. Mayer, head of MGM, hosted a dinner for influential leaders of the movie business at which the idea of a non-profit academy to promote movies was first discussed. On January 11, 1927, at the Ambassador Hotel, the Academy of Motion Picture Arts and Sciences was officially formed. Among its founding members were Mayer, Cedric Gibbons, Mary Pickford, Joseph M. Schenk, and Douglas Fairbanks, Sr., who became its first president. It was decided that the academy would generate respect for the movies if it presented annually a slate of "awards of merit for distinctive achievement." Quickly taking up a pen, Cedric Gibbons, MGM's top art director, sketched out a statuette for the award that was a kind of Art Deco man holding a crusader's sword and standing on a reel of film. This design was later given to sculptor George Stanley, who molded it almost exactly to Gibbons's original sketch. The first awards night was a friendly banquet, held at the Roosevelt Hotel on May 16, 1927. Fifteen awards were given out and everyone knew the winners in advance. The first winner of the Best Picture Award is the only silent film to ever receive the award: *Wings*, directed by William Wellman. The Best Actor, Emil Jannings, was chosen for his work in two movies, *The Last Command* and *The Way of All Flesh*. Best Actress Janet Gaynor won for her work in three movies, *Seventh Heaven*, *Street Angel*, and *Sunrise*, because in the first year, acting awards were given for the performer's yearly work, not just for a performance in a single film. The statuette, called The Academy Award, was later on dubbed "Oscar" by Academy librarian Margaret Herrick, who claimed the statue "looked like my Uncle Oscar." The name stuck.

To select the Best Picture, all craft branches are polled, and the top five films become the five nominees. For all the other awards, only the members of the craft branch itself are allowed to vote nominations. No more than five nominations are allowed in any category. After the nominations are set, every member of AMPAS is sent a ballot containing all nominations, and the entire membership makes the selections. Since 1941, a sealed envelope has been used and no one (except the accounting firm responsible for the balloting) has advance knowledge of the winners ("The envelope please . . .").

They never won: Greta Garbo, Edward G. Robinson, Howard Hawks, Raoul Walsh, William Powell, Myrna Loy, Lana Turner, Marlene Dietrich, John Garfield, and many more.

Three contemporary female stars who have been nominated but not yet won Oscar gold wait in the wings for that ultimate recognition of their acting abilities: Debra Winger, Winona Ryder, and Julia Roberts.

...in which colored filters ...associate movie color with Technicolor, ...Corporation was founded in 1915 and produced two full-length early features, *The Gulf Between* in 1917 and *The Toll of the Sea* in 1922. Special Technicolor sequences appeared in big-budget movies throughout the 1920s: *The Ten Commandments* (1923), *Ben Hur* (1925), and *The Phantom of the Opera* (1925). The Douglas Fairbanks swashbuckler *The Black Pirate* (1926) was a full-length Technicolor feature. These special sequences and isolated full-length movies were popular with audiences, so that by the end of the 1920s, filming in two-strip Technicolor became prevalent. Usually, two-strip Technicolor was used to film lavish musical sequences in the popular early sound films of the era, such as MGM's Oscar-winning *Broadway Melody* of 1929. When musicals lost their popularity temporarily, so did the two-strip Technicolor process.

In 1932 and 1933 Walt Disney introduced the use of the new, improved three-strip Technicolor process in his cartoon shorts, *Flowers and Trees* (1932) and *The Three Little Pigs* (1933). The three-strip process was a vast improvement over the two-strip because the latter had had no blue range: the sky and the sea were always roughly the same color, a rather odd shade of green. The new process, with its third strip representing the blue range of the spectrum, meant that color could seem more true and real. Three-strip was used in a short film with live people (rather than cartoon figures) in 1933–34 with *La Cucaracha*, and a full-length feature was soon shot in the process, *Becky Sharp* (1935). Outdoor location work in three-strip appeared with *The Trail of the Lonesome Pine* in 1936. With the release of such successful color films as *Gone with the Wind* (1939), *Jesse James* (1939), *Blood and Sand* (1940), and a series of musicals from Twentieth Century-Fox (*Down Argentine Way* and *Moon over Miami*, 1940 and 1941, respectively), color became an expensive-to-produce, but familiar aspect of moviegoing. Throughout the decades of the 1940s, 1950s, and into the mid-1960s, films were made in both black-and-white and color, and the two formats existed comfortably side by side.

Technicolor monopolized the field from 1932 until 1950, doing 90 percent of the color business, but in 1950 Eastman Kodak introduced Eastmancolor—a monopack system. Because the picture was recorded in three different layers on one strip of film, the process could be used in a regular black-and-white camera. In addition, the film and processing was less expensive than Technicolor. studios were able to develop their own processing systems; thus Metro Color, Warner Color, and Deluxe Color, did not represent new color systems, only individualized processing.

By 1958 only 25 percent of Hollywood films were shot in color, probably because television was major outlet for feature films, and it was still broadcasting in black and white. By 1967 75 percent feature films were in color, and by 1970 a full 94 percent were shot in color. For ideological, tech- ...and historical reasons, then, it took thirty-five years for color to become essential.

Three example (clockwise, fro one of the Technicolor Cor version of *Vanit* first full-length Technicolor; a short, *La Cu*

# Sound

Silent movies were never silent. There was always some sort of music, if only a piano player tinkling along up front as the images unfolded, and frequently there was a large orchestra, sound effects, or some type of noise, including the quaint practice of having actors stand behind the screen and speak the roles for the stars appearing on screen in the movie. Experiments in sound took place from the beginning of the invention of the motion picture. Thomas Edison, after all, invented the phonograph. From the very beginning of the creation of the motion picture, inventors were looking for ways in which they could integrate both picture and sound.

One of the great misunderstandings of film history is the popular idea that *The Jazz Singer* (1927; starring Al Jolson) was the first time audiences ever heard sound in a movie. Actually, many previous methods of bringing sound to picture had been tried, some of them brilliantly simple. For instance, there were companies of actors and sound-effects men who traveled with movies, providing "sound" on the spot. In 1889, Thomas Edison's assistant, Laurie Dickson, was seen on a small screen, entering the frame, raising his hat, and saying, "Good morning, Mr. Edison, glad to see you back. Hope you will like the Kinetophone. To show the synchronization I will lift my hand and count up to ten."

D. W. Griffith tried a genuine sound film in 1921, *Dream Street*, in which the sound came from a synchronized phonograph record that contained a special sound score. The stars sang as well as spoke during a few minutes of the film while music accompanied the remainder of the movie. Vitaphone was formed in 1926 to develop a sound-on-disk system, and a group of short subjects as well as a feature, *Don Juan*, starring John Barrymore, were released. On Christmas Day 1926, *The Better Ole* premiered featuring a synchronized musical score, plus all-talking short subjects starring Al Jolson, George Jessel, Elsie Janis and Willie and Eugene Howard. *The Jazz Singer*, premiering in 1927, was not an all-talking movie, but it did contain several song sequences and two scenes with dialogue. It also had a musical score. By the end of 1928, a full-length all-talking movie, *The Lights of New York*, was in circulation. These movies were all on the sound-on-disk system, while the sound-on-film system—the one that would survive—was heard in one-reel sound films as early as 1927. In late 1928 or early 1929, the first out-of-doors sound-on-film movie, *In Old Arizona*, premiered.

Most historians agree that the year in which sound really took over from silence was 1928. Movies had synchronized musical soundtracks, short dialogue sequences, sound effects—whatever could be managed quickly as the industry geared for change. 1929 was a year during which Hollywood had to learn how to make movies all over again, this time with sound. Every aspect of the filmmaking process was changed to make talking pictures, and the artists of the business began at once playing creatively with the new dimension. Directors such as Frank Capra and Rouben Mamoulian began experimenting with sound, and talented writers such as Ben Hecht created sharp dialogue, while producers raided Broadway theaters for new actors "with voices." By 1930 the new system had taken over, and by 1932, talking movies were simply taken for granted.

Above: Most people think of the 1927 *The Jazz Singer* (with Al Jolson and Eugenie Besserer, who plays his mother) as the first time any kind of sound was ever used in movies. Although this is historically inaccurate, *The Jazz Singer* remains one of the first times that sound reached the masses linked to a story movie, and people remembered it because of the great Jolson's rendition of such hit songs as "My Mammy," "Blue Skies," "Toot Toot Tootsie," and the joyous promise of his famous spoken words, "You ain't heard nothin' yet."

Right: Sound, color, and design combine for this spectacular moment from the Best Picture of 1984, *Amadeus*, an extraordinary presentation of Mozart's life and music.

# Widescreen

In the beginning, movies were like railroads: there was no standard gauge. The French studio Pathé used 28mm film while Biograph and Mutoscope used film that was 2 ½ inches high and 2 ¾ inches wide. There was 65mm and 9mm and the Lumière brothers had film with only one sprocket hole per frame. Thomas Edison, however, made his films on 35mm film with four perforations on each side of the film per frame. Because Edison was the man who sold the most motion picture equipment in the early days, his 35mm film became the standard internationally. There were various ways of making the image look wider: crop the top and bottom off the image; actually use a piece of wider, bigger film; try to stretch the image out when projecting it on the screen through a special lens; or project several images side by side across a wider screen. All were tried. All were used. Most people think of widescreen as an anamorphic process, however, such as that of the famous CinemaScope images created in the 1950s so that movies could compete with television. There were five widescreen techniques perfected and sold to moviegoers during the "widescreen decade" of the 1950s: Cinerama, a process that used three vertical 35mm images photographed by three interlocking cameras and projected on a special curved screen; Todd-AO, in which a 65mm negative was exposed onto a 70mm piece of film which was then projected on a large screen; CinemaScope, which used an anamorphic camera lens to squeeze an image horizontally onto a 35mm color negative, and then unsqueezed it with an anamorphic lens attached to the projector; Technirama, an anamorphic process that squeezed the image 50 percent in shooting and an additional 50 percent in printing—it photographed on a double-width negative—and it could be made into an excellent 35mm print or increased in size to a 70mm print; and VistaVision, which used a 35mm negative run horizontally through a specially designed camera to photograph a wider image on the film negative—it could be used to make an excellent print blown up to 70mm or reduced to 35mm.

As was true for both the introduction of color and synchronized sound, the widescreen processes of the 1950s were not entirely new, nor did they alone significantly alter the shape of the film industry. In 1922 there was Widescope, a two-lens system that anticipated the three-lens system of Cinerama in 1952. In 1929 a method like the later VistaVision was proposed, running the film sideways to widen the pictures. Various large formats were experimented with, including 65mm and 75mm, which was later used in the Todd-AO system of the 1950s. By the early 1930s there was a system using an anamorphic lens to squeeze the picture during recording and broaden it during projection. The larger formats did not only increase the picture size; in addition there was more space for the soundtrack. Stereo sound was proposed, using up to four tracks. The Academy of Motion Picture Arts and Sciences began to organize an investigation of the various processes, working toward industry cooperation as it had with synchronized sound.

In approximately 1952 3-D was introduced. Since the majors were not initially interested, a small independent company produced *Bwana Devil* (1952) in Natural Vision. The film was shot with two lenses, and then projected through two separate polarized filters. The audience wore polarized glasses to create the final 3-D effect. After the successful opening in January of 1953, UA bought the film and Warners began experimenting with 3-D, releasing *House of Wax* in 1953. Other studios followed suit, releasing approximately forty horror and adventure pictures in 3-D by 1955.

Although the popularity of 3-D did not last because of problems with synchronization and the discomfort of the glasses, CinemaScope and related widescreen processes were able to make a space for themselves in the industry.

In 1959 MGM remade its silent film hit *Ben Hur* (1926), this time bringing to it glorious color, magnificent settings, and a widescreen image that allowed for even more drama in the climactic chariot race, one of moviedom's most dazzling action sequences. This race was directed by the film's second unit director, Andrew Marton, and staged by the famous stuntman Yakima Canutt. Winner of a record-setting eleven Oscars, including Best Director for William Wyler, Best Actor for Charlton Heston (as Ben Hur), and Best Supporting Actor for Hugh Griffith.

# $8$ TRANSITION: THE TELEVISION AGE (1960–1980)

In 1946, America's romance with the movies was at its peak. Going to the movies was a national habit, and nobody really thought it was a habit that could be cured. After all, what would people do without movies? By 1956, only a decade later, attendance was half of what it had been in 1946, and the Hollywood studio system faced dramatic change and reorganization. It would soon disappear. What happened to the studio system of the golden age? The answer given to this question is always the same: it collapsed. This collapse—which conjures up the image of a great many buildings falling down—is seldom defined. And if it is defined, it is explained as having happened "because of television."

The real reasons are, as might be expected, more complex. Although it is certainly true that television initially drew audiences away from the big screen, it is also true that television kept film alive by showing old movies and, eventually, new movies on its own small screens. It is also true that the studios soon enough figured out that they must themselves go into the business of providing or making programs directly for TV. Television was a factor in the "collapse," but not the only factor, and in the end film and television became linked in business, sharing stars, directors, and production monies.

Although it is technically correct to say that the old Hollywood system collapsed and disappeared, it would be incorrect to say that nothing from the studios remained after. What really happened was the beginning of Hollywood's amazing ability to re-define itself. The movie business, pronounced dead more often than Count Dracula, has always managed to reorganize, repackage, and redistribute its assets just in the nick of time, rather like one of its own happy endings in which the U.S. Cavalry arrives to rescue the beleaguered settlers. The "collapse" of the studio system was actually a business restructuring, with power shifting away from the former studio bosses and over to directors and stars and ultimately over to agents and huge conglomerates that purchased the studios.

This power shift began in about 1950 and continued throughout the decade, with 1960 usually cited as the date by which the new had more or less replaced the old. Key factors contributed to the downfall of the studio system: the Paramount antitrust decrees (which brought about the end of studio ownership of theaters and their practices of block bookings); new competition from the film businesses of Europe; the House Un-American Activities Committee (HUAC and censorship changes); and the advent of television.

## Antitrust and the Paramount Decrees

> When the divorce decree came in, where the studios had to divorce themselves from the theaters and exhibition, they lost a certain amount of insurance at that time. Because when you owned the theaters, you knew that a picture would go out and make so much money. You could depend on it. Without the theaters, you didn't have that insurance.
>
> A. C. Lyles

**Previous pages: The use of the wide screen to bring exotic locales and spectacular scenery to moviegoers was one startling way in which television's twelve-inch boxes could not compete with the movies' 110-foot screens. This is well illustrated by British director David Lean's 1962 70mm epic, *Lawrence of Arabia*, which tells the story of a British army officer in Arabia during the First World War.**

During the 1950s television began to take its place as the source of original and creative drama—well written, well acted, and well produced and directed. Clockwise from bottom left: Anthony Quinn in the movie version of an original television production, *Requiem for a Heavyweight*; two frames from Sidney Lumet's film version of *Twelve Angry Men*, which was remade starring Henry Fonda; originally a television play, *Marty* (shown here in two scenes), starring Ernest Borgnine, won four Oscars, including Best Picture.

A primary factor in the collapse of the studio system was a legal decision: the famous Paramount decrees, in which the United States Supreme Court demanded that the studios sell their theaters. This took away their monopolistic control of both production and distribution, and that in turn took away their safety nets. Whereas studios had been able to experiment with new stars and offbeat stories, counting on sure-fire formulas to bail them out at the box office, now they had no security. Even though the old system *was* a system, not a freewheeling, experimental atmosphere, it had nevertheless allowed some room for development and growth. That safety margin was now gone.

The government had, in fact, focused on the trust practices in the movie industry for a long time. Encouraged by exhibitors, the government had been looking into the problem periodically since 1925, and more consistently since 1938. In 1939 the industry began to take the government's threats seriously and responded to the suits by creating a new Trade Practice Code. However, this code did not satisfy the government; it was ruled illegal within five months. By June 1940 an actual trial began. Fairly quickly the industry representatives signed "consent decrees," promising, among other things, to rent no more than five films in a block at one time, and to rent A features without forcing exhibitors also to book their B features, newsreels, or shorts.

While exhibitors and the government considered the consent decrees an improvement, they did not consider them sufficient. The issue was brought to the courts again, and the now famous Paramount consent decree case began in 1945. In 1948 the Paramount case and seven others—involving RKO, Columbia, United Artists, Universal, and several theater chains—went before the Supreme Court. The Court reversed a lower court decision in what came to be known as "the Paramount decrees" and called for a number of important changes in the movie industry's distribution and exhibition practices, each of which can be classified either as divorce or divestment of their theaters.

In order to carry out divorcement, or the end of oligopoly practices, the eight majors were required to accept four procedures. First, block booking was prohibited. Instead of forcing exhibitors to rent a number of films in one block if they wanted to get a particularly promising first-run film, the distributors now had to rent each film on an individual basis. Second, the distributors were forced to stop fixing admission prices. In other words, the exhibitor had the right to charge whatever price he or she wanted, no matter the film. Third, unfair runs and clearances were outlawed. Rather than refusing to rent to independent theaters located in an area controlled by the majors, the distributors now had to consider each theater separately. Fourth, discriminatory pricing and purchasing was ruled illegal. Rather than offering the best prices to their own theaters and those of other majors, each Hollywood company had to offer their films at the same prices to any theater.

The order to divest focused only on the industry's exhibition practices (probably because it was the independent exhibitors who had been instrumental in bringing this issue to the courts). In other words, each company was allowed to keep its production and distribution branches together, but was forced to divest itself of its theater holdings, including those pooled with other majors. Furthermore, no shareholder could con-

Opposite: Anne Bancroft and Patty Duke (as Helen Keller) both won Oscars re-creating their Broadway roles in the 1962 version of *The Miracle Worker*, originally made for television in 1957 and then again in 1979, with Patty Duke in the Bancroft role of Keller's teacher, Anne Sullivan.

The screaming woman (above) was a member of the audience of *The Tingler* (1959), starring Vincent Price, in which fear causes a slimy creature, which can only be subdued by screaming, to grow on people's spines. Electrical buzzers were placed under selected theater seats for this shocker.

Opposite: Cybill Shepherd and Ellen Burstyn played daughter and mother in Peter Bogdanovich's *The Last Picture Show* (1971). Based on Larry McMurtry's novel about life in a small Texas town and photographed in black and white by Robert Surtees, the story was set in the 1950s at the point in movie history when theaters began to close down and disappear, threatened by TV and challenged by competition from foreign filmmakers.

trol stock in both a production-distribution company and the exhibition company formerly associated with the parent company.

Despite the influence this decision seems to have when explained on paper, in reality the major studios were still able to maintain a significant amount of control over exhibition. Although RKO and Paramount signed consent decrees immediately and were given some leeway in their divestment proceedings, the other six majors fought the decision as long as possible, with Loew's-MGM signing its consent decree as late as 1952. Furthermore, the companies took their time obeying, not finishing their divestment proceedings until the late 1950s. During that time, the country's demographics were shifting substantially, and as a result, the courts allowed the companies additional time to decide which theaters to sell in order to get the best prices possible. As a result, they were able to hold onto the theaters made most profitable by the new demographics that emerged.

The majors continued to exert a great deal of economic control over the movie industry. However, this did not mean that the shape of the companies did not change significantly. It did. Of the majors, United Artists was the best prepared for the Paramount decision. Its former liabilities—no theaters and no actual studio space—became assets. It had no property to sell as the result of the antitrust decisions. Many of the other companies began to look like UA as they sold their theaters and some of their studio space.

Just before the antitrust decisions, the eight majors controlled 73 percent of domestic film rentals and owned 60–70 percent of the country's first-run theaters. While they *did* sell many of these theaters over the course of the next decade, they were able to keep some. As it turned out, because of the reduction in the number of movies being made, many of their smaller theaters probably would have closed anyway. While this was happening, between 1948 and 1954 almost three thousand drive-in theaters opened, and the majors were still legally able to own many of these. By 1966, then, the majors still continued to control as much as 71 percent of film rentals in the United States. Although the shape of exhibition shifted drastically during this period as a result of the antitrust decision (as well as the particular international situation following World War II), the majors managed to shift the area of profit in the film industry from the exhibition to the distribution branch.

The newly reshaped studios became only production-distribution companies. In order to shift economic power away from exhibition, since they were no longer exhibitors, too, they cut production and raised rental prices. Because they had to produce a "sure thing" at the box office in order to rent it to the now independent exhibitors, they made fewer films and the budgets of those projects went up. Furthermore, the production end of the business now had no incentive to fill the screens, and thus did not lose money if theaters had trouble filling their schedules.

At first, the majors were able to continue their control not only because of their ability to reduce product and increase rental costs, but also because it was so risky and expensive to start a production company. Thus, despite the fact that overall production went down, the Little Three stepped up production and independent production companies doubled between 1946 and 1956, reaching a total of 150 in the mid-1950s.

These new independents often rented studio space from the majors and then distributed the resulting movies through them.

The antitrust decisions were an important impetus in the collapse of the Hollywood studio system. Not only did the studios lose some of their former power, and their policies of exhibition, distribution, and production practices change, but there was more competition. Hollywood was no longer a closed factory system in which eight companies controlled all three branches of the industry. That "oneness"—the mark of the golden era—was gone.

## HUAC and Censorship Changes

The content of Hollywood films has always been regulated in one form or another; however, between 1947 and 1954 the House Un-American Activities Committee (HUAC) became indirectly involved in this kind of regulation. After the Second World War the United States' alliance with the Soviet Union ended, the Cold War began, and the "Red Scare" moved into full force. The HUAC members considered it their duty to purge the country of any Communist influences. While numerous industries were investigated by HUAC, because of Hollywood's high profile, it became the best known target of this infamous committee.

In 1947 the committee's purpose was threefold. First, it intended to prove that the Screen Writers' Guild had Communist members. Second, it hoped to show that these writers were able to insert subversive propaganda into Hollywood films. Third, J. Parnell Thomas, head of the committee, argued that President Roosevelt had encouraged pro-Soviet films during the war. Although none of these claims was ever substantiated, the committee's tactics worked to force many talented and creative people to leave Hollywood.

During the initial hearings so-called friendly witnesses were asked to testify. These people were allowed to read prepared statements and were treated with respect. They were not under suspicion, but, instead, were willing to testify about any Communist activity that they were aware of in Hollywood. Some of the best-known friendly witnesses were Jack Warner and

**Actor Adolphe Menjou prepares to testify before the House Un-American Activities Committee during the days of the notorious "Red Scare" in Hollywood.**

Louis B. Mayer, representing the studio heads, as well as Gary Cooper, Robert Taylor, Robert Montgomery, and Ronald Reagan, representing actors.

Nineteen "unfriendly" witnesses were subpoenaed. These were people whom the committee considered to be Communists. Although only eleven were called to testify, all their lives were deeply affected. German playwright Bertolt Brecht was the only one of the eleven to answer any questions on the stand. He claimed he was not a Communist, but after testifying he immediately left Hollywood to return to East Germany. The remaining ten became the famous so-called Hollywood Ten. One director (Edward Dmytryk) and nine screenwriters (John Howard Lawson, Dalton Trumbo, Albert Maltz, Alvah Bessie, Samuel Ornitz, Herbert Biberman, Adrian Scott, Ring Lardner, Jr., and Lester Cole) took the stand and refused to answer any questions, claiming their Fifth Amendment rights.

These ten witnesses knew they had three options. They could claim they were not and never had been members of the Communist Party (this would have meant perjuring themselves); they could admit or claim membership and then be forced to name other members (and this would have meant losing their jobs both because of their former membership and their dubious position as informers); or they could refuse to answer any questions (which is the choice they made). Although most lawyers would agree today that the Fifth Amendment gave them the right to choose this last option, the committee (and then the courts during appeals) did not agree. All ten were held in contempt and subsequently served between six and twelve months in jail, although one, Edward Dmytryk, later agreed to cooperate with the committee and did not serve his entire sentence. The remaining nine were blacklisted by the Hollywood film community and found themselves forced to use pseudonyms in order to sell scripts. ("Robert Rich," for instance, who won the Oscar for Best Screenplay for *The Brave One* in 1956, was actually the blacklisted Dalton Trumbo.)

Immediately after these ten men went before the committee, fifty Hollywood executives gathered for a two-day secret meeting. Knowing that they could face huge losses at the box office no matter what the committee's findings, they debated the best way to handle the situation. On November 24, 1947, they announced as a group that the Hollywood Ten were suspended without pay. Furthermore, they issued a statement that declared, "We will not knowingly employ a Communist or a member of any party or group which advocates the overthrow of the Government of the United States by force, or by any illegal or unconstitutional method."

While this statement was purposely worded ambiguously, in the end it served to encourage and condone a ten-year blacklist. From 1951 to 1954, HUAC, now directed by John S. Wood, again focused on Hollywood, compiling a list of 324 present and former Hollywood workers who supposedly were or had been members of the Communist Party. Whether or not these people admitted membership, they ended up on an unofficial blacklist. Even cooperative witnesses who named others or renounced their own former membership in the party were on the list. Of these 324 people, 212 were actively working in Hollywood during this time, and thus lost their jobs.

The production process was affected by these proceedings. Not only were the 212 workers lost at almost all levels of production (actors, writers, directors, technicians), but the content of the movies being made began to shift as well. Studios became even more cautious and aware of the public's reception of their films. Between 1947 and 1954 almost forty explicitly propagandistic anticommunist films were made in Hollywood. Despite the fact that nearly all lost money, the studios continued to put the products out, hoping to prevent boycotts. Furthermore, producers tended to shy away from films about social problems.

Pressure from banks also worked to limit the film industry during this period. During the war the banks were quick to lend money for film projects. The audiences were growing, while the products were becoming fewer as a result of the war. Simple supply and demand told the banks that just about any film would make a profit. However, after the war the audience began to turn to television in lieu of movies. Combined with the other changes, this meant that Hollywood films could not necessarily be assumed to turn a profit. Thus, as the banks became more cautious, they got more involved in monitoring the content of the films, pushing for conservative, safe ventures.

Yet, even as HUAC and the subsequent blacklist served to limit and control the content and system of production and financing of Hollywood films, other forces were working against censorship and tight studio control. Imported foreign films and independent productions distributed through Hollywood began to bypass the Production Code Administration.

In fact, foreign films never did go to the PCA. Instead, individual state censorship boards granted particular films licenses. As the number of foreign films being imported into the United States after World War II grew, more and more of their distributors ended up going to the courts to ensure their right to rent their films to exhibitors. The first and most important of these cases took place in 1952, when Roberto Rossellini's *The Miracle* was initially banned by New York censors as "sacrilegous."

Despite such contests, the Motion Picture Association of America (MPAA; formerly MPPDA) continued to enforce and rely on its production code. In fact, in 1951 new restrictions against mentioning abortion or drugs in films were introduced. Although most people either working in or distributing through Hollywood continued to shape their films to please the PCA, some did not. Otto Preminger was the best-known independent producer to challenge the code. In 1953 United Artists released his *The Moon Is Blue*, a film that dealt with seduction and adultery, without code approval. Although a few states did ban the film, and the producers did in fact go all the way to the Supreme Court over the ban in Kansas, the film was a great success, earning more than $3 million.

**Otto Preminger's 1955 movie *The Man With the Golden Arm* challenged the censorship restrictions regarding the depiction of drug addiction on the big screen. Frank Sinatra was the film's protagonist, who openly played an addict, showing his preparations for a fix, his drug paraphernalia, and his tortured attempts at withdrawal.**

**Opposite: French actress Brigitte Bardot was the sex symbol of the 1960s and one of the most successful foreign "imports." Known as "the sex kitten," she presented an image of pouty-mouthed, nubile femininity. Her films brought new sexual frankness and nudity to American screens, and her look influenced a new generation of American actresses, among them Jane Fonda.**

In 1955 Preminger again bypassed the code, this time releasing (again through United Artists) *The Man with the Golden Arm*. The *hero* of the film (played by Frank Sinatra) was a drug addict, and this had been deemed an offense by the MPAA. Again, the film was a financial success. By this time, the PCA realized that if it wanted to maintain *any* control over Hollywood product, it would have to revise its code. Changing—a little in 1953, a little more in 1954, and finally a great deal in 1956—the code came to reflect the kind of movies that were going to be produced anyway.

While the specifics of these censorship and self-censorship changes may not have led directly to specific production, distribution and/or exhibition changes, they helped to define the changes going on throughout the film industry during these years. As films seen in the United States increasingly were produced by non-Hollywood workers, the content of the films changed. Furthermore, distributors (whether they were the Hollywood studios or not) were forced to carry these films because they had fewer titles to choose from, and, perhaps more important, because they realized that these films would make a great deal of money. This in turn created new appetites and interests in the audience and tended to splinter it into smaller, more specialized groups. Lastly, exhibitors rented these films for the same reason distributors offered them. They needed to fill their screens and then to fill their seats.

The HUAC political investigations removed talented individuals from the system and affected the kinds of films being made while the new censorship systems began to splinter the audience from one mass group into smaller specialized groups. Although one was a repressive force that drove talent away (HUAC), and one was a nonrepressive force that loosened censorship and created new audience interests, both contributed to the collapse.

## New Competition from Europe

During the silent film era, movies were an international business, as titles could be easily translated into another language, and foreign language versions of big movies were often shot simultaneously alongside the American version. In 1927, 65 movies were imported into the United States from foreign countries and distributed widely throughout America. Although the coming of sound created the need for dubbing or subtitles, by 1935 the number of imports had increased to 225 titles and rose to a pre-World War II peak of 298 in 1938. During the 1940s the number of imports declined due to the war. By 1942 the number was 33, and in 1943 only 20.

Because these films were available only in big cities, people often forget that such a large number of foreign films were available in the United States prior to World War II, but a glance at *Variety* reviews confirms the regular flow of imports available. Within a period of a few weeks during 1935, *Variety* reviewed the openings of *Pêcheur d'Island* (France), *Passing of Third Floor Black* (Britain), *So Ein Maedel Vergisst Man Nicht* (Germany), *Pepo* (Armenia), *Border* (USSR), *Csunay Lany* (Hungary), *Larsson I Andra Giftet* (Sweden), *Don Quintin El Amargao* (Spain), and *Dopo Una Notte D'amore* (Italy), among others. These films are not famous today,

and most people think of foreign imports as only such classics as *The Cabinet of Dr. Caligari* (1919), *The Rules of the Game* (1939), *The Battleship Potemkin* (1925), and *The Italian Straw Hat* (1927). However, all kinds of foreign films were regularly imported into the United States, particularly from the very strong German film industry with its artistically creative Ufa Studios.

In the first few years after World War II, the United States did not import many films because most European countries had not yet recovered from the war's devastation and had not returned to full film production. However, as time went on, more and more foreign films became available, and by 1952, the number of imports was back up to 220 titles. In fact, many of the Hollywood majors organized their own importation systems. Thus, they were able to provide films for exhibitors but did not have to risk the production costs and time themselves. Seeing a foreign movie with subtitles—once a big-city or museum experience—became possible throughout the entire United States.

In 1950 there were fewer than 100 foreign film or art houses in America. By 1956, there were more than 220 theaters specializing in new foreign films and re-released Hollywood "classics." In addition, approximately 400 more theaters ran these kinds of films on a part-time basis. By 1963, 800 foreign films were being shown yearly in 500 U.S. art houses, and by 1965 there were over 600 art theaters in the United States. In fact, for much of the 1960s there were more foreign than domestic films in distribution in this country. According to David Cook, "Between 1958 and 1968, the number of foreign films in distribution in the United States would actually exceed the number of domestic productions, often by a ratio of two (and, sometimes, three) to one."

It is important to point out, however, that some of these "foreign" films were partially financed by Hollywood. Not only did Hollywood studios control much of the distribution of foreign films in this country, they also managed to coproduce films in European countries. For example, François Truffaut, one of the filmmakers who defined French cinema of the 1960s, had partial financing from a United Artists' subsidiary based in France—Les Artistes Associés—for a number of his post-1966 films. Thus, despite the fact that on the surface it seems these French films created competition for Hollywood, it was entirely to the latter's economic advantage to import Truffaut's films.

While it took a few years for other countries to start exporting to the United States following the war, America immediately began exporting. During the war, many European markets were closed, and as a result, Hollywood had a tremendous backlog of films ready to play in foreign markets. It is important to understand this in terms of the relationship Hollywood has always had with the international film community. Because much of the cost of film production is in the initial construction of a master negative, the cost of additional prints is negligible. Thus, Hollywood has always worked to maximize its distribution base internationally. Initially various countries resisted, creating import quotas; however, these measures only served to slow the inevitable effects of Hollywood's influence and control.

Part of the reason Hollywood was able to export so effectively was because of the U.S. State Department's cooperation and help. In fact, the U.S. government considered Hollywood films, depicting their own representations of the pleasures of a capitalist system, good propaganda tools, especially for countries in which a Communist takeover

François Truffaut, a French film critic and director who revered American movies, became in the 1960s a darling of American critics and art-house audiences with such films as *The 400 Blows* (1959). It was the first in a series of largely autobiographical films, telling the story of a neglected Parisian boy who drifts into a life of petty crime, played by Jean-Pierre Léaud.

or victory was feared. Thus, the State Department often interceded on behalf of Hollywood studios, arguing that because the United States did not have any import quotas, European countries were restricting free trade while the United States was not.

In the years following World War II, most countries limited the amount of money the United States could take out from them. In 1948 Great Britain required that no more than $17 million earned by U.S. film companies leave Great Britain in any one year. This meant that approximately $40 million of U.S. film companies' profits remained frozen in Great Britain each year. In the same year, France set the limit at $3.6 million and restricted imports to 121 films annually. Italy and Germany instituted similar provisions.

Initially, the film companies experimented with investing their frozen funds in wood pulp, whiskey, furniture, and various other commodities in order to resell the products for U.S. dollars. However, what has come to be called "runaway production" quickly developed. In other words, the Hollywood companies began to shoot their films in Europe rather than in the United States. Not only did this enable them to use their frozen funds, but they also were able to use "authentic locales," find cheap labor and sets, and avoid some U.S. taxes. This brought a big change to the studio system because it meant that not all Hollywood movies were being made in Hollywood. "Hollywood" went international.

The studios began setting up coproductions with a variety of other countries. For instance, a studio might receive funding from three different countries, covering up to 80 percent of the production costs. While these practices began slowly, with only 19 U.S. films being produced as runaway productions in 1949, by 1969 183 such U.S. films were produced. Because overall production also went down during this period, those 183 films represented approximately 60 percent of Hollywood output in the late 1960s. The major increase actually took place during the 1960s, with the percentage of U.S. films produced abroad moving from 35 percent in the first half of the decade to 60 percent at the end. The use of foreign funds by U.S. companies increased during this period as well. In the 1950s approximately 40 percent of these companies' revenues for runaway productions came from abroad; by the early 1960s it was up to 53 percent.

As its own productions went down and American banks became tentative about lending money, Hollywood looked elsewhere for films and for financing. Finance, production, distribution, and exhibition all shifted away from the old studio system. It happened in a way that allowed the major Hollywood companies to maintain their control, but only by changing the old studio system into something quite different. What has been called a "collapse" might better be called a "reorganization of business methods."

## Television and Hollywood

Another factor was influencing film in the United States in the years just after the close of World War II—the emergence of commercial television. While many still believe that television was directly responsible for the changes taking place in Hollywood after the end of the war, television was really only one factor influencing the changes. It was, however, an important factor in redefining the studio system's methods of daily operation. In the long run, Hollywood and the television industry actually worked together in symbiosis, rather than in competition.

Television had been in the experimental stage since 1928 in the United States; however, the first big push for commercial television did not come until 1939. By this time Radio Corporation of America's (RCA) system was developed enough for its subsidiary, National Broadcasting Company (NBC), to broadcast the World's Fair from New York. Despite the potential of this event for creating a large audience, there were only 200 television sets in the area capable of picking up the transmission.

After the war, the number of television sets around the country increased steadily. From 200 sets in the New York area in 1939, there were 172,000 sets nationwide in 1948, and by 1949 the number hit the 1 million mark. At the same time, the number of stations went from seventeen to forty-one, and the number of cities with transmission capabilities increased from eight to twenty-three. Finally, by 1950 there were 4 million sets nationwide.

An oversimplified view has grown up about Hollywood's reaction to TV. It says that movie-industry people pretended television would go away and that audiences would return to the movies. The public, they thought, "would get tired of television." "People would want to go out to socialize." "Women would want a chance to get out of the house" (assuming they were there in the first place). "The quality of television would not be as high as that of film." In truth, most evidence indicates that the Hollywood studios did *not* try to pretend television would go away. Instead, they tried to get involved in it themselves from the very beginning. In fact, as early as 1938, a major Hollywood studio (Paramount) *did* become involved with television. At that time Allen B. DuPont Laboratories was heavily involved in television experimentation and research. Paramount invested enough money in this company to maintain a powerful voting interest. Furthermore, in the early 1940s Paramount owned the first experimental station in Chicago and the first commercial station in Los Angeles.

During the 1950s television spread quickly around the country, and Hollywood found ways to stay involved despite antitrust sentiment. By 1954 there were as many as 32 million sets nationwide. In 1955 half the U.S. homes owned one television set. In 1956 the estimated average viewing time per television household was more than five hours per day. By the end of the decade 90 percent of the homes in the United States were equipped to receive television transmissions.

Columbia was the first Hollywood studio to begin producing for broadcast television. As one of the Little Three it was hard hit by the declining movie audience and the death of its former strength, B features. As it turned out, Columbia's experience with the quick pace and small budgets needed for B movies made the studio particularly suited for television production. Columbia's new subsidiary—Screen Gems—went into commercial television production in 1950 and then television film production with "Ford Theater."

At the same time, literally hundreds of independent television production companies began to spring up. Renting space from the so-called poverty row studios (Monogram, Republic, Columbia), most of the independent companies were unable to survive past one or two projects. They died because it was hard for independents to get financing, and it was expensive to produce the one-hundred-plus episodes needed to

Dale Evans and Roy Rogers pose with an issue of *TV Guide*, presumably to tell us that even cowboy stars have to find out when *Bonanza* is on.

take a show to syndication where it could actually begin to make a great deal of money. Just one television season in the 1950s lasted thirty-nine weeks, requiring a great deal of money, time, and risk to produce an entire season's worth of shows. (Desilu Productions, Inc., Ziv-TV Programs, Inc., and Official Films, Inc., represent some of the companies that were able to last.)

In the mid-1950s the majors joined Columbia and the independents in television production, thus driving out any of the remaining struggling independents. Disney, in fact, led the way with *Disneyland* in 1954. The series was a success, and other Hollywood studios began television production with similar shows. *MGM Parade*, *Twentieth Century-Fox Theater*, and *Warner Brothers Presents* followed the same principle but were not successful and quickly died out.

The failure of the first television production ventures did not discourage the Hollywood studios, however. The new subsidiaries—Twentieth Century-Fox Television Productions, Universal International Films, Walt Disney Productions, RKO Television Corporation, Screen Gems, Republic Pictures' Hollywood TV Service, and Warner Brothers' Sunset Productions—all moved into television production, with RKO and Republic becoming entirely television production studios by 1958 and $6 million of Columbia's $88 million of gross receipts coming from television production in the same year.

The major television networks were actually happy to have Hollywood's involvement. In fact, these networks began to function as distributors, much as the Hollywood studios were beginning to function primarily as distributors of motion pictures. Thus the networks financed many shows and were then able to set prices and establish fairly long-term contracts. In 1955, 20 percent of prime-time and 40 percent of daytime television was produced in Hollywood. By the end of the decade, 90 percent of all prime-time shows were emanating from the Hollywood-based production companies. In the early 1960s approximately 30 percent of Columbia's, Warner Brothers' and MGM's revenues were from television.

The Hollywood studios did not only produce for television, they also sold a great deal of old product to it. Although exhibitors threatened to boycott studios who sold to television, RKO, which had withdrawn from film production in 1955, and thus became unaffected by this threat, sold its entire pre-1948 library for $15 million. Warner Brothers sold next in 1956 for $21 million. By 1958, 3,700 pre-1948 Hollywood films had been sold by the Hollywood studios for a total of $220 million. At this time these films made up 25 percent of sponsored television time on non-network channels.

By the 1960s the cooperative relationship between Hollywood and television was firmly established. In fact, as more and more companies worked both in film and in television production, the distinction can be considered to be arbitrary in some ways. After debates with the Hollywood guilds about shares from television broadcasts of post-1948 Hollywood films were settled in 1960, these films began to be rented or sold to television. In 1961 NBC capitalized on these new films, becoming the first network to broadcast Hollywood product produced for theatrical release and showcasing the deal with the successful *NBC Saturday Night at the Movies*. Networks came to rely on these films, prices went up, and the studios realized that they had undersold their pre-1948 product.

As television's popularity threatened the big screen, Hollywood inevitably made movies that criticized TV: *Champagne for Caesar* (1950; top) was a delightful comedy that poked fun at quiz shows with big prizes; *A Face in the Crowd* (1957; above) warned us that cynical people could use it as a political weapon, manipulating viewers to vote for unscrupulous candidates who posed as nice guys.

The creation of fantasy worlds was always a particular talent for designers of Hollywood's enormously successful musical films. All of the studios produced musicals. This page: The MGM biographical story *The Great Ziegfeld* (1936) put hundreds of beautiful young women and an equal number of tuxedoed men on a huge wedding-cake structure to the tune of "A Pretty Girl Is Like a Melody." Inset: In 1964 Disney's *Mary Poppins* took the no-nonsense governess into a fantasy dream of a carousel in a park on a "jolly holiday."

Opposite: One of the most successful movies at the box office in the history of the motion pictures, *The Sound of Music* (1965) delivered to the audience many different pleasures: the hit songs from a Broadway success; magnificent on-location scenery in the Swiss Alps; a sentimental saga based on a true story; a leading lady, Julie Andrews, who was an Oscar-winning favorite; children, dogs, nuns, and lovers; and outstanding production values, as in this beautiful silhouette of Christopher Plummer and Julie Andrews in a tender moment.

# A Day in the Studios, 1960: What Had Changed?

What all these changes added up to was a simple fact: it was the end of mass production of movies. Instead of grinding out a large number of features per year, the studios began making the equivalent of handcrafted movies: only a few per year, and each one a very big deal. Television assumed the burden of mass production of entertainment. Movie production in the United States decreased. In 1940 Hollywood produced over 450 movies. By 1955 the number was down to 254. In 1960 it was 160, and by 1970, 137. In 1945 Hollywood spent $402 million on production but in 1955 only slightly more than $250 million. (Because the admission prices had doubled in that decade, and because the population had grown, actual receipts were up from $735 million in 1945 to $1.28 billion in 1956, however).

As the studios made fewer movies, they needed fewer people on the payroll. Since there was overseas money to be spent, and since new technological developments made location shooting easier, movies began to be made *outside* the studios, frequently in foreign countries. If my imaginary 1938 film *The Royal Road to Romance* was going to be made in 1965, cast and crew would relocate to the actual streets of Paris for shooting. And if you did not need the carpenters, designers, architects, painters, and plasterers to build the streets of Paris for you—or any other streets, cities, houses, or offices that you could find already built on location—why did you need these people under contract and on the payroll? The studios began to cut back on their large departments for art direction, costuming, research, and special effects.

Since star vehicles were not being churned out—as many as two or three per year for "hot" properties—studios also didn't need stars under contract. Furthermore, the stars *wanted* their freedom, the right to choose their own material, and better working conditions. At the beginning of the 1950s, stars still had to face exhausting days that began at six A.M. and lasted until eight P.M. or later. They still had to answer fan mail, pose for stills and glamour layouts, and spend Sundays learning their lines. They still had to work on Saturdays. On February 1, 1957, a new union contract eliminated working Saturdays, giving stars a normal five-day work week. By the end of the 1950s, stars and directors had asserted themselves after facing massive layoffs from the studios during the decade. Talent was no longer readily and cheaply available.

The relationship of the stars to the studios changed. In 1945 there were 790 actors and actresses under contract to the major studios. By the mid-1950s there were only 209. Where 340 writers had been under contract, there were now only 67 so employed. Security for performers was gone, but a new freedom replaced it. Stars began to choose what they would do and what they would not do, and so did writers and directors. Even more significant, most of these key creative people were represented by a handful of large agencies (MCA and William Morris, for example), and these agencies began to become increasingly important, to exert more and more leverage in the business.

The men who ran the movie studios were suddenly more like the 1950s concept of "the man in the gray flannel suit"—a corporate entity that did civic service and worried about the stockholders. Many of the ragtag, colorful old tycoons who had pioneered the business were fired, bought off, or removed from power. These men were the original "movie moguls" of the studio system, whose tenures dated from the silent era:

M\*A\*S\*H (Mobile Army Surgical Hospital) was an irreverent success directed by Robert Altman starring Donald Sutherland and Elliott Gould as two doctors living a wild existence in a medical unit during the Korean War. With an Oscar-winning screenplay by Ring Lardner, Jr., and creatively overlapping dialogue, the movie (1970) was a black comedy about the futility of war that appealed to Americans during the Vietnam era. Its popularity was such that it was translated into an even greater success on television. The series, starring Alan Alda, ran for a record-setting eleven years.

Louis B. Mayer, the son of an immigrant laborer, turned a junk dealership into a profitable scrap-metal business and then became a movie theater owner and ultimately the head of powerful MGM; Harry Cohn, the head of Columbia Pictures, was the son of an immigrant tailor who was first, among other things, a chorus boy, a shipping clerk, a pool hustler, and a fur salesman; Carl Laemmle, whose schooling consisted mainly of being put in charge of supervising short products in his family's business, Universal Pictures, while still in his teens; William Fox, who supported his family as a child by selling newspapers and candy, went to work in a garment center sweatshop at the age of eleven; Jack Warner, whose father was a peddler who put all his sons to work when he acquired a nickelodeon. These men were educated in the streets and on the job, and they brought to the business their considerable experience in salesmanship, tough negotiations, and finding a product the public wanted. When they left the business, the studio system was cut loose from the early days of film, the growth period in which the business was defined and shaped. The corporate employees who followed them were more likely to be university-educated rather than street-educated.

A visit to a typical studio in the early 1960s would find it still there, with the same buildings and the same guard at the gate. The offices were still busy, but greatly reduced in activity. The sound stages might not be in use, or they might be used for television production. The head of the studio might not even be on the lot. He might be at Cinecittà in Rome, checking up on the studio's big-budget costume drama that was being shot over there with an international cast that he had assembled by dickering with agents from all around the world. He was not planning on coming back to Hollywood soon because, well, why should he? He was going to Spain, to negotiate for the Yugoslav army to play Napoleon's troops in the big battle scene that was going to be filmed there in widescreen, stereophonic sound, and vivid Technicolor. He was planning to use an American director of cinematography on that film but would hire a crew of Italians to build the sets. In a sense, Hollywood was no longer in Hollywood. It was anywhere and everywhere. It had become a concept, or a label, rather than a geographical place.

My fictional 1938 movie, *The Royal Road to Romance*, if made in the 1960s would not only be a completely different story, but would also be made within a completely different system:

Charlton Heston and Sophia Loren were stars who could fill the epic screen with their physical beauty and larger-than-life personalities. Here they play lovers for whom politics will always interfere with personal happiness in *El Cid* (1961), one of the decade's most magnificent widescreen costume dramas, directed by Anthony Mann.

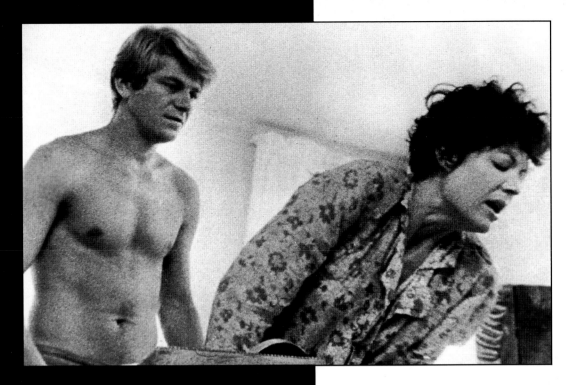

*Seconds* (1966) is a cult favorite among movie aficionados for its remarkable camera work by James Wong Howe (left). The movie is the story of an unhappy middle-aged businessman who buys a "new life" and is transformed into Rock Hudson. Hedonistically released into a whirl of sex, alcohol, and drugs, he finds only temporary happiness. This distinctive film was directed by John Frankenheimer.

John Cassavettes made underground film history with his highly personal and independent films that broke with Hollywood traditions. *Faces* (inset; 1968) became successful with the general movie-going audience largely due to fine acting performances from Seymour Cassel, Geena Rowlands, Lynn Carlin, and John Marley.

- It would be shot in Technicolor, on locations in Rome, Paris, and Budapest. It would be in CinemaScope with stereophonic sound.
- Its story would be reversed, so that the prince was a princess, played by Sophia Loren, and the con woman would be a con man played by William Holden.
- The clothes worn by Loren would all be designed for her by Givenchy, who would be hired separately—no studio contract.
- No sets would be built, and the great masquerade ball would be shot in Monaco with the use of the gambling casino and great hall provided by the royal family in return for the film's being donated as a premiere to benefit their children's hospital.
- Financial backing would come from Monaco, Sophia Loren's husband, Carlo Ponti, and Paramount Pictures in the United States.
- Vittorio de Sica would direct because otherwise Loren would not accept the role.
- Brackett and Wilder's original script would be updated by a writer of Holden's choice because otherwise Holden would not accept the role.
- A publicity firm would be hired to handle all marketing under the direction of Ponti, with Loren and Holden agreeing to share top billing, but with Loren's name on the right side of the screen and all posters.
- The Givenchy clothes, along with two Harry Winston diamonds, a tiara, and a sable coat, would be given to Miss Loren at film's end.
- William Holden's family would be flown to all locations and accommodated in first-class hotels at no charge.

Hollywood was Hollywood partly because those who worked there were shrewd business people. The creative question for them in the 1960s was, what could compete with

television? The first thing to do seemed to be follow the old adage, "If you can't lick 'em, join 'em." Hollywood kept on making comedies, romances, dramas, westerns—the same kinds of movies it had always made. It just made fewer of them for *less* money. The second thing was to start making television themselves, and to sell their movies, both old and new, to television. The third thing it did was immediately to take an on-screen attitude toward the "little black box." This attitude came in two flavors: critical (television will destroy your family and civilization as we know it) and humorous (this little device is ludicrous and can never give you what we can give you).

In the former category are such films as Elia Kazan's *A Face in the Crowd* (1957), in which Andy Griffith, a down-on-his-luck hillbilly, becomes first a big television star and then a dangerous demagogue. In the latter are such comedies as *Champagne for Caesar* (1950), which ridiculed quiz shows; *Dreamboat* (1952), which satirized the fact that most of television consisted of nothing but reruns of old movies; and *Callaway Went Thataway* (1951), which made fun of the fact that in television's early days, old films, such as those of the former cowboy star Hopalong Cassidy, were used to fill programming voids, resulting in a nationwide "Hopalong" craze among young viewers.

One of the best examples of how Hollywood satirized television on its own big screen takes place in *Will Success Spoil Rock Hunter?* (1957). The movie's hero, played by Tony Randall, walks out on an empty stage and directly addresses the audience. First he stands in the standard ratio black-and-white frame. Then, by the magic of movies, he pushes the screen out on both sides to its newer, wider CinemaScope format and adds glorious Technicolor. In case the viewer could not appreciate this, he shows "the average television screen" in the middle of the vast expanse, just to let people contemplate that teeny, tiny thing they sat home watching when they could be out seeing the gigantic, colorful panorama in front of them. The point was sensible: what was the point of going out to the movies if you had something similar at home? Movies needed to think about what television could not do, and what television could not do was part the Red Sea, fly you to the moon, make the Roman Empire fall. Television could not provide a viewer with *spectacle*.

Hollywood went big, or BIG!, to compete. It was the era of COLOSSAL!, GIGANTIC!, EPIC! Technology that had been possible almost from the invention of the movies—color and widescreen—was now emphasized and made financially feasible in order to provide moviegoers with something they could not find at home on their television sets. Since TV in those years was mostly in black-and-white, the number of color movies made in the studios increased. As color TVs became common, almost all movies were made in color. The black-and-white film, once a stable of the old studio system, became a rare artistic event, as when Peter Bogdanovich boldly chose to shoot *The Last Picture Show* (1971) in black and white.

Widescreen formats—CinemaScope, Cinerama, VistaVision, SuperScope—made the viewing screen enormous. 3-D brought a dimensional aspect to the screen, so that phantom hands seemed to reach down and grab viewers, all of whom were wearing strange little glasses that helped create the effect. For *The Tingler* (1959) theater seats were actually wired to give the audience a little jolt of excitement, and stereophonic sound blasted the eardrums with noise that made it seem that the orchestra was sitting in the same building.

Above: *They Shoot Horses, Don't They?* was released in 1969 and directed by Sydney Pollack, it told a hard-luck tale of the Depression, in which desperate people danced literally all night and all day for prize money in marathon contests. Michael Sarrazin and Jane Fonda portrayed an aimless young man and a self-destructive woman who end up nowhere in a no-win situation.

Opposite: Warren Beatty and Faye Dunaway brought style and panache to their portrayals of Bonnie Parker and Clyde Barrow in 1967's *Bonnie and Clyde*, directed by Arthur Penn. The movie was widely praised for its freewheeling cinematic style, which spawned a decade of lesser imitations. It was also heavily criticized for its violent ending in which the two notorious bandits of the Depression were gunned down in a slow-motion barrage of blood and bullets.

> *"TV taught me to think quickly on my feet. To prepare. To plan. To know what I want to do when I get to work in the morning so that I can accomplish the job. TV for me wasn't an art form. It was a job."*
>
> Steven Spielberg

Movies went all out being BIG!, and budgets had to keep pace. Hoping to create an "I've got to see that" situation for audiences, the studios spent lavishly on these huge films, not only in production, but also in the costs of advertising and promoting them. Great costume dramas such as *Quo Vadis* (1951) from MGM and the widescreen *The Robe* (1953) from Twentieth Century-Fox were released in the early 1950s, and massive epics such as *El Cid* (1961), *The Fall of the Roman Empire* (1964), and *Lawrence of Arabia* (1962) came along in the 1960s. Lavish musicals like *Gigi* (1958) and detailed re-creations of historical events such as *The Longest Day* (1962) were big box-office hits. "Movies Are Bigger and Better than Ever," became a motto that replaced the original, simpler one, "Movies Are Better than Ever."

At the same time, however, something else was taking Hollywood forward to its next phase of change. Quietly, rather calmly, television was encouraging live-action drama and allowing a group of talented young men and women the opportunity to experiment and create. Directors such as Robert Altman, Arthur Penn, Sydney Pollack, Sidney Lumet, John Frankenheimer, Franklin Schaffner, Delbert Mann, and John Cassavetes began by working in television. Fresh actors and actresses—including Gena Rowland, Peter Falk, and Robert Redford—trained in theater and method performance, began to have an impact in both media. Writers such as Paddy Chayefsky turned their talents to the small screen. Working with small budgets in an atmosphere of optimism—they were, after all, the pioneers of a new creative medium—they brought an intensity and a desire for innovation. For them, television was a place to learn, a school that just happened to broadcast their lessons out to millions of Americans. Ultimately, because of the industry's money, facilities, and distribution systems, these people all worked in the Hollywood movie world, bringing with them the things they had learned in the early days of television. These television people became the artists who would dominate moviemaking in the 1970s. As Arthur Penn put it, they combined "the irreverence of television with the technique of film." They contributed intimacy, smallness, and delicacy of performance to the films being made. They were determined to break with patterns of the past, and they wanted to make important movies about important subjects. They wanted to make films about acting as well as stardom. Their movies reflect this desire: *Marty* (1955), originally a television drama, remade as a low-budget movie about ordinary people who have no beauty or glamour, but who still need love and reassurance; *Twelve Angry Men* (1957), also originally a television drama, the story about a jury's deliberations in a tense and claustrophobic room; *The Miracle Worker* (1962), an adaptation of a successful stage play, the story of Helen Keller.

If Hollywood had just been doing BIG! movies, with no alternatives, it might never have withstood the changes it was facing. The contributions of "the TV generation" brought the business forward, keeping it connected to the audiences who were watching television, growing up on television as a daily habit.

**Meryl Streep and Robert Redford fall in love in director Sydney Pollack's sumptuously photographed *Out of Africa* (1985), which won numerous Oscars, and demonstrated Hollywood's ability to use out-of-studio location photography (in Kenya's Rift Valley) to bring a "classic" lusciousness to the screen.**

# 9 HOLLYWOOD NOW: THE FILM SCHOOL GENERATION (AFTER 1970)

By the end of the 1960s, the old Hollywood system had ended, and the "television generation" was gaining momentum. Starting in the 1970s and continuing through the 1980s, a generation of film school–trained talent arrived in the business and conglomerates took over the studios, resulting in new circumstances for the studios and the film industry.

# The Film Schools

"The idea was that all of these young filmmakers were going to be able to express themselves and they were going to be filled with great ideas that would change the world and give us great works of art."

John Milius

In 1960 there was not a single school in the United States that offered an advanced degree in film studies. By 1967, 200 American colleges and universities offered approximately 1,500 courses in film and television, and within eleven years, by 1978, over 1,000 schools listed 10,000 such courses. Throughout the 1970s film study was developed as a serious discipline. By 1980 16 schools were offering doctoral work, 76 were offering master's degrees, and 227 offered the bachelor's degree. Over 44,000 students were pursuing degrees in some type of film and/or television study or in some closely related area. An even larger number of students—estimated at 200,000 by the American Film Institute (AFI) in its *Guide to College Courses in Film and Television*— were taking courses in film study even though they were not majors in the field. In a twenty-year span, film studies became one of the liberal arts in colleges and universities, and related courses in film in the humanities also developed rapidly. In the beginning, enterprising faculty members would offer a "film appreciation" course, in which classics of silent film and of the 1930s would be screened and discussed according to the primary concern of the instructor: politics, history, or literature. By the mid-1960s, there were majors offered in film and television in New York (at NYU and Columbia) and Los Angeles (at USC and UCLA), and these programs were largely directed at the profession of filmmaking. They provided technical training for a relatively small number of students. During the 1960s the interest in film study in academia expanded rapidly to reflect the sudden focus of interest in the media by the students. The 1960s was a period of unrest in universities as students challenged authority and curricular requirements that seemed to them outmoded. As students turned away from the old, teachers found film courses to be a successful drawing card, so that many teachers trained in other disciplines suddenly became "film teachers." Film study sprang up in many different departments on many different campuses: art departments, English departments, theater departments, government departments. Students in film courses were being taught by professors who themselves had never taken a film course, and who certainly did not have advanced degrees in the subject. Today, film programs of all types exist: production, history, theory, and various amalgamations of all three. According to the 1990 AFI guide, there are 556 institutions offering film courses to a

**Previous pages: In 1982 Steven Spielberg directed a movie about a ten-year-old boy who hides a creature from another planet in his house, trying to help the alien "return home." The movie, *E.T. The Extra-Terrestrial*, became one of the greatest box-office hits in the history of the motion pictures, a kind of *Wizard of Oz* of its day in which a child's innocence and the alien's longing for home touch moviegoers of all ages. This image, which combines the ordinary (a boy on a bicycle) with the extraordinary (E.T., hidden in the basket, lifting the bicycle to safety with his alien powers) perfectly illustrates the film's magical quality.**

Three movies that captured the essence of the 1960s: *Big Wednesday* (top, 1978; retitled *Summer of Innocence* for TV screenings), is a John Milius film that re-created the California surfing world of the 1960s. *Easy Rider* (above, 1970), in which two laid-back bikers take to the road to search for the "real" America was the first film directed by Dennis Hopper. Director Bob Rafelson's *Five Easy Pieces* (left, 1970) stars jack Nicholson as a talented musician who drops out of the success drive to work an oil rig.

total of 67,131 students, taught by 3,910 faculty members, both full-time and part-time. It was inevitable that this amazing growth would eventually influence Hollywood, and, ultimately, what appeared on the screens of neighborhood movie theaters. It began to happen by the 1970s, when more and more new employees were arriving for work in Hollywood, fortified by degrees from film schools.

Where once studios had B-movie production units, in which newcomers could learn the craft of filmmaking, now they had a distant (and unrelated) adjunct, the film schools, which were complemented in 1969 by the AFI's conservatory for filmmaking, stressing narrative techniques that Hollywood had perfected in its history. Out of these schools came a new breed of directors, young men who loved watching movies, who loved making them, and who drew on a deep knowledge of the medium in their own work.

"The signal thing that's unique about our generation is that it was the first generation to come out of film school, and primarily, previous generations had come out of television, theater or newspapers depending on which generation you refer to. But the group of filmmakers who came into their own in the 1970s were by and large products of film schools, which implies a number of things. A knowledge of film history. Some sort of political awareness."

Paul Schrader

Like their counterparts who came before them, the television generation, these new-comers brought with them enthusiasm, imagination, energy, and the determination to do it their own way. What was different about them was something new to the business: the self-conscious awareness of the history of film. These people had grown up watching movies from all over the world. They were movie-literate. Furthermore, they had studied filmmaking in an intellectual atmosphere, discussing the relevance of specific cuts or camera movements and questioning the influences of technological developments, censorship constraints, and studio business practices. Typical and most influential of this generation were Martin Scorsese, George Lucas, Steven Spielberg, and Brian DePalma. Godfather to them all was Francis Ford Coppola, and godfather to Coppola a great independent filmmaker, Roger Corman.

Corman was a low-budget filmmaker who hired young talent and gave them free rein. He provided a freewheeling, efficient outlet for newcomers to filmmaking. Working for Corman was not unlike making a low-budget student film. The filmmakers needed imagination and a knack for playing with the medium in order to combat limited financial resources. Corman's production system became the rough equivalent of the old B units of the big Hollywood studios: he provided beginners with a training ground. Where newcomers to Hollywood had once made films for B units in the golden era, and then for television in the transition era, they now made them in film schools. After that they came to Hollywood to work for Roger Corman. His cheaply made genre pictures—westerns, horror films, motorcycle and gangster movies made for American International Pictures—became the learning ground for Scorsese (*Boxcar Bertha*, 1972), Dennis Hopper (*Easy Rider*, 1969), John Milius (*Dillinger*, 1973), and Coppola (*Dementia 13*, 1963), as well as for Jonathan Demme, Peter Bogdanovich, and Jonathan Kaplan. Milius has remembered his experience at AIP:

Francis Ford Coppola's *The Rain People* (1969) starred James Caan as a simple-minded football player and Shirley Knight as a pregnant runaway wife in a low-budget "on the road" movie of the sort that young filmmakers made away from the constraints of the Hollywood studio factory.

For us, there was a certain kind of openness. There actually was no pretension. We had a lot of fun. Everybody got to do everything. The thing that applied from student filmmaking to professional filmmaking was to make what you had go as far as it was possible. To try and get it to look as much like a big film as possible. And to never sit there and say "I need more."

There was a solidarity among the young directors, as Steven Spielberg has noted:

George, Marty, Francis, and I . . . It was a golden age of filmmaking because we were all single, ambitious, and we were in love with film. We're still in love with film, but we're no longer as ambitious, and none of us are single. I think once we started getting married and having kids, we began to fraction and then we began to divide and we began to go into our own lives and our own lifestyles. But when I was in my twenties and they were in their twenties, we were all kind of married to each other.

The first film school generation made films that spoke directly to their own peers, other young people, who were the primary moviegoers of the 1970s. These directors became the celebrities of their era, as another film-school concept, the "auteur" theory—in which film directors were respected as artists—also became the prevalent theory of creative control in filmmaking.

Auteur theory had been loosely formulated by a group of five young Frenchmen who had attended regular showings of old movies of all types, from all nations, in a small, fifty-seat theater (the Cinemathèque Française in Paris).

These passionate film fans—François Truffaut, Jean-Luc Godard, Eric Rohmer, Jacques Rivette and Claude Chabrol—became the center of an emerging film culture as they wrote about the films they saw in a new film journal, *Cahiers du Cinema.* Later, they became celebrated filmmakers themselves, forming the basis of what critics refer to as the French New Wave, an explosion of new films that began in 1958.

Godard, Truffaut, and the others who wrote for *Cahiers du Cinema* revolutionized critical and academic thinking about movies because they challenged accepted ideas about what films belonged in the accepted list of "great works." At that time, there was a general feeling that European films were art, but that most Hollywood films were not. Because Hollywood movies were the products of a large business concern—whereas European ones were often subsidized by their governments—many critics took the stance that Hollywood could not itself produce art. The French challenged this idea. They suggested that commercially made Hollywood films by such directors as Howard Hawks, Alfred Hitchcock, John Ford, Samuel Fuller, Vincente Minnelli, and others were also art. Andrew Sarris, an influential American critic and teacher, brought the

Marlon Brando in the title role of *The Godfather* (1972) presents his daughter, played by Talia Shire, in the opening sequence of the movie, directed by Francis Ford Coppola. Based on the best-selling novel by Mario Puzo, it was the first of three movies about the violent world of a Mafia family headed by the grand patriarch Don Corleone (Brando). This trilogy stands as one of Hollywood's most magnificent epic presentations, from the original in 1972 to Part II in 1974 and Part III in 1990, with the actors aging naturally over time, giving credibility to the truth of the decades covered in the story itself.

idea to America in his seminal book *American Cinema* (1968), successfully challenging Americans to take their own cinema seriously.

The new young directors who had gone to film school were a group who did not want to write the great American novel. They wanted to make the great American film. They had a passion to learn, and they asked themselves the question, how can you express things in purely cinematic terms? Their approach to movies was analytical, and their models were the great American and European films of the past.

In a sense, there was no other way for them to learn. How do young people practice their craft in a medium like film, which is, as someone once said, the only medium in which the artists can't afford his or her own tools? One way to learn was to study the masters, and the film school graduates did just that. They learned by analyzing the work of John Ford, Howard Hawks, Anthony Mann, Alfred Hitchcock, Frank Capra, Ernst Lubitsch, and Josef von Sternberg. They brought this knowledge into Hollywood, where their films were consciously cinematic. As Scorsese explained:

> I carry those images inside me. Those old films. Those films were a part of my reality day by day. I didn't just analyze them. I was affected by them. I related to them emotionally.

The film school generation's definition of themselves, however, although one of great respect for Hollywood's past, was that they were there to break with tradition and tear film loose from rigid studio control. In shooting his 1969 feature *The Rain People* on the road, Francis Ford Coppola remarked, "If we can do this in Nebraska, there's no reason to be in Hollywood."

They mixed the traditions of Hollywood and European film and documentary film and experimental film together freely. Having studied all the forms, they felt open to all kinds of movies, and they brought a new eclectic approach to Hollywood. In addition, they were, like most of their audience, young. They knew what the people who went to the movies thought and felt, and they threw out the old traditions, reinterpreted the old genres, and found new kinds of stories to tell about groups of people who had seldom been seen in the Hollywood movie before. Instead of rejecting this surge of youth, Hollywood, in Paul Schrader's words, welcomed it:

> The signal event for the film industry from our generation was *Easy Rider*, which just happened to coincide with several big-budget studio flops: *Hello Dolly*, *Paint Your Wagon*, *Star*, and *The Molly Maguires*. Small films like *Five Easy Pieces* and *The Last Picture Show* all were making money, and those big studio films weren't making money. Studios wanted to plug into what young people wanted to see, tap the *Easy Rider* market. So the studios opened their doors to the people from the film schools, because the men who ran the studios were no longer sure what the audience wanted to see. That's where and why a lot of us walked in.

The film school directors needed the distribution and exhibition systems of Hollywood, as well as the financing. In the end, studios, the powerful assimilators, snapped up the film school generation also. When George Lucas once described himself in a conversation with Paul Schrader as not connected to Hollywood because he lived in northern California's Marin County and had built his production facility, Skywalker Ranch, there, Schrader informed him, "I hate to break this to you, George, but you *are* Hollywood."

Film schools stressed different approaches—for example, that technique was not as important as what the movie said or that only personal expression in cinema mattered. Ultimately, however, these approaches meshed and intermingled, and the film schools sent forth a generation of directors who made polished, personalized films that had something to say. These young people were anxious to make movies, and making movies cost money, so Hollywood was inevitably a destination for them. Although breaking into the movie business has always been difficult, film students who had learned how to make films on a shoestring, and who had new ideas and new attitudes to sell to the moviegoing public, were attractive to the industry. These young people would work for low salaries just to have the opportunity to make movies, and they were often uncritical of Hollywood since they respected its history and its products.

Typical of these young people who had learned their skills in school and who had original ideas to bring to American screens were four men who became the most successful and respected: Francis Ford Coppola, George Lucas, Martin Scorsese, and Steven Spielberg. They would become what they dreamed of becoming: auteurs whose works would be studied by the generations of film school students who would follow them. Each of the four had his own distinctive approach to the medium.

## Francis Ford Coppola

Coppola studied film at UCLA, where he won the Samuel Goldwyn award for his screenplay *Pilma Pilma*. After finishing school, he went to work for Roger Corman, who in 1963 allowed him to direct his first feature, *Dementia 13*. He gained attention with a light-hearted, youthful film, *You're a Big Boy Now* (1967), and as a result of its success, went on to make *Finian's Rainbow* (1968), a big-budget Hollywood musical, and *The Rain People*, an inexpensive road picture. Coppola's reputation was made with his 1972 epic, *The Godfather*, which was the first of a three-part story about a Mafia family. The *Godfather* saga, along with *Apocalypse Now* (1979) and *The Conversation* (1974), are Coppola's most celebrated movies. His style is operatic, and he has remained true to his desire to make films that, although epic in sweep, are personal in point of view.

## George Lucas

George Lucas was a prize-winning student at the Cinema School of the University of Southern California. He became a protégé of Coppola's after graduation and affirmed his mentor's faith in him with his success in directing *American Graffiti* (1973), an autobiographical movie about adolescent life in the 1960s. His biggest success, however, was *Star Wars* (1977), a unique and entertaining science-fiction movie that broke all box-office records and spawned two sequels. Lucas's work reflects his interests in sci-fi, comic books, and technology, and he presents viewers with heroes who know who they are and who can take decisive action in overcoming evil.

George Lucas put the memories of his youthful years cruising up and down his hometown streets in cars, honking at his friends, drag racing, and picking up girls in the nostalgic coming-of-age movie *American Graffiti* (1973), starring Richard Dreyfuss. Set in 1962, the movie effectively used hit songs from the period on the soundtrack, and it helped to make the careers of several young players besides Dreyfuss: Ron Howard, Harrison Ford, Suzanne Somers, Candy Clark, and Cindy Williams.

Two of the earliest films from members of the film-school generation were George Lucas's first full-length feature, *THX-1138* (top), a 1970 sci-fi story about a society of robot-like creatures for whom sex is forbidden and everybody looks alike, and *Who's That Knocking on My Door?* (1968), Martin Scorsese's first full-length picture, an autobiographical story about a streetwise New Yorker (Harvey Keitel, in his film debut), inhibited by his strict Catholic upbringing.

## Martin Scorsese

Martin Scorsese has both a B.S. and an M.A. in filmmaking from New York University, where he has also taught various courses in filmmaking and film history. After making several prize-winning student films and cosupervising the editing of *Woodstock* (1970), Scorsese, like Coppola before him, was hired by Roger Corman in 1972 to direct a low-budget feature, *Boxcar Bertha.* The success of this film led him to a career that has been marked by one successful film after another: *Mean Streets* (1973), *Taxi Driver* (1976), *Alice Doesn't Live Here Any More* (1975), *Raging Bull* (1980), and *Age of Innocence* (1993). Scorsese's career alternates personal films about his Italian-American background and the violent world of New York City streets with more commercial enterprises such as the remake of the 1962 thriller *Cape Fear* (1991). His best work considers the plight of a modern hero cut loose from a traditional value system. He trains an almost documentary-like skill onto specific worlds and characters, particularly those of his Italian-American background. Scorsese's love of film has been channeled into extensive work on behalf of film preservation and film study.

## Steven Spielberg

Although Spielberg studied filmmaking briefly at California State College, he was already a prizewinning director at the age of twelve. His success with a short movie, *Amblin'* (made in 1969), led to a contract at Universal Pictures, where he began directing TV episodes and made-for-TV movies. His big breakthrough was *Jaws* (1975), which became one of the biggest box-office draws of all time. Spielberg's strong visual sense and his remarkable storytelling gifts have made his box-office record the most remarkable in the history of the business. He directed *Raiders of the Lost Ark, E.T.,* and *Jurassic Park,* three more of the biggest hits of all time. With *Schindler's List* in 1993, Spielberg has been acclaimed as one of the today's greatest artists. He has continued the great American tradition of audience-driven, deeply involving storytelling.

At the same time that these film students were defining the art of the new Hollywood film, first in terms of low-budget filmmaking, then in terms of personal visions, the studios provided an opposite: the blockbuster. A blockbuster is a movie that is an extraordinary box-office success, and someone said that means "a movie that an audience is willing to go out and see more than once." It is also a movie with a product tie-in that becomes an industry unto itself, such as *Batman* (1989) with its Batman toys and games. In this regard, the Hollywood studio system was still functioning as an efficient money-making machine, while at the same time it was absorbing the young film school generation. Soon enough, the film school generation were directing, writing, and producing blockbusters.

The sale of goods that have advertising potential prior to a film's release became a driving force behind marketing strategy in Hollywood. Motion-picture marketers buy an average of five times as many gross rating points (indicators of the quantity and quality of audience reached during a specified period of time) as any other marketers of packaged consumer goods. Radio stations played and record stores sold songs and albums related to the movies. *Saturday Night Fever* (1977), followed by *Flashdance* (1983) and *Dirty Dancing* (1987) are examples of dance films that were quite successful following the preselling method—other films have also benefited. Music videos also became a prominent form of "free publicity."

Because of the importance of the sale of film-related goods, Hollywood began to develop marketing programs in the early 1970s as an important aspect influencing the success or failure of a film. Marketing schedules often began even before a film was scripted. Potential audience members would be asked about their preference for stars or genres, and the resulting data would be organized demographically. The results informed distributors not only of which films were likely to be popular, but also helped select the appropriate advertising media. Marketers used this information to decide which of the film's elements to emphasize and which to disguise. Images advertising the film would be displayed on books, albums, and clothing. And, of course, television and newspaper media were bombarded.

The film school generation found success in all aspects of Hollywood: directing small, personal films *and* blockbusters, music videos *and* television ads, with lavish marketing *and* without. They are creatures of their own times, comfortable with the big screen and the small, educated to have high artistic goals, but comfortable in the world of commerce. Where the sale of theaters and competition from Europe had freed the studio business structure and released it from being locked into Hollywood, the young, talented, and well-educated members of the film school generation helped to free it artistically. They took Hollywood on the road, gave it new faces and new political attitudes, and they meshed its classical style with other filmmaking traditions.

## Conglomerate Takeovers

The conglomerates gave Hollywood something it needed, too: new sources of money. By the mid-1960s Hollywood studios had incurred tremendous losses due to a significant decrease in box-office returns. In 1969 Twentieth Century-Fox reported a loss of $77 million and in 1970 a loss of $65 million. MGM reported deficits of $72 million in 1969 and, following the forced sale of real estate and other studio assets, a loss of $17 million in 1970. Other studios reported similar losses. By the early 1970s, MGM, once the most prestigious studio, had ceased distribution, and Warners, United Artists, Paramount, and Universal had become subsidiaries of diversified conglomerates. (In 1960 the major studios released a total of 184 features, and by 1970 that number had been decreased to 153. By 1980 the figure was only 102. Of course, the studios were also importing films that had been backed with American money, as

*New York, New York* (1977), with Liza Minnelli and Robert De Niro was director Martin Scorsese's homage to the Hollywood musicals of the past. Photographed largely on sets at a time when the majority of films were shot on real locations, the film conciously presented a designed musical world, unfolding from the end of World War II to the end of the Big Band era.

Harrison Ford descends into the pit of snakes in Steven Spielberg's *Raiders of the Lost Ark* (1981), another of the smash box-office successes for Spielberg. The director's affection for the slam-bang pace of the old Saturday matinee serials was the inspiration for this tale of an archaeologist who is really an adventurer out of the pages of comic books and boys' adventure books.

well as purchasing independent features for release, but the bottom line was that fewer films were being made.)

It is exactly the accumulation of such considerable losses that made Hollywood studios particularly attractive to conglomerates looking to expand and diversify. Because of their financial instability, shares in a studio could be bought relatively cheaply. However, the instability was deceptive because such studio assets as furniture, costumes, and real estate still maintained a fair market value. Therefore, conglomerates could buy shares at little expense and then sell studio property in order to refinance the company or to pay off loans incurred by the holding company during takeover. These transactions could be executed with little or no hindrance to the operation of the studio. Moreover, refinancing the company was often part of a larger program to enhance production.

Furthermore, with the acquisition of film libraries, the value of which swelled quickly with television's growing need for programming, a holding company could gain a certain amount of control over both the film and television industries, paving the way for conglomerate involvement in the entertainment market as a whole and linking it to related industries such as travel and resort hotels. Owning a studio would almost certainly raise the value of shares in any holding company, whereas merely investing in a blockbuster was always a high risk. Conglomerates—big corporations—began buying into the movie business.

The studios benefited from these conglomerate takeovers. Following a period of frightening instability and uncertainty, they could now count on financial stability through both good and bad seasons. Furthermore, wealthy conglomerates became a new source of steady funding for production. A holding company was likely to have "extra" funds for investment in film production, thus the amount of money studios had to borrow from banks, though still needed, was significantly reduced. With interest rates constantly rising in the early 1980s, internal investments were not only less costly, but also self-fortifying. Given that the means of Hollywood is for the most part borrowed, internal investments spared the studios drastic cuts in production costs.

Yet despite the changes that occurred over the past thirty years, only the former definitions of "Big Five" and "Little Three" became meaningless. Universal, Paramount, Warners, Columbia, and Twentieth Century-Fox are still in business. RKO has gone; and MGM and United Artists, which became MGM/UA, are in limbo. Disney, not originally part of the Big Five or Little Three, has moved into place as a true studio now making feature films for all audiences instead of just making animated movies aimed at the children's market. Each of the studios, except Disney, has become involved in some way with a conglomerate.

John Travolta made movie history in this ice-cream-man's white suit, dancing his nights away to the tune of the Bee Gees in the 1977 *Saturday Night Fever*, a story of a Brooklynite whose life takes on meaning only when he's the center of attention at the local disco.

## Universal Pictures

In the 1960s Universal-International, by then a subsidiary of Decca Records, found itself in serious financial difficulty. Decca was ready to sell Universal; and the Music Corporation of America (MCA), divesting itself of its original agency operation, took control of more than half of the shares in Decca and Universal. Universal City Studios, Inc., consisting of separate motion picture and television divisions, became a subsidiary of MCA, Inc., the company that was formed through the Decca-MCA merger. Later, NBC signed a contract with MCA's Universal for the production of a series of feature films for television that would be theatrical releases. As a result, the television and film industries had formed a new and powerful bond. MCA became a precursor to the huge cross-media conglomerates of the 1970s and 1980s.

In 1985 MCA bought a substantial share of the Canadian-based Cineplex Odeon theater chain, which had previously obtained Plitt theaters and had subsequently bought from the Almi Group the RKO Century Warner Theaters (including the Cinema Five chain in Manhattan). Thomas Pollock, a Hollywood entertainment attorney, became president of Universal in 1986, and in 1990 MCA was taken over by the Japanese company Matsushita.

## Paramount Pictures

Gulf & Western, a company dealing mainly in metals, chemicals, and electrical products, merged with Paramount Pictures in 1966. Paramount, now a subsidiary of Gulf & Western, maintained its own management, but many employees were laid off. In 1993, Paramount became the prize to be won in an extraordinary takeover fight between Sumner Redstone's Viacom Corporation and former studio head Barry Diller's home-shopping network, QVC, which Viacom finally won.

## MGM and UA

Though Metro-Goldwyn-Mayer and United Artists are considered operationally separate entities as of this writing, their histories coincide considerably in conglomerate Hollywood. Transamerica, Inc., a company dealing primarily in insurance and real estate, bought UA in 1967. The corporation held UA for more than ten years with little change in production practice. But by the late 1970s, UA executives Arthur Krim and Robert Benjamin grew leery of the profitability of conglomerate ownership. Krim and Benjamin, along with Eric Pleskow, William Bernstein, and Mike Medavoy (the top five executives of UA), made a mass exodus to form Orion Pictures in 1978. Because of their previous success, the five had no problem collecting the money needed to form the new studio. Warner Communications, Inc., allowed Orion to use its distribution facilities for a flat fee, without compromise of control over any aspects of production, marketing, or distribution. Orion was thus able to enter into the Hollywood system as an equal competitor with the major studios. This was the first time in Hollywood history that an agreement of the sort was made. Orion found box-office success with two comedies starring Dudley Moore, *10* (1979) and *Arthur* (1981), as well as critical acclaim with a series of Woody Allen movies. In 1982 Orion merged with Filmways, Inc., a production company founded by Martin Ransohoff, and the merged company produced the Academy Award–winning hit *Amadeus* (1984).

In 1969 MGM was bought by real-estate tycoon and resort hotel owner Kirk Kerkorian. The number of employees at MGM was cut dramatically and payroll for those remaining was reduced by 35 percent, studio merchandise was auctioned off, the English studio was sold, New York offices were moved to the West Coast, and 75 percent of the studio's real-estate holdings were put up for sale. With the profits, Kerkorian expanded his already extensive investment in resort hotels.

By 1973 MGM had stopped distributing. Domestic distribution was licensed to United Artists and foreign distribution to the Cinema International Corporation, the joint force of Universal and Paramount for overseas distribution. The motion-picture production operation was sold off by shares to stockholders in 1980 (now under the name of the MGM Film Company).

Having lost its most successful executives to Orion Pictures and thus suffering a major downfall in production, United Artists became a subsidiary of MGM Film Company in 1981; and in 1983 the name of the parent company was changed to MGM/UA Entertainment Company. Ted Turner, the Atlanta broadcasting mogul (founder of the Turner Broadcasting System and CNN), bought MGM/UA for $1.5 billion in 1986, at which time he sold the UA half back to Kerkorian, where it became part of his Tracinda Corporation. Turner's motivation was to attain ownership of the MGM library of old films to be broadcast on his "super-station," the national cable programmer WTBS, and his new station, TNT. The MGM motion picture and television production and distribution divisions, along with its home entertainment branch, were sold back to Kerkorian; and the MGM Culver City studio and MGM Laboratories were purchased by Lorimar/Telepictures, Inc.

This mass of transactions left Turner with only the MGM library, including pre-1948 Warner Brothers and RKO films. Kerkorian integrated his holdings in UA to form MGM/UA Communications, Inc. United Artists Pictures and MGM Pictures were left as separate production and marketing entities while the two television divisions were combined to form MGM/UA Television. In 1989 a failed attempt was made by the Quintex Corporation of Australia to obtain MGM/UA.

### Warner Brothers

Nearly all the assets of Warner Brothers Pictures, Inc., were acquired in 1967 by a subsidiary of the Canadian-based Seven Arts Productions Ltd.; the name of the company was changed to Warner Brothers/Seven Arts. (The acquisition did not include Warners' extensive library, which had been purchased by United Artists in 1956.) In 1969 the infant company was purchased as a whole by Kinney National Services, headed by Steven J. Ross. Kinney National, a conglomerate operating in parking lots, modular homes, and mortuaries, instigated major changes in Warner Brothers/Seven Arts, including a drastic cut

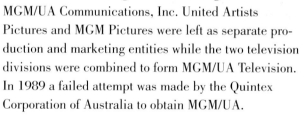

**The hot romance and passionate dancing of Patrick Swayze and Jennifer Grey in 1987's *Dirty Dancing* turned a low-budget, non-star movie into an unexpected megahit. The story concerned a sheltered young woman (Grey) and her introduction into the real life of people who have to work for everything they have (Swayze and his friends) when her family takes a vacation at a Catskills resort in the 1960s.**

in the number of employees, the lease of studio space, a move of New York departments and their executives to Hollywood, and a significant decrease in the percentage of motion pictures shot in Hollywood. The name of the holding company was changed to Warner Communications, Inc. (WCI), in 1971. By the late 1970s, WCI's holdings included Elektra, Atlantic, and Asylum records; the Wolper Organization (a television producer); Panavision; half of Burbank Studios; Atari, Inc.; portions of Warner Fragrances, Coca-Cola Bottling Co. of New York, and Bausch & Lomb; and 95 percent of the New York Cosmos professional soccer team.

In the early 1980s the name was changed back to Warner Brothers. WCI experienced financial difficulty in the early 1980s because of losses incurred by the videogame subsidiary, Atari. Consequently, the ailing division was sold and WCI redirected its efforts into its film and television production organizations while maintaining music recording and publishing interests.

In 1989 Time, Inc., and WCI made an $18 billion merger involving an exchange of stock and thus formed one of the largest communications companies in the world. By the end of 1989, Time-Warner had subsidiaries in Australia, Asia, Europe, and Latin America. The new company is one of the largest magazine publishers in the United States, with assets that include *Time, Life, Sports Illustrated, Fortune,* and *People.* Time-Warner also owns the book publishers Warner Books; Scott Foresman; Little, Brown; Time-Life Books; and the Book-of-the-Month Club—as well as the record company Warner Brothers, and a cable television operation which includes American Television and Communications Corporation, HBO (including HBO Video), and Cinemax.

**Twentieth Century-Fox**
In the late 1960s, the primary changes taking place at Twentieth Century-Fox were managerial reorganizations. Following a nearly catastrophic failure with *Cleopatra* in 1963, Darryl F. Zanuck became president, replacing Spyros P. Skouras, who was then named chairman of the board. Skouras retired in 1969 and Richard D. Zanuck became executive vice-president in charge of worldwide productions.

In 1971, once again battling financial turmoil, Twentieth Century-Fox found itself being bid upon by Walter Heller International Corporation as well as by Broadway producer David Merrick, and just escaped losing studio control in a bitter proxy fight.

The tremendous debts incurred during this period were paid off through a refinancing of the company. All of Twentieth Century-Fox's theaters in South Africa were sold, hundreds of employees were expelled, and thousands of props and other items of merchandise from its warehouses were auctioned off. In 1972 the majority of Twentieth Century-Fox's East Coast personnel moved to the West Coast, concentrating distribution, publicity, advertising, promotion, and general accounting in one location.

In 1981 Twentieth Century-Fox merged with a company owned by Denver oil baron Marvin Davis. Production declined again, and in March of 1985, Rupert Murdoch bought a 50-percent interest in the studio. In September of that year, Murdoch bought the remaining interest and Twentieth Century-Fox became a part of his Australia-based News Corporation Ltd.

In 1977 George Lucas made movie history with the release of his megahit *Star Wars*, a futuristic story about a space princess, an intergalactic hero, and a bunch of robots. First of a successful trilogy about the same characters, the film won seven Oscars and starred Mark Hamill, Carrie Fisher, and Harrison Ford.

In 1985 the hyphen in Twentieth Century-Fox was dropped. In October 1985 Twentieth Century Fox Film Corporation, Fox Television Stations, Inc., and Fox Broadcasting Company were consolidated into Fox, Inc. Murdoch thus had the means of production and distribution of films for both theatrical and television release, as well as ample outlet for exhibition. In 1989 Joe Roth, an independent producer and director, was hired as chairman of the major filmmaking unit of Fox, Inc., and the unit was renamed Fox Film Corporation. Joe Roth became the first motion-picture director to run a major Hollywood studio since Lubitsch ran Paramount in 1935; however, he left Fox in 1992 to set up his own production unit at Disney.

## Columbia

In the early 1960s Columbia pictures experienced a substantial decline in theatrical production financing. However, the burden was eased considerably through a massive investment in successful British film productions. (The release of *Lawrence of Arabia* [1962] and *Oliver* [1968].)

In the early 1970s, a former Wall Street banker named Herbert Allen, Jr., purchased control of Columbia Pictures and became president. In 1982 Columbia Pictures was purchased by Coca-Cola for about $750 million. With sponsorship from Coca-Cola, Columbia Pictures joined financial forces with Home Box Office and CBS to form Tri-Star Pictures, which was to develop as a separate entity from Columbia. The impetus behind the development of Tri-Star pictures was a recognition by all three participating companies that cable television would be an immense success and therefore would need a large volume of films for broadcast. Original productions by Tri-Star were intended for theatrical, network-television, and cable-television release. In 1985 Columbia Pictures acquired the Walter Reade Theater chain while Tri-Star began bidding on the theater chain of United Artists Communications, Inc. During the mid-1980s, Coca-Cola had acquired a number of other media operations, including Columbia Pictures Television, Merv Griffin Enterprises, and Loew's Theater Management Corporation (which at the time owned 635 screens in 180 locations); in 1987 Coca-Cola had restructured its entertainment holdings to form Columbia Pictures Entertainment, Inc.

Formerly separate entities of operation, Tri-Star Pictures was made a unit of Columbia Pictures in 1989. Later that year Columbia was purchased by Sony for $3.4 billion.

## Disney

Originally a company that produced animated cartoons and features aimed at the youth market, the Walt Disney company moved into major-studio position when it began making successful live-action family-oriented features during the 1960s. Financial instability and a decline in the quality of Disney motion picture and television productions threatened the company's future following its founder's death in 1966. Some degree of equilibrium was maintained by the Disneyland theme park in California, however. In 1971 Walt Disney World was built in Florida and has had a comparable success. But in the same year Walt's brother Roy died, leaving no family member in charge of the operation. In 1983 Disney founded Touchstone Pictures, a subsidiary intended for the production of films for an adult audience.

In 1989 Disney acquired Henson Associates, Inc., and is currently attempting to obtain the rights to characters like Kermit the Frog and Miss Piggy for use in its parks, television programs, and motion pictures. Also in that year a Florida production facility began operation, and production was doubled through the creation of a new division named Hollywood Pictures. In 1992 Disney opened EuroDisneyland near Paris, its fourth theme park, and in 1993 it purchased a successful independent film company, Miramax.

### Independents

"Independent films are the most important things there are in our country, in the USA. They're the lifeblood of the filmmaking industry. They set the new standards and they set the trends and they have the wildest ideas and the most interesting stories."

Sam Raimi

The changes taking place in Hollywood in the studios due to conglomerate takeovers also affected independent production. The conglomerates forged new relationships with television and the international world, as well as with the government, and this in turn stimulated the growth of independent production. Of course, Hollywood had never been without some form of independent production. In the days of silent movies, there were no majors and everyone was independent. From Carl Laemmle's use of the Independent Motion Picture Company to challenge the Motion Picture Patents Company's attempted control of the industry in the 1910s to David O. Selznick's various independent companies operating in the late 1930s and early 1940s, someone in Hollywood has always been called an "independent."

In fact, between 1934 and 1939, 38 percent of the films released were not produced by the majors. However, many of these films were B pictures—shorts, newsreels, and the like. The A features that made the most money were 95 percent of major-studio productions. Furthermore, there were only about ten independent companies covering the remaining 5 percent of these A features. Nevertheless, the number of independent companies producing features grew during the 1940s. In 1945 there were forty companies, in 1946 there were seventy, and by 1947 ninety-three independent companies were producing features.

Part of the reason for this growth was the banks' willingness to loan money to motion picture companies. Around 1939 the banks determined that *any* film was bound to return at least 60 percent of its cost. Thus, it became relatively easy for an independent to secure financing, even if he or she had not made a film before. The bank would put up the "first money," or about 60 percent, and the production company would have to cover the rest with money or credit from the distributor, the lab, or a finance company. In addition, salary deferments might help to ensure "completion money"—additional funds the banks required as protection against going over budget. During this time, in fact, the *banks* came to compete with each other in order to give

Robert Redford directed and narrated, but did not appear in, the 1992 critical success *A River Runs Through It*, based on Norman McLean's autobiographical novel about how his preacher father taught him and his brother the art of fly-fishing while they were growing up in rural Montana.

Few women directors have had the success of Susan Seidelman with her 1985 hit, *Desperately Seeking Susan*. An offbeat story about a bored housewife played by Rosanna Arquette, who pretends to be a freewheeling spirit. The comedy was partly successful due to the presence of Madonna, who became a superstar while the film was in final production.

film companies loans. Thus, at times they would lower their interest rates and/or raise the first money to 75 or 80 percent of the negative cost.

After the war the number of independents increased even more. In 1949 they made up 20 percent of the major Hollywood studio and distribution companies' releases. By 1957, 57 percent of Hollywood's distributed product was independently produced, with the number jumping to 65 percent in 1958. In 1959 the percentage stayed the same; however, as many as 165 full-time independent companies (as compared to the 10 working in 1939) produced these films.

This unprecedented growth in independent production took place for a number of reasons. First, between 1946 and 1950 all the majors (except MGM) got rid of their stock players. In 1946, as a whole, the majors had 598 actors, 160 directors, and 132 producers on staff, while by 1957 they had reduced the number to 196 actors, 58 directors, and 65 producers. With the reduced production, the companies were happy to let these people go and the workers were just as pleased. New tax laws were taking large chunks out of income, while a lower tax was levied against capital gains. Thus, these stars (actors, directors, and producers alike) incorporated themselves into independent companies, and as a result managed to keep more of their money for themselves. Furthermore, the reduction in major studio production left a lot of screens empty. While some theaters were closing, and others were showing foreign films, still others needed product to fill their programs. And thus, there was an increased market for independent films. Lastly, new markets were opening up as drive-ins became popular, creating a largely teenage audience that enjoyed pseudo-B (self-consciously B) features made by independent companies.

Despite the potential for shifts in content and economic control that the growth of independent companies represents, in the end the size of the industry and the established command of the majors prevented many power shifts. 1946 represented the peak income year for the movie industry, but by 1947 attendance was already dropping, as were profits and security. The competition between banks disappeared, and they lowered their first money loans to 50 percent of the negative cost. Furthermore, the Federal Reserve Board cautioned the nation's banks against their inflationary lending policies.

The growth of independent production of this type ironically helped to keep the major studios strong during the conglomerate era. This was because, by the 1950s, for an independent moviemaker to obtain funding from a bank, he or she already had to have a major distribution company lined up for the movie. No bank would back a production that had no outlet for reaching an audience. Obviously, that kind of distribution could only be obtained from the major Hollywood studios. Thus, the studio could exert some control over the production. Sometimes independent productions borrowed their financing directly from the distributor (or studio) instead of going to the bank. If the studio was going to exert control anyway, why not get the funding directly from them and save steps? Either way, the studios remained in strong positions of control and influence.

# 10 HOLLYWOOD TODAY AND THE CUTTING EDGE

"I think every generation changes Hollywood. That's just part of life. It keeps rolling over. You could say the Playhouse 90 generation changed Hollywood, or the Ben Hecht generation changed Hollywood, or the German expatriate generation changed Hollywood. We all changed Hollywood. Maybe the Spike Lee generation is going to be the legacy of the nineties. We are all Hollywood filmmakers because that's where they have the money."

Paul Schrader

When it comes to moviemaking in America it's important to understand that no matter what changes occur, "it's just the same old story." Hollywood's ability to assimilate is nothing short of frightening. Over the years, the movie studios have been threatened by legal decisions, government interference, depressions and recessions, world wars, and technological developments, but the movie business has always survived. Hollywood has withstood competition from foreign films, television, cable, and independent productions. Somehow it always manages to suck these entities up, changing its methods of production, distribution, and exhibition—the three key factors in its business operation—in order to assimilate any new threat.

This is what is still happening today. Although everyone is talking about "the threat" of interactive television, CD-ROMs, virtual reality, video editing, digital systems, and the rise of the independent film (again!), Hollywood as a thriving system of business remains in place. There are still studios, although power has shifted over to influential agents, and stars have gained the freedom to forge their own deals. Movies are not just seen on big screens, but also on television, on videotape, and on laser disks. Although movies from all over the world flood the market, Hollywood is still there. However changed, however diminished, however reorganized, the studios are still coping with their three key problems: production, distribution, and exhibition.

What is different today about producing movies? How does today's system work? Let's set up a hypothetical comparison:

1935: Suppose Louis B. Mayer, head of Metro-Goldwyn-Mayer, has purchased a humorous book about a feuding couple who end up falling in love. The man is a hayseed and the woman a sophisticated New Yorker. They meet when he inherits a piece of property on which she is trying to exploit the oil rights. The book is a comedy, called *Mr. Black and Miss Blue.* Mayer loves the book and wants to make the film with Jean Harlow and Gary Cooper, but he wants Frank Capra to direct it. Capra is under contract to Columbia Pictures. Mayer calls Harry Cohn, the head of Columbia, and offers a deal: "If you loan me Capra to direct *Mr. Black and Miss Blue,* I'll loan you Clark Gable and Joan Crawford to star in that movie you're having trouble casting, *Strange Moments.* What do you say?" Cohn says yes, and after much haggling back and forth, Gable and Crawford are sent to Columbia and Capra comes over to Metro. Six months later, both films are finished and ready to release. Capra wins the Oscar, and Columbia has a flop.

1965: Frank Capra becomes interested in remaking *Mr. Black and Miss Blue.* He has purchased the original rights from MGM, and he calls producer Sam Spiegel and discusses it with him. Spiegel says he'll produce it, if Capra will change the location from a Texas Ranch to an Italian villa. They can change the problem from oil rights to one of a small winery being threatened by a hotel chain that wants to tear out the grape arbors and build condos. If the whole thing can be shot in Italy, Spiegel can get international backing and a distribution deal shared between Paramount in the United States and Cinecittà in Rome. Furthermore, if Capra will rewrite Miss Blue into an Italian, they can get Sophia Loren, and then her husband, Carlo Ponti, will put up some of the money. Capra is enthusiastic. He is Sicilian, and he and his wife can take a trip to his homeland on their way to the location shooting. Capra wants coproducer credit and wants to bring an American crew. Cinecittà says no to the American crew.

Previous pages: **Sex, Lies, and Videotape** became a breakthrough independent hit in 1989 when the film won for first-time writer-director Steven Soderbergh the top prize at the Cannes Film Festival. Starring James Spader, Peter Gallagher, Andie MacDowell, and Laura San Giacomo, the movie is a tangled tale of sex, love, and marriage.

As the decades go by, the public continues to select the individuals it wants to see on the screen, a process that is both unpredictable (Whoopi Goldberg, a nontraditional leading lady)...

... and predictable (Julia Roberts, the traditional beauty associated with Hollywood stardom).

Capra must use an Italian crew or it won't finance. These negotiations take ten months. Rewrites take eight. The film takes another ten months to shoot and is finally released in 1968. Starring Sophia Loren and William Holden (who owed Spiegel a picture), it is called *The Battle of the Villa Called Love.* Loren's participation is guaranteed by the backing of the film by Ponti, although she demands star billing and requests that she do no promotion work. For an extra $500,000 Holden agrees to do five American talk shows to promote the film. Capra has a flop.

1989: The rock star, Madonna, watches an old movie on television called *Mr. Black and Miss Blue.* She loves it. She calls "her people" and asks them to look into it for her. Her people call her agent, and her agent calls Frank Capra's agent, who is retired, to ask about the rights to the movie. The rights have been purchased by Ted Turner, so Madonna's agent meets Ted Turner's agents to discuss the possibility of purchasing the rights. Turner sells. Madonna's agent now begins to call the agents of several top male stars, of several top directors, and of several top screenwriters. He begins to put together a package. After a year, he finds a costar for Madonna—a newcomer named Jake Watson that he is representing—a director, Rob Reiner, who loves Frank Capra and who is also under contract to the agent's home agency, and his fifth set of screenwriters. (Madonna has not liked any of the new scripts.) Finally, Madonna's agent says he thinks they ought to sell it as a "concept" and forget about the script for now. The agent sells the film, with Madonna as star and Reiner as director. The concept is that Madonna, playing a rock star, will be on a tour bus that breaks down in a small town in Texas where she will meet a cowboy. Later, they will fall in love, and Madonna will sing six songs, three of which are guaranteed to be of her own composition. There will be six rock videos, to be released before the film, one at a time, and a soundtrack album. Columbia Pictures buys the deal, not recognizing that it was originally its own property. A sixth set of screenwriters is hired to "update the concept." They think Madonna should not be a rock star—it's too obvious. It is decided that Madonna will play a nun, and Watson will be a minor league baseball player. Madonna refuses to play a nun so it is decided she will be *pretending* to be a nun. (The agent sells it as "*Sister Act* meets *Bull Durham.*") Madonna will be a disguised famous rock star trying to get back in touch with real people. Watson will be moonlighting as a bus driver, and the film will be called *Miss Blue Regrets.* The advertising campaign is in the works with T-shirts showing Madonna in a nun's habit lifting her skirts to reveal fishnet stockings and a pair of red sequined spike heels. This project is still in development.

This hypothetical comparison of an imaginary film from 1935 with one from 1989 illustrates the shifting power structure in the changing systems of production in Hollywood from the 1930s to the 1980s. First, studio bosses controlled stars and properties, and films were made in the small-town neighborhood of Hollywood. Next, films went international and talent went free-lance. Directors and stars decided what they would do, and films were made anywhere and everywhere. Today, powerful agents package deals for superstars, and the deal is everything. The deal also includes more than just the movie—also records, videos, T-shirts, etc.—and the advertising campaign may be written before the script is finalized.

Inevitably, the "purchase of Hollywood" by conglomerates resulted in prominent changes in industry practice. Work was no longer as steady as it was in the golden age.

In the modern era, movies that become hits in America may be the homegrown product, such as the 1987 *The Witches of Eastwick*, with big-name stars Jack Nicholson, Cher, and Michelle Pfeiffer, or international imports, such as Kenneth Branagh's version of Shakespeare's *Much Ado About Nothing* (1993), starring a cast of excellent British and American actors.

The conglomerates were more interested in what would be profitable quickly, rather than long-term contracts, which might mean supporting an artist or other crew member who was not profitable. Hollywood actors, writers, producers, and camera crews found themselves visiting the unemployment lines. On the other hand, this reduction of structure opened up the doors to new talent.

The phenomenal success of the low-budget cult film *Easy Rider* in 1969, directed by thirty-three-year-old Dennis Hopper, had inspired studio executives to take a chance on youth-oriented movies. The administrators of the new Hollywood requisitioned films that were more appealing to a new generation of entertainment consumers. In 1972 young filmmakers such as Martin Scorsese and Brian DePalma directed *Boxcar Bertha* and *Get to Know Your Rabbit,* respectively. Movies such as *American Graffiti* (directed by George Lucas), *The Paper Chase* (James Bridges), and *Mean Streets (*Scorsese) were released in 1973. This preference for youth was not restricted to artists. Between 1968 and 1973 the new generation had likewise been handed the reins of power. The studios sought out young executives whose perspectives on popular culture were more closely linked to those of a new generation of paying customers. Many of these rising executives were former agents who in the new Hollywood became highly valued attendants to film production.

Suddenly it was the time of the influential agent, or the era of the deal. The studio's power was diminished, and new players took control.

## The Agent

"Agents don't have power in themselves. Their power is ceded to them by their clients."

Rick Nicita

During the Golden Age of Hollywood an agent referred clients to studio executives who then decided whether or not to offer a contract to the talent. The agent's duty ended there. In the age of conglomerates, with studios avoiding long-term and even short-term contracts as much as possible, the agent became the entity who managed talent, often having a fair amount of control over their future. At one time uncooperative agents were dismissed by studios. Today nearly the opposite is true. The studio cannot operate without the agent's resources. It is not surprising then, that even during the economic crisis of the 1960s and 1970s, no Hollywood agency went out of business.

On the other hand, agents can no longer depend on a weekly commission from a studio and so must collect enough talent to be able to mediate a number of different jobs. Today's agent has to work longer and harder to secure work for clients; however, with the increasing number of independent artists becoming more and more important to studios under conglomerates, the agent usually has a line on numerous opportunities.

In the 1970s agency packaging became a common phenomenon. "Packaging" means selling as one unit a group of the elements needed to produce a film. This practice was sometimes used by the agent to secure jobs for clients whose talents were not in demand, requiring the studio to hire the unknowns if they were interested enough in the stars. This practice has led to the term "creative agent," for the agent who is ambitious enough to put together such packages has to be imaginative. In the early days of conglomerate takeovers, studios found relief in the creative agent's experience with the cinema.

Today's agent is also more strictly regulated than those commissioned by the early studios. The Agency Code of Fair Practice states that all Hollywood agents are under the jurisdiction of the California State Labor Code, and before he or she can begin practicing, a formal application must be completed, including information leading to the would-be agent's financial stability and background. The agent is also required to maintain satisfactory space for conducting business, and movement of offices must be approved by the Labor Commission. (The golden age agent probably conducted business from the nearest telephone booth.) The Artists' Management Guild is an organization set up for the mutual protection of agents and their clients.

In the beginning of the agent's heyday, there were a few large agencies and many small ones. If any of the smaller agencies were to represent a successful artist, one of the bigger agencies would try to steal the talent by offering "sweet" deals. If the attempt was unyielding, the larger agency would simply bid to buy the artist's contract or even to buy the agency as a whole. (This practice resembles conglomerate takeovers of studios and other entertainment organizations.) In fact, following the corporate capitalist model, agencies began to turn to conglomeration. For example, by 1977, having merged with David Begelman's Creative Management Associates, Marvin Josephson Associates had bought Ashley Famous Agency and was in control of a radio station, the Sol Hurok Organization, some minor agencies, and most important, International Creative Management (ICM, whose only substantial competitor was the William Morris Agency), and was making a profit of over $3 million annually. Though agencies are forbidden to invest in motion picture productions (oddly, agencies in the 1970s were not forbidden to invest in video production), ICM extended itself into these interests via its clients—actors, writers, and directors who had invested in projects they were working on. For instance, ICM collected 10 percent (the traditional agent fee at the time) of 54 percent of the profits from *Jaws*, the 54 percent being the total from all their clients.

For the most part film agreements are now mediated by the agent. The agent handles actors, writers, directors, and often various other crew members, and he or she has likewise begun the practice of buying the rights to books and plays. So in the new Hollywood, the agent has the resources to organize a production even before the studio has reviewed a prospectus. Because of this, productions of both the independent and studio class are dependent upon the agent. As agent Rick Nicita has explained:

> There are a few exclusive deals around Hollywood. By exclusive, I mean a deal where the actor is contracted to do their next several pictures for a given studio. Those deals are very hard to sustain . . . to sustain in a happy way. Most of them have very, very rocky periods. Other than that, everybody is basically a free agent, and it's pretty much of a free-for-all. When a studio gets a good script, it's wide open as to who they're going to go to. All the agents in town are scrambling to get that offer for their clients, and the studios want to get the most bankable stars. That number of bankable stars is growing fewer and fewer every day. No matter what a studio's prior relationship really was with a given star, in the absence of a long-term contract, it's

Above: A low-budget, independent success directed by a woman was the 1989 movie *True Love*. Nancy Savoca directed and co-wrote the "this is real life" story about an Italian wedding in the Bronx. Authentic and never condescending, *True Love* stars Annabella Sciorra, Ron Eldard, and Aida Turturro.

Top right: Spike Lee brought to the screen the life of Malcolm X in 1992, with Denzel Washington playing the title role. The epic traces the rise of the controversial black leader from train porter to hustler to religious convert to, ultimately, high-profile national political figure.

Right: Independent filmmaker Jim Jarmusch directed the 1989 *Mystery Train*, starring Masatoshi Nagase, Youki Kudoh, and Screamin' Jay Hawkins. In the story, three foreigners, all staying in a Memphis fleabag hotel, cope with the memory of Elvis and struggle with the mystery of American music, pop culture, and Southern life.

just starting from ground zero again. "Here's our script, please take a look." This makes for, shall we say, anxiety on all levels, including the artist, who has nobody on the inside that they can really rely on.

Thus, the agent has to be the actor's link to the business because the actor truly is removed. I think it's one of the few businesses in the world where the acquiring of money is as far removed from the goal as it is. Because if you think about the money, your career will not flourish. The artist has to think about what they want, what brought them there, what makes them satisfied, what they think the public will want.

In my opinion, the role of the agent is not to make the client the most money possible. I'm not a business manager, I'm not a financial adviser, I'm not their banker. I'm trying to allow them the most choices, constantly. The idea of the career is to go like that. When they are able to do every possible part, then I feel I've truly done my job; nothing is unavailable to them. All the pressure in this business on the actors is to put them into as small a box as possible; an absolutely caged-in, typecast situation where they only do one thing. And so all the actors are trying to push that out and that's the constant battle. The good thing about being in a hit movie is the recognition. Your salary goes up and you will be offered more of that kind of movie. But then you turn around on the actor's behalf and say, well he was a big hit in an action movie, how about this romance? And they go, he's not romantic, he does action movies. So you're cursed by the success of it. The phrase *bankability* is starting to disappear, at least on the domestic side of things. Where

**David Lynch, enjoying a huge success from his television series, *Twin Peaks*, released a 1990 movie entitled *Wild at Heart* to a less successful box office. Starring Nicholas Cage, Laura Dern, Diane Ladd, Isabella Rossellini, and Willem Dafoe, the film lived up to Lynch's reputation as a man who could create a bizarre synthesis between American pop culture and an intellectual, more European style of filmmaking.**

you hear it is on the foreign side, which is more and more important, because at this point, half and soon more than half of theatrical revenues are going to be coming from foreign sources. On the American side, the word bankable isn't used too much any longer because you rarely hear of a gross predicted. Nobody makes a movie thinking, oh this will be modest, do about 30 or 40 million. They can't think that way. The economics are too big. They have to hit a couple of home runs to pay for all the failed movies because of the negative costs and the print and advertising costs. So you get very few movies that have a modest financial aim to them. They all either overtly or slightly below the surface have a blockbuster fantasy. Somebody or some people in the studio, the makers, financiers of the movie are going to bed thinking, this is it. Not, we're making a good little movie here, but this is *it*. The public's going to ride this one and take it all the way.

A studio is reluctant to spend money. They're reluctant to do something that doesn't quite add up on paper, that doesn't give them some secure feeling; well, we have an action star in an action movie; can't go wrong. And they can't really feel, aw, we'll take that chance because we have our action star for his next three action movies, and you never know because if he improves his career, we will benefit. No, in this one-shot thing, if he improves his career, he will probably cost us twice as much next time around. So we're not going to be the ones who make his or her career better. There's nothing in it for them. They don't want to take the chance.

## The Producer

The agent, with newfound experience and authority in motion-picture production, became a prime candidate for the position of production head, or producer, in the new Hollywood. Producers are rarely salaried or part of the studio staff. Although most Hollywood producers today are independent, their roles have not changed much since the days of studio contracts. One major change, of course, is the producer's new relationship with the agent, because, in general terms, their responsibilities are quite similar.

Another difference comes about if the independent producer is likewise financially independent. In this case there are far fewer restrictions placed upon the producer, at least during production. Unlike the studio producer, or even the independent producer sponsored by a studio, the independently wealthy producer is entitled to a share of profits. But, in the early years of the new Hollywood even the "wholly independent" producer was dependent upon the studios not only for distribution and marketing because the majors had powerful sales organizations, but also for financing because banks would not have been likely to lend money without a guaranteed release by a major studio. Today, however, distribution operations exist that are not owned by major studios and are not members of the Motion Picture Association of America. In 1988, nearly 70 percent of the total number of films released were distributed by these independents.

The independent producers will buy story material themselves, to be repaid by a purchasing studio. Special deals concerning payment over a period of time are made with writers and other filmmaking members who are aware that most independent

Director Alan Parker's 1987 *Angel Heart* barely avoided an X-rating, and did so only because he was willing to take a few seconds out of one of its hottest sex scenes. The story is about a small-time detective (Mickey Rourke) who is hired by a mysterious man (Robert De Niro) to find a missing person. Rourke embarks on the search, which turns out to be more than he bargained for. Along the way he meets Lisa Bonet, Charlotte Rampling, and Brownie McGhee.

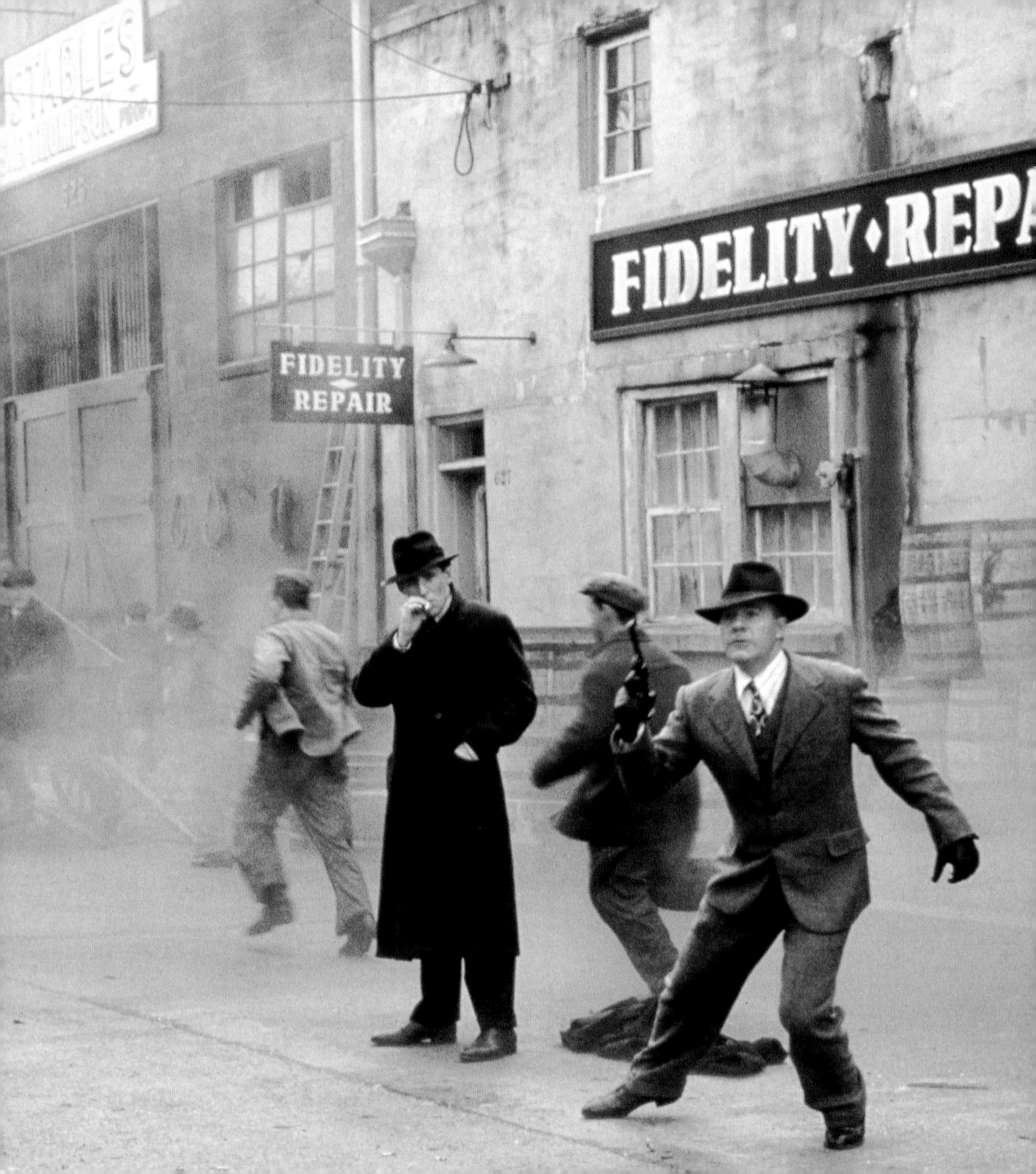
STABLES
FIDELITY REPAIR
FIDELITY REPA

The Coen brothers, Ethan and Joel, drew on their knowledge of American gangster pictures for *Miller's Crossing* in 1990. Gabriel Byrne plays an Irish mobster with a twisted kind of loyalty to his boss, kingpin Albert Finney. The movie also stars John Turturro and Marcia Gay Harden.

producers are unable to offer the sort of initial funds that a studio might. In the old Hollywood, a producer on a studio's staff remained employed even after a failed film. But in the new Hollywood, because the independent producer uses personal funds, one failure could actually mean the end of a career. Again, the result is that even the so-called independent producer is dependent upon forces other than intuition.

Mace Neufeld and Robert Rehme are two of the most successful creative producers in the film business today, having produced such hits as *Patriot Games* (1992) and *The Hunt for Red October* (1990). They have what is called an "exclusive contract" with Paramount Pictures, which means that whatever projects they develop during the term of the contract have to be for Paramount. If they develop projects that Paramount decides not to do, they must put them on the shelf until the contract ends, or ask Paramount to give them a waiver to set the project up with another studio. This "exclusive contract" has advantages and disadvantages. The advantage is that Paramount pays all the overhead of the Neufeld/Rehme Company, including all their personnel and development costs. Paramount advances Neufeld/Rehme guaranteed fees against what they expect the films to earn over the term of the contract. This gives Neufeld/Rehme financial security and a direct connection to film production and distribution. Lesser producer deals are called "first look" arrangements or "housekeeping" arrangements. In the former, a studio would guarantee the defrayment of some of the producer's overhead costs and/or provide an office in return for the "first look" or first opportunity to say yes or no on whatever was developed.

## The Director

The role of a director in the new Hollywood is different from that of his counterpart in the golden age. The abolishment of long-term contracts is the primary difference. New opportunities are offered for a greater number of directors to make it into the Hollywood scene, but at the same time the new, independent directors often do not have any significant control over their own work. A finished product has to be approved by the producer and corporate employer, who are free to make any changes they feel are necessary. The same was true in the old Hollywood, but the "corporate employer" then was a businessman whose interests included profit—but who lived, breathed, and loved the production of motion pictures. It is not clear that the same is true today. The director's cut is still not necessarily the final cut. (This brings up the famous example of "Alan Smithee," who "directed" *Death of a Gunfighter* in 1969. Smithee is a pseudonym created originally because *Death of a Gunfighter* was directed by two different men, neither of whom felt it reflected his own work. Smithee is now used whenever a director wishes to disclaim a film.

Losing control, of course, is less likely to happen to a director whose credits include hit after hit. Such a director has gained greater control over his or her work, making demands that include higher salaries as well as final say in the finished product. (In 1987 members of the Director's Guild threatened a strike that could have had

devastating effects in a year when both production and sales were up by quite a margin. A settlement was arranged and production continued to increase for the 1988 Christmas season.) Directors have become celebrities, and often today audiences go out to see the "new Woody Allen" film or the latest "Spielberg" or "Scorsese." Although such men as Frank Capra, John Ford, and Alfred Hitchcock were well known in the golden era—with Cecil B. DeMille possibly the most famous of all—most audiences were attracted to a film because of its stars or its genre designation.

This reflects the changes that overtook the film business in the 1960s, but it also reflects the changes in the audience. During the 1960s, when the study of film in schools began to expand, audiences became more sophisticated in their understanding of the medium itself. The concept of "auteur" more or less defined the director as the single main artist of filmmaking. Directors became stars. Their faces began to appear on the covers of magazines, and they became the subject of television interviews and documentaries. It was inevitable that the new and more serious attitude toward film as a medium that accompanied the expansion of film schools would change the way critics and audiences approached a movie. It became chic to discuss the director of a movie, rather than its stars, and the movie business began to look for new, young directors who could be turned into box-office favorites the way the old stars had been.

Young directors, like producers and executive staff members, have been solicited by the owners of the new Hollywood. This is not to say that the veterans have been expelled completely, but, again, the impetus behind the younger look is the corporate perception of youth's affinity with what sells. In the early years of the cinema the theater was a primary source of motion-picture directors. In the 1960s and 1970s television became the primary source because corporate managers approved of its rapid and economical shooting methods; the quality of production was less demanding than film. Television talent was very accessible to the executives, for they did not have to leave their home or office to "discover" a new artist. In the late 1960s, with the growing popularity of the made-for-television movie compounded by considerable decreases in motion-picture production for the cinema, television became a more steady source of employment for directors, many of whom chose to stay in that industry.

## The Writer

The writer in the new Hollywood has increased opportunities and more prestige. No longer is the writer restricted exclusively to one studio, and few writers are under contract on a work-every-day-on-what-is-assigned basis. (In the golden age, writers were under such contracts and were herded together in the "writers' building." Jack Warner called them "shmucks with Underwoods.") The increased influx of free-lance scripts being submitted has created a need for a new person, the story analyst, who reads submissions and passes on a summarized version to producers and corporate managers, who then make final decisions. Staff writers are hired to "fix" whatever studio heads may suggest is wrong with a script. Staff writing is one avenue by which screenwriters make themselves known in Hollywood, but the road is long as staff writers cannot be particular about the kind of work they do and often have to make changes which they find offensive. In order for the writer to have control over aspects of production, the writer must own the work a studio wants and then demand directorial rights as part of the asking price.

Like the director, the screenwriter in the new Hollywood has a much better chance of being employed but sometimes sees a final product that hardly resembles the original screenplay. And, again, the main difference in the effects that such changes have on the body of films produced is that for the most part the new conglomerate owners do not have the kind of experience or even love of film that the old Hollywood tycoons had. In recent years, however, with increases in production and, hence, a rising need for stories, the writer has taken the opportunity to make certain demands. In 1988, less than a year after directors threatened a walkout, a twenty-two-week Writer's Guild of America strike slowed production down considerably. The conditions to be met included a larger percentage of the profits derived from the sale of one-hour television shows.

## The Star

Stars, like most or all other artists involved in the production of motion pictures, are no longer kept under contract by major studios. Consequently, the studios are no longer the impetus behind the creation of a public image for a particular personality. The time, money, and effort spent promoting a personality now come from the artists themselves, or from their agents. At the same time, the abolishment of contracts left the artists freer to make decisions, and many of them began developing production companies of their own. Moreover, with the increased number of independents, the star in the new Hollywood had gained a significant amount of bargaining power. Generally, distribution often hinged on the bankable star in the first years following the golden age, because banks were always more likely to lend money on the strength of a star's image than on that of a director, producer, or writer.

The new studios at first became attracted to a phase of "starless" films (mainly foreign and avant-garde) and attempted to eliminate the star altogether. But Hollywood has never been able to sever its bonds to stars because the public likes them, and stardom can in fact be created even more rapidly in today's multimedia world. The accessibility of television, radio, and even print has greatly facilitated and sped up the creation of a star image. In 1990, a star's average asking price for a lead role—in which the star is billed above the title of the film—was upwards of $10 million.

Television became a primary source of developing fresh talent in the new Hollywood. Mary Tyler Moore, John Travolta, James Garner, Goldie Hawn, Lily Tomlin, Ted Danson, Clint Eastwood, and Burt Reynolds all had their first big successes in TV. The reverse also occurred. Former big-name screen stars—Fred MacMurray, Doris Day, Jane Wyman, Loretta Young—began their careers in film and then moved to television. This generally happened during a period of decreased production of film releases coinciding with a particularly stable period in television. The source for Hollywood stars, however, burst wide open with personalities coming from sports (O. J. Simpson), comic theater (Richard Pryor), dramatic theater (Meryl Streep, Al Pacino, Faye Dunaway, Glenn Close), dance (Mikhail Baryshnikov), and music (Diana Ross, Kris

Above: *Daughters of the Dust* (1991), directed by a young black woman, Julie Dash, found a wide audience with its story of slave descendants who live on islands off the coasts of South Carolina and Georgia, maintaining their West Indian ways just after the turn of the century. A combination of historical fact and imaginative storytelling, this movie proved that American audiences are ready for new kinds of movies.

Opposite: Cult hero John Waters continued his offbeat appeal to audiences with a taste for black humor in 1994's *Serial Mom*. Kathleen Turner portrays a particularly up-to-date American mother; dissatisfied with the results of her parent-teacher conference, she does what most parents feel like doing—she runs the teacher over in the school parking lot. The mainstream success of John Waters reflects the broadening taste of American moviegoers.

Kristofferson, Madonna, Sting, David Bowie, Mick Jagger, Bob Dylan). But the public's taste is as fickle and varied as ever. In the 1990s there has been a return to favor of the classic British stage actor: namely, Anthony Hopkins, Kenneth Branagh, Emma Thompson, Natasha Richardson, and Daniel Day-Lewis. Stars today come from everywhere. A movie may present the NBA basketball star Shaquille O'Neal as a leading man (*Blue Chips;* 1994) or an unknown Vietnamese refugee as its leading lady (Hiep Thi Le in *Heaven and Earth;* 1994). On the other hand, actors such as Clint Eastwood and Burt Reynolds are still important and popular figures thirty years after their debuts, with Eastwood a major film star and Reynolds an award-winning television personality.

• • •

The effects of these major changes concerning the "players" (producer, director, writer, and star) are twofold. First, with the abolition of long-term studio contracts stipulating salaries, the producer, writer, and director are now entitled to royalties. In 1960, over 12 percent of sales to television went to these talents. This, of course, puts a considerable economic strain on the studio, which leads to the second major difference in the new Hollywood: the "hyphenate"—the writer-producer, the producer-director, the writer-director, and, ultimately, the writer-director-producer, or even the writer-director-producer-star.

Initially, directors were forced to take on the tasks of producers who opted not to be on the site of production. This, however, proved beneficial to directors, who gained greater control and who no longer worked under the constant supervision of the producer and the interests dictated by corporate mandates. Similar transitions were made by writers whose words were constantly being altered by directors and producers. Finally, the writer-producer-director (and sometimes actor) has become the most common of filmmakers in the new Hollywood. The conglomerate owners, who were at first unwilling to allow this amount of authority to one artist soon recognized its economic value—one artist is less expensive by far than three or four. Still, critics have suggested that though the name has become common, the amount of freedom that the writer-director-producer (and sometimes star) has is far from complete. Filmmakers still deal with resistance to the inclusion of personal convictions in the cinema.

What we see is that the structure of the new Hollywood is quite dramatically different from the old. The major studios have increasingly turned to working with independent artists. In fact, the studios have steadily decreased the number of their in-house productions. This allows for a great deal more opportunity for outsiders or unknowns. It also creates a greater sense of freedom for each of the artists involved in production. Although production is different, however, the studios still maintain distribution operations, so that an independent artist has first to convince the studio that the film is worth financing and distributing. The three key components of filmmaking—production, distribution, and exhibition—still define how Hollywood works as a business.

**One of the biggest box-office stars of the 1990s, Tom Cruise stretches himself with roles such as that of Dustin Hoffman's brother in *Rain Man* (1988).**

## Production

Ownership by conglomerates meant changes and shifts in production practices. Some people feel that the changes in the studio system that have been described have led to a dwindling commitment to cinema itself. In the golden age, studios had concentrated on an assembly-line mode of production. They made movies and nothing else. They were in the movie business, period. Today's diversification, critics argue, has diminished quality. Well, certainly it has diminished the number of films produced in the new Hollywood. The revamped studios are now concentrating on distribution.

Conglomerates appreciate the practice of purchasing and releasing movies made by others because it eliminates the risk (and cost) of producing pictures from scratch. The holding company can invest a minimum amount of cash in an independent production, thus creating a cash flow that is attractive to investors. Regardless of the success or failure of the film, the studio will collect a set distribution fee, which in itself will probably cover any expenses incurred. Moreover, if the film is even only a moderate success the company is likely to make a profit.

But the studios under conglomerates are nevertheless motivated by proposals with blockbuster potential. The mentality is "bigger is better." The more money spent on a film, the more attractive it is thought to be to audiences. (Keep in mind that the conglomerate is motivated more by great cash flow than large profits.) The independent artist is not likely to be able to handle the kind of production costs that the studio can. Now releasing fewer films, the company needs to insure substantial returns from at least one or two hits per year, filling in the schedule with independent productions that can bring in a large box-office return. Thus, the studios have not given up production completely. The search for the big hits also means that the company is in search of an executive who can supervise them. An executive with a record of successful productions will probably be let go if a string of flops ensues, but he will almost always be hired at another studio.

Following the sale of studios to conglomerates, the need arose for a shift in production trends. A new plan was devised to raise money by inspiring box-office receipts following the "bigger is better" frame of mind. But box-office receipts did not increase at a rate commensurate with accumulating debts, and, thus, costlier films threatened the future of the major film corporations. Banks who were lending money for film production feared having to finance studio losses and subsequently urged the companies to cut overhead, share facilities, and decrease the number of costly films produced.

The number of films produced *did* decrease—only 120 in 1975, but, contrarily, investment in individual pictures steadily increased. "Bigger is better" meant bigger than what had preceded it. Current box-office successes often dictated the content for new films—the idea was to produce a film that was exactly like, yet completely different from, what was currently popular. One might compare this to the evolution of genres in the golden age, but the lesser number of films produced today in addition to the shorter duration of trends are prominent differences.

Decreases in the number of productions led to a product shortage in the mid-1970s. Theaters began closing due to lack of product, or they turned to pornography,

Another male star of the 1990s, Tom Hanks won the Oscar for his role as a lawyer with AIDS in *Philadelphia* (1993). Both Cruise and Hanks have alternated playing comedy/adventure and serious dramas throughout their careers.

which offered less discriminate distribution terms. The majority of drive-in theaters closed as the land upon which they were built became more valuable to real-estate speculators than to the theater owners. As an added blow to production funding, investment in independent productions as a tax shelter was outlawed in 1976.

By the end of the 1970s, the Hollywood-conglomerate connection had proven quite fruitful. Independent productions were contracted to fill in distribution schedules while blockbusters were being produced in-house. Furthermore, in the 1980s, though the majority of drive-in theaters had closed, the total number of screens in the United States began increasingly rapidly. Multiscreen theaters were being built in malls all around the country. In addition, conglomerates continued to buy entertainment industries, such as network and cable television, video distribution, airlines, resort hotels, etc. All these changes meant a need for an increase in the number of films produced. Between 1983 and 1985 production increased by about 150 percent. The new trend is dozens of smaller-budget films aimed at adult audiences, and fewer blockbusters. (In fact, a smaller-budget film is more likely to make a profit. *Star Wars* (1977) returned about ten dollars for every dollar invested, whereas *American Graffiti* (1973) returned fifty dollars.) Box-office returns also increased in the 1980s. This increase reflects a rise in ticket prices, but overall attendance has gone up since the 1970s.

Revisions to the Motion Picture Production Code have also had a notable effect on film production and distribution in the United States. Following the extensive violations to the pre-censorship code that occurred during the post–World War II era, the code was discarded completely in 1968 and replaced by the Code of Self-Regulation of the Motion Picture Association of America—the rating system. This code is directed by the Classification and Rating Administration, which is supervised by the MPAA, the National Association of Theater Owners, and the International Film Importers and Distributors of America. The rating system allows for adjustments in criteria according to social changes and industry pressure. This move instigated criticism, ranging from those who believe its leniency sanctions permissiveness to those who voted for the abolishment of any censorship code altogether.

The original ratings included "G" (suggested for general audiences), "M" (suggested for mature audiences), "R" (restricted, persons under 16 not admitted unless accompanied by adult guardian), and "X" (persons under 16 not admitted). Films not submitted for rating were screened under an "X" rating. In 1970, "M" was changed to "GP" (general audience, parental guidance suggested), and the age limit for "R" and "X" was increased to 17 in 1972. "GP" was revised as "PG" (parental guidance suggested, some material may not be suitable for preteenagers). A fifth rating, "PG-13" (parents are strongly cautioned to give special guidance for children under 13), was added in 1984. A new rating, "NC-17" (no children under 17 admitted), was subsequently added to the code of self-regulation.

As the restrictions clearly reveal, a given rating anticipates a given audience. Studios and marketers thus stipulate the MPAA rating required in prefilming contracts for major releases. On the average, the greatest number of first-runs fall into the PG and R category, which in itself reveals the industry's perception of the market as mainly adult. However, revenues collected from G- and PG-rated films have proven that there is an extensive market for these pictures. Moreover, a complex relationship exists between the restrictions of the rating system and the quality of films produced.

## Distribution and Exhibition

Despite these changes in Hollywood in the 1960s and 1970s, the relationship between distributor and exhibitor has remained one of mutual dependence. Theatrical first runs have sustained their importance even with the advent of network and cable television and videocassettes. Though attempts have been made to establish independent distribution operations, the major studios have maintained a fair amount of control over distribution. In 1970, twelve of thirteen films released were distributed by major studios, because only they had the kind of cash needed to cover costs. Consequently, distributors took advantage of exhibitors' dependence upon them by executing contracted deals well in advance of the actual completion of a film. "Blind bidding," as this practice is referred to, forced exhibitors to accept films without seeing any portion of a final product. The National Association of Theater Owners ventured to interfere, but little action was taken at the time. Today, distribution companies are regulated by the United States Department of Justice. No more than three films can be blind bid per year.

The four most common methods of first-run booking are: (1) An *exclusive first run*, an opening that occurs in only one theater in any major metropolitan area (this was previously the most common of the methods used, but a greater concentration of audience participation moving into suburbs has motivated first-run bookings for a larger market); a *limited first run*, or releasing a first run in a few theaters, only in metropolitan areas; *multiple first runs*, showing only in a small number of theaters braced by an extensive advertising campaign; and the most common, the *blockbuster*. (This method begins with a massive marketing campaign and is followed by release in many theaters on the same day, securing a fairly large audience before critical word of mouth can stifle attendance.) Occasionally a first run is tested in previews prior to national release or released in an area of the country where a special interest is popular. A film may also be pulled from distribution in the first days of its first run, remarketed emphasizing different aspects, and subsequently re-released.

Today, exhibitors are able to assert a certain degree of control. Exhibition being essential, theater circuits have been able to dictate negotiated rental terms to distributors, giving themselves an advantage over independent exhibitors in terms of which films they can offer. In addition, they have demanded boundaries of time and space within which the same film can or cannot be shown. Furthermore, in metropolitan areas, exhibitors orchestrated a division of products among themselves ("product split"), so that they would not be competing against each other in bidding, thus forcing distributors to moderate their terms. With exhibitors taking the upper hand, distributors began to make higher demands. In 1975, distributors required 70 percent of gross before house overhead was deducted in addition to prompting exhibitors to raise admission fees. Studios (distributors) likewise demanded advance payment for anticipated blockbusters, especially during peak seasons. Minimum runs were also set—twelve weeks for a blockbuster with the revenue percentage split alternating in favor of the exhibitor the longer the film ran. The theater profits by this practice if the proposed blockbuster proves successful. Otherwise, the theater runs the film to nearly empty chambers. These terms could be set up to a year in advance without any recourse for the exhibitor if the film is a failure. "Four walling," a practice in which distribution companies paid exhibitors a rental fee for theater space on a weekly basis (usually

Top: The huge box-office hit *The Hunt for Red October* (1990), starring Alec Baldwin as an American intelligence agent and Sean Connery as a Russian submarine commander who may or may not be planning to defect, was created from a best-selling book by Tom Clancy.

Above: Cher and Olympia Dukakis, who won Oscars for their performances in *Moonstruck* (1987), a heartwarming movie about an Italian-American family.

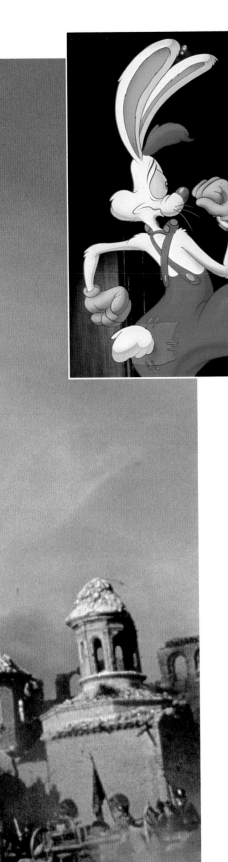

Movies continue to play with special effects, as in *The Adventures of Baron Munchausen* (far left; 1989), in which a fabulous liar's stories are brought to life. In *Who Framed Roger Rabbit* (left; 1988), live actors interact with animated characters when Bob Hoskins and Christopher Lloyd do battle with one another while cartoon character Roger Rabbit tries to help out the good guys.

during slow periods) became common in the late 1960s and 1970s. Exhibitors collected only the rental fee, handing all profits to the distributor. This practice was judged unfair restraint of trade by the Justice Department and outlawed in 1977.

Inconsistency in the number of films produced led to a shifting of terms between distributors and exhibitors. With the growing popularity of the multiplex, exhibitors required a greater number of films. In 1985, General Cinema Corporation, the nation's largest circuit, built 125 new screens at a cost of $22 million, bringing the total number of U.S. screens to 22,000. But the studios continued to believe that they should maintain as low a rate of production as possible. This meant that independent productions were in great demand. As stated earlier, a studio could make a considerable profit by simply investing small amounts of money in independent productions requiring a set distribution fee.

Since the mid-1980s, it has become common for holding companies of major studios to buy exhibition operations. For example, Gulf & Western acquired Mann Theaters and Festival Theaters in 1985, and the Canadian based Cineplex-Odeon acquired Plitt Theaters in 1988. As a result of the fewer number of exhibitors due to consolidation of theater ownership, major distributors themselves have turned to centralization of domestic operations, dropping from an average of twenty branch offices per studio to nine in 1987.

Production, distribution, exhibition, and marketing practices in the new Hollywood are constantly changing due to the ever-growing motivation for conglomerates to invest in multimedia operations. This has, and will continue to have, an effect not only on the quality and quantity of motion picture production, but also on the status of the various human elements involved. Majors continue to merge in various different ways with corporations whose interests are tangentially related to the cinema such that film production is but one unit of a much larger operation. Buying major film companies as well as other media operations, including television (cable and network), print, and radio, puts large corporations in a position of having an elaborately structured control over the total entertainment market. These new giant media firms have the power to squeeze out smaller firms, creating an oligopoly much like that which was outlawed in the 1940s by antitrust regulations, but on a much larger scale.

What then are the antitrust implications? In 1970, major studios brought a civil suit against ABC and CBS for developing theatrical filmmaking branches for the purpose of television productions. The claim was "conspiratorial monopoly used to private advantage in violation of the Sherman and Clayton antitrust acts." However, we know that television studios have continued to produce theatrical, made-for-television films. The irony of this action is that by the mid-1980s studios had come not only to produce and distribute films, but many also now own theaters, manufacture and sell videocassettes for public use, and simultaneously lease these to pay-cable operations. Later they syndicate them to network television stations, which are often themselves owned by the studios. Neither Columbia nor Universal were halted from acquiring theaters, and Paramount now owns the Trans-Lux theater chain. When in 1989 Paramount and Warner joined to buy some five hundred theaters, the Federal Court dismissed antitrust implications against them suggesting that this purchase will not restrict competition. Warners is, however, required to keep its theater operation separate from its various other interests. So it seems that although regulations forbidding cross ownership *within* media have been written, the conglomerate that owns *across* a business and the media has found a safeguard.

"Virtual reality" was simulated for moviegoers in the 1992 cult hit *The Lawnmower Man*. Loosely based on a Stephen King story, the movie cuts through familiar horror film territory in its plot. A crazy scientist (Pierce Brosnan) needs a victim for his experiments in "computer instruction"—and who does he see outside his window? The grinning idiot who mows his lawn. And thus familiar genres continue to entertain.

# Conclusion: What's Next?

As the one hundredth birthday of the movies comes and goes, it is interesting to think about the next hundred years. What will the bicentennial celebration bring? What massive changes in production, distribution, and exhibition? Will there be studios and independents, and how will the players change positions on the board? Well, what we have seen is that, although the world changed hugely in the hundred years since cinema was born, and technology emerged and new names and faces came along, Hollywood found a way to keep on making audience-driven films that stressed story and character. There's no reason to expect the bottom line to be any different in 2095 than in 1995.

The truth is that Hollywood just tries to make movies that people want to see. How they do this changes, and what they make shapes itself to the events of the day. What everyone in the elaborate system wants, from the studio head to the lowest employee, is to be associated with a success. To have a hit. And how does that happen? To conclude, here are the words of wisdom on that subject from some of today's most successful hitmakers and starmakers: "Nobody knows. Nobody really knows. That's why the crap game is so uncertain. Every bit as much as ever. More so," says agent Rick Nicita; "No one knows what's going to be a hit," says Steven Spielberg; "Moviemaking is far from an exact science. A movie is a very, very, very chancy art form. You're telling a story and painting a portrait with so many different elements, any one of which can go wrong, that it's a miracle when it comes out as a first-class film. It's not one on one, like a painter with his canvas. It's the director, and will the star be happy with reading the lines, and will the cinematographer make it look right, and what will the sets be like. . . . When you finally get it all done, will it get messed up in the sound mix or the music score? A hit movie, a good movie, is more a miracle than anything else," elaborates producer Mace Neufeld.

Today, Hollywood is in yet another process of assimilation: incorporating the new venues of videocassettes, laser disks, and cable television, and providing mainstream distribution and exhibition for minority voices. Minorities have been traditionally marginalized in Hollywood films, but the arrival of the 1990s seems to indicate that this may be beginning to change. During the 1980s, a small group of minority filmmakers began to receive both critical acclaim and box-office success: black filmmakers Spike Lee (*She's Gotta Have It* [1986], *Do the Right Thing* [1989]), John Singleton (*Boyz N the Hood*, 1991), Allen and Albert Hughes (*Menace II Society*, 1993), and Mario Van Peebles (*Posse* [1993] and *New Jack City* [1991]); women directors Jane

Two young black filmmakers brought to mainstream audiences the look and feel of black communities in two influential movies: John Singleton depicted life in a black section of central Los Angeles in his directorial debut at the age of twenty-three with *Boyz N the Hood* (opposite; 1991); and Spike Lee, whose 1989 *Do the Right Thing* (above) showed the black community of Bedford-Stuyvesant in Brooklyn, where a white-owned pizza parlor flourished.

Campion (*The Piano*, 1993), Randa Haines (*Children of a Lesser God*, 1986), Amy Heckerling (*Look Who's Talking*, 1989), and Susan Seidelman (*Desperately Seeking Susan*, 1985); and gay filmmakers Gus Van Sant (*Drugstore Cowboy* [1989] and *My Own Private Idaho* [1991]), Todd Haynes (*Poison*, 1990), and Tom Kalin (*Swoon*, 1992). It remains to be seen whether or not this new assimilation is sincere enough to provide a true outlet for minority voices, but when such films make money, Hollywood is always interested. The second assimilation—that of videocassettes, laser disks, and cable TV—is related to the assimilation of minority voices, as these new outlets for films have provided avenues of showing work that might not have made as much money without the added exhibition outlet of cable and home videos and laser machines.

The future of the cinema is not really in doubt, as it seems that with cable television's many channels to fill, there is more interest in filmed stories now than ever before. It's not a question of whether or not stories will continue to be told visually and distributed and exhibited to individual viewers. And it's not a question of whether or not the audience will still be important. Movies will be seen, and the ones the public likes will be hits. The questions about the future of cinema have to do with technological developments, venues, methods of distribution, and, of course, the aesthetics and content of the finished films.

Who knows what will happen? In the year 2050, Mr. and Mrs. America may go out to the movies at a gigantic movie theater in which they will be projected into the film via a virtual reality presentation, or by individualized seat controls, laser beams, and heat and light and smell simulations. On the other hand, maybe they'll stay at home, having long since forgotten what celluloid was. They'll sit around projecting their laser disk system onto their automatic wall system that provides seventy-foot projection, stereophonic wraparound sound equal to Dolby, and a literally tactile three-dimensional experience. Maybe they won't ever buy anyone else's movie. Maybe they'll sit at individualized computers and create their own. Mrs. America can re-create *Casablanca* and place herself in the Ingrid Bergman role. Mr. America will make up his own movie, a story about how he drove a wagon train west in 1882.

Whatever happens, you can bet Hollywood will be in there somewhere, three steps ahead of the game, hard-selling the software, the hardware, the movie ware, or the whatever ware—and making up new versions of the old stories, with one eye on the audience and one eye on the cash register.

"What is the audience in the mood for at a particular time. Noone really knows until it happens. By and large, you just make the film and make it as good as you can and that's it. Put it out there and then it's up to the audience. It's their responsibility to like it or not."

Clint Eastwood

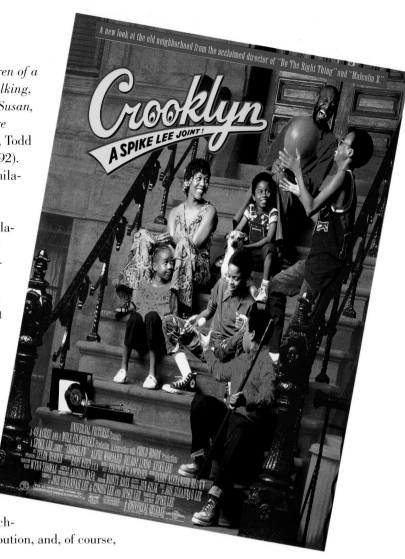

Above: Spike Lee's 1994 feature, *Crooklyn*, is a coming-of-age story set in his old neighborhood in Brooklyn.

# INDEX

Page numbers in *italics* refer to captions.

## NOTES

1. For a thoroughly detailed, accurate, and readable history of the silent film era, three volumes of *The History of the American Cinema*, edited by Charles Harpole, are highly recommended. The definitive study of the beginning of cinema, these volumes trace the technological, industrial, and artistic growth of the medium. Volume 1, *The Emergence of Cinema: The American Screen to 1907*, by Charles Musser, covers the period discussed above.
2. This period is covered in Volume 2 of *The History of the American Cinema: The Transformation of Cinema, 1907–1915*, by Eileen Bowser.
3. Volume 3, *An Evening's Entertainment, the Age of the Silent Feature Picture, 1915–1928*, by Richard Koszarski, details the growth.

## BIBLIOGRAPHY

**The Silent Era:** Bowser, Eileen. *The Transformation of Cinema: 1907–1915.* Vol. 2 of *The History of the American Cinema.* Edited by Charles Harpole. New York: Charles Scribners' Sons, 1990; Koszarski, Richard. *An Evening's Entertainment, the Age of the Silent Feature Picture, 1915–1928.* Vol. 3 of *The History of the American Cinema.* Edited by Charles Harpole. New York: Charles Scribners' Sons, 1990; Musser, Charles. *The Emergence of Cinema, the American Screen to 1907.* Vol. 1 of *The History of the American Cinema.* Edited by Charles Harpole. New York: Charles Scribners' Sons, 1990. **Technology: Sound, Color, Widescreen:** Basten, Fred E. *Glorious Technicolor: The Movies' Magic Rainbow.* New York: A. S. Barnes and Co., 1980; Belton, John. *Widescreen Cinema.* Cambridge: Harvard University Press, 1992; Carr, Robert E. and R. M. Hayes. *Wide Screen Movies: A History of Wide Gauge Filmmaking.* Jefferson, N.C.: McFarland, 1988; Fielding, Raymond, ed. *A Technological History of Motion Pictures and Television.* Berkeley: University of California Press, 1967; Geduld, Harry M. *The Birth of the Talkies: From Edison to Jolson.* Bloomington, Ind.: University of Indiana Press, 1975; Walker, Alexander. *The Shattered Silents: How Talkies Came to Stay.* London: Elm Tree Books, 1978. **Film History and General Reference:** Allen, Robert C. and Douglas Gomery. *Film History: Theory and Practice.* New York: Alfred A. Knopf, 1985; Balio, Tino, ed. *The American Film Industry.* Revised edition. Madison, Wis.: University of Wisconsin Press, 1985; Bordwell, David, Janet Staiger, and Kristin Thompson. *The Classical Hollywood Cinema: Film Style and Mode of Production to 1960.* New York: Columbia University Press, 1985; Ceplair, Larry and Steven Englund. *The Inquisition in Hollywood: Politics in the Film Industry, 1930–1960.* Berkeley: University of California Press, 1979; Conant, Michael. *Antitrust in the Motion Picture Industry: Economic and Legal Analysis.* Berkeley: University of California Press, 1960; Daly, David Anthony. *A Comparison of Exhibition and Distribution Patterns in Three Recent Motion Pictures.* New York: Arno Press, 1980; Dick, Bernard. *Radical Innocence: A Critical Study of the Hollywood Ten.* Lexington, Ky.: University of Kentucky Press, 1989; Donahue, Suzanne Mary. *American Film Distribution: The Changing Marketplace.* Ann Arbor, Mich.: UMI Research Press, 1987; Edgerton, Gary R. *American Film Exhibition and an Analysis of the Motion Picture Industry's Market Structure, 1963–1980;* Finler, Joel W. *The Hollywood Story.* New York: Crown, 1988; Gomery, Douglas. *Shared Pleasures: A History of Movie Presentation in the United States.* Madison, Wis.: University of Wisconsin Press, 1992; Handel, Leo A. *Hollywood Looks at its Audience: A Report of Film Audience Research.* Urbana, Ill.: University of Illinois Press, 1950; Huettig, Mae E. *Economic Control of the Motion Picture Industry.* Philadelphia: University of Pennsylvania Press, 1944; Izod, John. *Hollywood and the Box Office, 1895–1986.* New York: Macmillan, 1988; Kindem, Gorham, ed. *The American Movie Industry: The Business of Motion Pictures.* Carbondale, Ill.: Southern Illinois University Press, 1982; Marlowe, Frederic. "The Rise of Independents in Hollywood." *Penguin Film Review* 3 (August 1947): 72–5; Monaco, James. *American Film Now: The People, The Power, The Money, The Movies.* New York: Oxford University Press, 1979; *The Motion Picture Almanac.* New York: Quigley Publishing Co., 1984–1990; Perry, Louis B. and Richard S. Perry. *A History of the Los Angeles Labor Movement, 1911–1941.* Berkeley: University of California Press, 1963; Pye, Michael and Lynda Miles. *The Movie Brats: How the Film Generation Took Over Hollywood.* New York: Holt, Rinehart & Winston, 1979; Schatz, Thomas. *The Genius of the System: Hollywood Filmmaking in the Studio Era.* New York: Pantheon Books, 1988; Stanley, Robert H. *The Celluloid Empire: A History of the American Movie Industry.* New York: Hastings House, 1978; Wasko, Janet. *Movies and Money: Financing the American Film Industry.* Norwood, N.J.: Ablex Publishing Co., 1982; Wasko, Janet, ed. *Hollywood in the Age of Television.* Boston: Unwin Hyman, Inc., 1990. **Film Noir:** Shadoian, Jack. *Dreams and Dead Ends: The American Gangster/Crime Film.* Cambridge: MIT Press, 1977; Silver, Alain and Elizabeth Ward, eds. *Film Noir: An Encyclopedic Reference to the American Style.* Woodstock, N.Y.: Overlook Press, 1979. **Combat:** Basinger, Jeanine. *Anatomy of a Genre: The World War II Combat Film.* New York: Columbia University Press, 1989; Dick, Bernard. *The Star Spangled Screen: The American World War Two Film.* Lexington, Ky.: University of Kentucky Press, 1985; Isenberg, Michael T. *War on Film: The American Cinema and World War I, 1914–1941.* Rutherford, N.J.: Associated University Presses, Fairleigh University Press, 1981. **Screwball Comedy:** Paul, William. *Ernst Lubitsch's American Comedy.* New York: Columbia University Press, 1983; Sikov, Ed. *Screwball: Hollywood's Madcap Romantic Comedies.* New York: Crown, 1989. **Westerns:** Hardy, Phil. *The Western: The Complete Film Sourcebook.* New York: William Morrow and Co., 1983. **Stardom:** Dyer, R. *Stars.* London: British Film Institute, 1979; Gledhill, Christine, ed. *Stardom, Industry of Desire.* New York: Routledge, 1991; Haskell, Molly. *From Reverence to Rape: The Treatment of Women in the Movies.* New York: Holt, Rinehart & Winston, 1974; Sklar, Robert. *City Boys: Cagney, Bogart, Garfield.* Princeton, N.J.: Princeton University Press, 1992.